Law, Politics, and Responding to Injustice

This book examines the issue of injustice, and our responses to it, in a range of contemporary contexts.

In her ground-breaking book *The Faces of Injustice* (1990), Judith Shklar draws attention to our tendency to view injustice as an abnormality. Of course it is not: injustice is ubiquitous. But how should we respond to it? The book brings together leading legal and political theorists to explore the nature of injustice, its relationship to law, and responses to it, in a variety of contexts. Their chapters cover issues such as protest, resistance, violence, the moral obligation to obey the law, civil disobedience, democratic reform, and transitional justice. They all, though, share a concern to examine such issues through a Shklar-inspired focus on injustice.

This book will appeal to academics and advanced students in law, politics, and philosophy.

Coel Kirkby is Senior Lecturer at The University of Sydney Law School, Australia.

Wojciech Sadurski is Challis Professor of Jurisprudence at The University of Sydney Law School, Australia.

Kevin Walton is Associate Professor at The University of Sydney Law School, Australia.

Law, Politics, and Responding to Injustice

Edited by Coel Kirkby,
Wojciech Sadurski
and Kevin Walton

Routledge
Taylor & Francis Group
a GlassHouse Book

First published 2025
by Routledge
4 Park Square, Milton Park, Abingdon, Oxon OX14 4RN

and by Routledge
605 Third Avenue, New York, NY 10158

Routledge is an imprint of the Taylor & Francis Group, an informa business

A GlassHouse book

The Open Access version of the introduction was funded by University of Sydney Library.

British Library Cataloguing-in-Publication Data
A catalogue record for this book is available from the British Library

Library of Congress Cataloging-in-Publication Data
Names: Kirkby, Coel, editor. | Sadurski, Wojciech, 1950– editor. | Walton, Kevin (Law teacher), editor.
Title: Law, politics, and responding to injustice / edited by Coel Kirkby, Wojciech Sadurski, and Kevin Walton.
Description: Abingdon, Oxon [UK] ; New York, NY : Routledge, 2025. | Includes bibliographical references and index.
Identifiers: LCCN 2024035844 (print) | LCCN 2024035845 (ebook) | ISBN 9781032676111 (hardback) | ISBN 9781032676166 (paperback) | ISBN 9781032676159 (ebook)
Subjects: LCSH: Justice, Administration of—Political aspects. | Transitional justice. | Justice (Philosophy)
Classification: LCC K2100 .L39 2025 (print) | LCC K2100 (ebook) | DDC 340/.114—dc23/eng/20240806
LC record available at https://lccn.loc.gov/2024035844
LC ebook record available at https://lccn.loc.gov/2024035845

ISBN: 978-1-032-67611-1 (hbk)
ISBN: 978-1-032-67616-6 (pbk)
ISBN: 978-1-032-67615-9 (ebk)

DOI: 10.4324/9781032676159

Typeset in Sabon
by Apex CoVantage, LLC

Contents

Contributors

Jonathan Crowe
University of Southern Queensland
Australia

David Dyzenhaus
University of Toronto
Canada

Patrick Emerton
Deakin University
Australia

Duncan Ivison
University of Manchester
United Kingdom

Coel Kirkby
University of Sydney
Australia

Ting-an Lin
University of Connecticut
United States of America

Colleen Murphy
University of Illinois
Urbana-Champaign
United States of America

Jayani Nadarajalingam
University of Melbourne
Australia

Nicole Roughan
University of Auckland | Waipapa
Taumata Rau
Aotearoa New Zealand

Wojciech Sadurski
University of Sydney
Australia

Eddie Synot
Griffith University
Australia

Ashwini Vasanthakumar
Queen's University
Canada

Kevin Walton
University of Sydney
Australia

Introduction

Coel Kirkby, Wojciech Sadurski and Kevin Walton[1]

In her book *The Faces of Injustice*, Judith Shklar draws attention to our tendency to view injustice as 'a prelude to or a rejection and breakdown of justice, as if injustice were a surprising abnormality'[2] and reminds us that '[m]ost injustices occur continuously within the framework of an established polity with an operative system of law, in normal times'.[3] Injustice is ubiquitous. But how should we respond to it? The present book brings together leading theorists of law and politics to explore this question in various contexts. Their chapters make important contributions to ongoing debates about the nature of injustice, its relationship to law, and political responses to it. Each is inspired by Shklar's important work on injustice, and several go so far as to build on her views through close engagement with them, thereby adding considerably to recent scholarship on her thought.[4]

In the opening chapter, David Dyzenhaus starts from Shklar's observation about the constant presence of injustice in established legal orders. He also starts from another of her observations—an apparently 'Hobbesian' one: 'Without juridical institutions and the beliefs that support them, there can be no decent, just, or stable social relations, but only anxiety, mutual mistrust, and insecurity'.[5] Dyzenhaus then explores the relationship between these two observations from the perspective of those who are subject to a legal order. Their experience, he says, shows that some types of injustice are incompatible with such an order because these injustices create tensions within the order that it can resolve only by justifying its claim to authority over those subject to it. If it cannot justify this claim due to the incompatibility of its ideology with the legal form, as in the case of Nazi Germany, though not in the case of antebellum America, Dyzenhaus concludes that it is not a legal order

1 We thank Rachael Li and Samuel McIntyre for editorial assistance with the chapters in this collection.
2 Judith N Shklar, *The Faces of Injustice* (Yale University Press 1990) 17.
3 Judith N Shklar, *The Faces of Injustice* (Yale University Press 1990) 19.
4 See, eg, Samanatha Ashenden and Andreas Hess (eds), *Between Utopia and Realism: The Political Thought of Judith N. Shklar* (University of Pennsylvania Press 2019).
5 Shklar (n 2) 18.

DOI: 10.4324/9781032676159-1

at all but merely a system of prerogative power, one in which human rights lawyering is impossible. He characterizes the cases of Nazi Germany and antebellum America differently from Shklar. He also challenges her hostility to legal theory, which, for him, when understood as concerned with normative legitimation, elucidates distinct aspects of the experience of injustice, not only in Nazi Germany and in antebellum America but elsewhere, too, such as in apartheid South Africa and in what Dyzenhaus calls the 'parallel state' of Israel and the Occupied Territories.

Shklar's focus on injustice is Duncan Ivison's topic in the second chapter. More precisely, he examines two increasingly popular claims, which together constitute what he calls 'the asymmetry thesis': first, that injustice is easier to detect than justice and, second, that liberal theorizing should begin with injustice. Ivison looks closely at Shklar's work and related work by Amartya Sen and Philip Pettit before suggesting that injustice can take at least four forms—moral, discursive, distributive, and political—of which any politically salient injustice is an intricate amalgam. Ivison concludes that, even if injustice is easier to detect than justice, theorizing about injustice is difficult, as Shklar herself appreciates, and must involve the development of a complex understanding of democratic liberalism that reifies neither justice nor injustice.

In the third chapter, Colleen Murphy considers the experience of injustice. For Shklar, this experience is individualized. For Murphy, however, it is conditioned by group-based identities in deeply divided societies, including the United States. Murphy proceeds by examining the moral permissibility of contempt by victims for other members of the political community who have wronged them. She argues that contempt depends on conditions that are absent in deeply divided societies, in which incommensurable narratives of different groups about victimization preclude accurate judgments regarding the character of individuals as members of a political community. She insists that contempt must be avoided in such contexts—contexts in which engagement with others through processes of transitional justice is needed.

One of the principal themes of this book is the capacity of liberal democracy to address injustice. Duncan Ivison obviously considers it in his chapter. It is Eddie Synot's concern, too. In the fourth chapter, Synot asks how the tensions in the relationship between Aboriginal and Torres Strait Islander peoples and the Australian state ought to be resolved. He considers two possible responses: first, the limited accommodation of Indigenous peoples by the liberal state and, second, the absolute refusal by Indigenous peoples to engage with colonial institutions. According to Synot, the first response proceeds from a universal ideal of justice for free and equal subjects that neglects the reality of the injustice experienced by Indigenous peoples, whereas the second overlooks the potential for Indigenous peoples to participate in structural reforms that enable genuine recognition. For him, both must be rejected in favour of continual engagement with justice claims through democratic processes.

Nicole Roughan also examines the injustices that Indigenous peoples experience, of which, she remarks, Shklar's treatment is lacking. Roughan's specific concern in the fifth chapter is the displacement of Indigenous legalities by state law. For Roughan, the distribution of the status of legality in response to competing claims to it is a question of justice that cannot be answered without abstraction. Like Dyzenhaus, then, she defies Shklar's scepticism about legal theory. Roughan argues that law is mere domination unless it permits the distribution of the status of legality through institutions of 'inter-legality' that enable relations between different—state and Indigenous—legal orders.

A significant feature of Roughan's chapter is her contemplation of the distinction between the concrete and the abstract. Other contributors reflect on it, too, not least Patrick Emerton and Jayani Nadarajalingam in their chapter, which is the sixth. Emerton and Nadarajalingam reject Karl Marx's claim that the liberal state, which grants all citizens the same abstract rights, is unable to overcome the concrete divisions between human beings. For Marx, there is no liberal path to human emancipation. According to Emerton and Nadarajalingam, however, key elements of John Rawls's liberal theory can be understood as aspects of a continuing and, indeed, never-ending historical process (in the real world), one that is propelled by principled political action (by real actors), of increasing recognition by the liberal state of particular claims of justice. They illustrate their argument with the example of the developing application of the Fourteenth Amendment of the United States Constitution.

Ashwini Vasanthakumar's starting point in the seventh chapter is Shklar's emphasis on the need to pay closer attention to the numerous victims of injustice. Vasanthakumar considers their moral duties. Whereas Murphy argues that victims have a duty not to treat other members of the political community who have wronged them with contempt, Vasanthakumar focuses on their duties to repair their self-respect and to assist others in the absence of institutional responses. She develops an account of these duties, including their interactions, in contexts of structural oppression. She then replies to the objections that they are, first, too burdensome and, second, implicated in victim-blaming.

In the eighth chapter, Jonathan Crowe examines another moral duty—the duty to obey the law. He asks how the widespread injustice that Shklar highlights bears on it. Crowe turns to legal theory—more specifically, natural-law theory—to provide a detailed account of this duty. He argues that it depends primarily on the law's salience as a mode of social coordination, its reasonableness, and its capacity to promote common goods. Although extremely unjust laws lack these qualities, Crowe stresses that less unjust laws need not. He concludes that obedience to some unjust laws might be obligatory. He adds that this possibility highlights the extensive power of governments to harm their subjects individually and collectively by imposing a moral obligation to obey unjust laws on them.

Like Vasanthakumar, Ting-an Lin, whose chapter closes the book, focuses on structural injustice. Unlike Vasanthakumar, however, Lin explores an institutional response to it. Having clarified the moral demands on those who share responsibility for structural injustice, she identifies some practical challenges to meeting these demands: psychological and epistemic barriers, the absence of mechanisms for coordinating collective action, and the considerable time and effort that must be expended. She claims that neither guidelines for moral reasoning nor appeals to disruptive politics as alternative ways of implementing responsibility for structural injustice can overcome these challenges. She then recommends deliberative mini-publics as a more promising means of generating the structural reforms that are needed to rectify injustice.

Chapter 1

The legal experience of injustice

David Dyzenhaus[1]

In *The Faces of Injustice*, Judith Shklar criticizes the 'normal model' of justice, which views injustice as 'a prelude to or a rejection and breakdown of justice, as if injustice were a surprising abnormality'.[2] Her central insight is that

> the real realm of injustice . . . does not stand outside of the gates of even the best of known states. Most injustices occur continuously within the framework of an established polity with an operative system of law in normal times.[3]

She adds a second, Hobbesian insight: 'Without juridical institutions and the beliefs that support them, there can be no decent, just, or stable social relations, but only anxiety, mutual mistrust, and insecurity'.[4] Since juridical institutions and their supporting beliefs may be necessary but insufficient to prevent injustice, the insights are consistent. Moreover, the centralization of power in the modern legal state gives to elites powerful instruments to do injustice they would otherwise lack.

My chapter enquires into this consistency, not as a matter of abstract logic, but of the logic of the legal experience of those in the 'jural community'—the

1 This chapter develops the argument of my *The Long Arc of Legality: Hobbes, Kelsen, Hart* (CUP 2022). I thank for comments and challenges: the audience at a workshop at the Faculty of Law at the University of Genoa; the organizers of the Online Lecture Series on the Rule of Law and Democracy at the Normative Orders Research Center of the Goethe University, in particular my two commentators, Chiara Destri and Uwe Volkmann; the audience at Escuela Libre de Derecho (Mexico City), in particular my commentators Adriana Ortega and Diego Garcia Ricci; the audience at the New York University Colloquium on Legal, Political, and Social Philosophy, in particular the convenors Jeremy Waldron and Sam Scheffler; the audience at my 'Julius Stone Address' at Sydney University; and Damian Cueni and Megan Pfiffer for written comments.

2 Judith N Shklar, *The Faces of Injustice* (Yale University Press 1990) 17.

3 Judith N Shklar, *The Faces of Injustice* (Yale University Press 1990) 19.

4 Judith N Shklar, *The Faces of Injustice* (Yale University Press 1990) 18.

DOI: 10.4324/9781032676159-2

community of persons subject to the operation of a system of law. That experience is in part a normative experience—an encounter of a legal subject with authority—so not with what HLA Hart famously called 'the gunman situation writ large', the image in John Austin of the sovereign as an 'uncommanded commander' whose commands backed by sanctions instill a habit of obedience in its subjects.[5] It is an encounter with the state's authority as well as with its power to deploy sanctions.

I examine here how operative systems of law make possible and even legitimate legalized injustice. My focus is not on Shklar's 'best of known states', but on some prominent examples of legalized injustice in her work and in particular on the role of human rights lawyers in combatting the injustice. I argue that certain kinds of injustice create tensions within a system which, if not resolved legally—that is, by using the system's own procedural and substantive resources—change the system from one kind to another or to a system of legally unmediated, prerogative power.[6] As I will show, there are ideologies that are very difficult or even impossible to implement through law since legal form—the formal quality of law that is the mark of an operative system of law—either resists or is incompatible with them. Put differently, if such ideologies are implemented, they will either strain or shatter legal form, with the result that the experience of injustice will no longer be legal. The victims of this kind of injustice will be subject not to law, but to legally unmediated power.

Section 1 sketches four 'ideal types' of state, which together mark the continuum of legality. The 'Rule-of-Law State', in which public officials stay within the limits of their legal authority, is at one end of a continuum of legality, while the 'Dual State' marks the end at which a state falls off the continuum because legal officials are subject to overrule by officials with legally unlimited authority. So long as an actual state is on the continuum, human rights lawyers can find resources in the law to contest the oppression visited by law on their clients, but they must deal with the fact that their participation in the legal order legitimates the very regime of injustice they struggle against.

Section 2 explains why the philosophers of law whom Shklar regarded as involved in a 'tiresome' 'family quarrel' about the relationship between law and morality are better understood as attempting to grapple with that process of legitimation.[7] In her view, these philosophers—the 'legalists'—are wedded to a methodology that ignores context and history, as well as to an

5 HLA Hart, 'Positivism and the Separation of Law and Morals' in *Essays in Jurisprudence and Philosophy* (OUP 1983) 59. See Norberto Bobbio, *Teoria Generale del Diritto* (G Giappichelli Editore 1993) 3: '*l'esperienza giuridica è un'esperienza normativa*' (emphasis in original).

6 I use 'operative system of law' and 'legal order' synonymously.

7 Judith N Shklar, *Legalism: Law, Morals and Political Trials* (Harvard University Press 1986) 106. See also Judith N Shklar, 'Political Theory and the Rule of Law' in *Political Thought and Political Thinkers* (Chicago University Press 1998) 21.

'ideology' that effects a 'divorce of law from politics . . . designed to prevent arbitrariness'. In addition, they regard politics 'not only as something apart from law, but as inferior to law' because '[l]aw aims at justice, while politics looks only to expediency'.[8] *The Faces of Injustice* adds her main insight. Even within the legal orders of liberal constitutional democracy, a political system she wholeheartedly endorsed, those who adopt the normal model neglect the ubiquitous experience of injustice.

However, on my account, when context and history get more attention, the beliefs Shklar mentions that 'support' juridical institutions turn out to be the institutions' product. In *The Faces of Injustice*, she remarks in passing on a 'curious division of labor' in that philosophy 'ignores iniquity, while history and fiction deal with little else', and she suggests that political theory could fill this gap because 'it lives in the territory between history and ethics'.[9] I agree, but add sociology, taking my cue from Austin's command theory of law and the habit of obedience of subjects that is both a mark of and sustains operative systems of law.[10] I argue that the area of disagreement between the philosophers of law discussed in Section 2 is far from tiresome when reconfigured as being about the 'political sociology of obedience' in that the acceptance of legal subjects is constitutive of legal order.[11] For there to be such acceptance, the officials of an order who implement, enforce, and interpret its law must be capable of answering the legal subject who asks an official, 'But, how can that be law for me?' The order must, that is, be capable of vindicating its claim to wield legitimate authority to those who are subject to it. Once the legal subject becomes a central—even *the* central—figure for philosophy of law, it becomes exactly the kind of inquiry Shklar thought it should be. She complained once in a follow-up essay to *Legalism* that philosophers of law tend to produce ' "legal", legal theory'. But, with the addition of the political sociology of obedience, legal theory becomes 'political, legal theory', thus fully recognizing, as Shklar urged, the 'social ethos upon which any viable legal system must be based'.[12]

8 Shklar, *Legalism* (n 7) 111.

9 Shklar, *The Faces of Injustice* (n 2) 16.

10 John Austin, *Lectures on Jurisprudence or the Philosophy of Positive Law* (5th edn, John Murray 1885).

11 On a related theme, see Ilaria Cozzaglio, 'Legitimacy between Acceptance and Acceptability: A Subjects-First View' (2022) 48 Soc Theory Pract 61.

12 Judith N Shklar, 'In Defense of Legalism' (1996) 19 J Legal Stud 1, 57. For 'political legal theory', see David Dyzenhaus, *The Long Arc of Legality* (n 1). For a similar idea, see Jeremy Waldron, *Political Theory: Essays on Institutions* (Harvard University Press 2016), arguing that political theory pays too little attention to questions about political process, political institutions, and political structures. Waldron remarks, at 7, that '[b]ad things happen mostly in the dark, in Fuller's account, and unjust aims do not have the same coherence as good ones', which he says is 'an intriguing hypothesis, but the consensus in legal philosophy is that it cannot be pushed very far'. My aim here is to disturb that consensus.

1. Types of state and human rights lawyering

In 'Political Theory and the Rule of Law', Shklar offered what she thought of as a refutation of Lon L Fuller's 'inner morality' of law.[13] Fuller argued that, if the powerful wish to rule by law, they will find that they must comply by and large with eight formal principles of legality: generality, promulgation, non-retroactivity, clarity, non-contradiction, possibility of compliance, constancy through time, and 'congruence' between official action and declared rule.[14] Congruence, which he regarded as the most complex, required that rule by law respects procedural principles to do with the legal subject's right to get an authoritative determination from an impartial and independent official, for example, a judge, as to whether a particular action was within the limits of the official's authority.[15] A system that fails completely to meet one of these principles, or fails substantially to meet several, would not, in his view, be a legal system. It would not qualify as government under law—as government subject to the rule of law. Moreover, Fuller claimed that in such a system a 'bond of reciprocity' would be established between ruler and ruled such that the inner morality of law would be manifested, and that '[e]very departure from the principles of law's inner morality is an affront to man's dignity as a responsible agent'.[16]

Shklar responded that Fuller's inner morality is 'perfectly compatible with governments of a most repressive and irrational sort' since 'the very formal rationality of a civil law system can legitimize a persecutive war state among those officials who are charged with maintaining the private law and its clients'. In her view, that was 'certainly the case in Nazi Germany, whose legal caste was perfectly ready to ignore the activities of the new court, police and extermination system as long as the "inner morality" of their law could remain unaffected'.[17] She cited in support of her claim the German lawyer

13 Shklar, 'Political Theory and the Rule of Law' (n 7) 33.

14 Lon L Fuller, *The Morality of Law* (rev edn, Yale University Press 1969) 33–44.

15 Lon L Fuller, 'The Forms and Limits of Adjudication' in Kenneth I Winston (ed), *The Principles of Social Order: Selected Essays of Lon L Fuller* (Hart 2001) 101.

16 Fuller, *The Morality of Law* (n 14) 162.

17 Shklar, 'Political Theory and the Rule of Law' (n 7) 33. *Legalism* and *The Morality of Law* both appeared in 1964, so Shklar's critique of Fuller focused at that time on his 'Positivism and Fidelity to Law: A Reply to Professor Hart' (1958) 71 Harv L Rev 630. In 'Political Theory and the Rule of Law', Shklar refers to the sections of *The Morality of Law* summarized above, as well as to Fuller's essay 'The Forms and Limits of Adjudication' as it appeared in the 1978–79 Harvard Law Review. Fuller never responded in print to Shklar. However, his heavily annotated copy of *Legalism* shows that he thought, rightly in my view, that she often was in complete agreement with his main points. (I thank Ken Winston for correspondence on this topic and for sending me Fuller's copy.) Indeed, in *Legalism*, Shklar, citing the Nazi order and Fraenkel (at 208, n 120), said that 'a study of totalitarian politics' can make a 'great contribution to legal theory; in showing the impossibility of thinking of law as something just "there"—a given entity filled with varying values, but still a solid system to

and political scientist Ernst Fraenkel's *The Dual State* as one of the 'few older studies of the Third Reich that remains valid'; and she suggested that '[t]he paradox of slavery, that made the slave both a human person and the property of another, created a "dual state" in pre-Civil War America as well, and it was just as irrational'.

> No-one can be three-fifths of a human being and two-fifths of a thing as the federal ratio had it in the original Constitution. Nor is the prohibition against murdering slaves, since they were people, compatible with their non-person status before the rest of the legal system, not to mention the exclusion from the guiding principles of the political order as a whole.[18]

But this irrationality, she claimed, 'may be a model of "inner morality"' and 'may well serve to render irrationality more efficient and more attractive to those who benefit from it'. The dual state, she concluded, 'remains a constant possibility in our century'.[19]

Shklar was right in her evaluation of Fraenkel's classic study, and what seemed to her the possibility of the Dual State recurring has become something like a reality in our time.[20] However, Fraenkel's book in fact shows why Fuller's 'inner morality' of law is *in*compatible 'with governments of a most repressive and irrational sort'. A Dual State does not give rise to a *legal* experience of injustice but to an experience of prerogative rule. That fact opens a window into the legal experience.

a. The Dual State, the Rule-of-Law State, and American slavery

For Fraenkel, the Nazi state was a Dual State because it consisted of two states side by side: the 'normative state', which contained whatever remained of the law and institutions of the Weimar legal order together with the statutory regimes enacted after 1933 and implemented through those institutions, and the 'prerogative state', which consisted of the apparatus of the Nazi

be dissected integrally and in isolation' (at 207). One had to see that 'certain ideologies and regimes are radically incompatible with any sort of stable rules' and that the 'political ends that law can serve' are 'relatively limited' (at 207–08). Nazism was an 'actively anti-legalistic ideology' (at 208). For an illuminating treatment of these themes, see William E Scheuerman, 'Law and the Liberalism of Fear' in Samantha Ashenden and Andreas Hess (eds), *Between Utopia and Realism: The Political Thought of Judith N Shklar* (University of Pennsylvania Press 2019) 47.

18 Shklar, 'Political Theory and the Rule of Law' (n 7) 33.

19 Shklar, 'Political Theory and the Rule of Law' (n 7). For Shklar's further reflections on this theme, see Judith N Shklar, *American Citizenship: The Quest for Inclusion* (Harvard University Press 1991).

20 See Cora Chan, 'From Legal Pluralism to Dual State: Evolution of the Relationship between the Chinese and Hong Kong Legal Orders' (2022) 16 LEHR 99.

Party wherein the leader's will (his actual will or his will as interpreted by subordinate officials) was the ultimate source of authority.[21]

Fraenkel contrasted the Dual State with the Rule-of-Law State, one governed in accordance with Fullerian principles.[22] Since an official in the prerogative state could override the normative state whenever this was considered in the interests of the Nazi Party, he concluded that the rule of law did not obtain in Nazi Germany.[23] Indeed, it was barely possible to be a lawyer, let alone a human rights lawyer, because the contours of the normative state both shrank and became more porous, the latter the result of a process Fraenkel charted that hollowed out the normative space from within. For officials in the normative state were constantly tempted to make prerogative-like decisions to avoid being overruled by officials in the prerogative state.

What then of Shklar's example of the Dual State in the legal institution of slavery in the pre–Civil War US? A slave-owning society is like a Dual State in that enslaved persons live in a space where prerogative rules, although private individuals, not state officials, wield their legally delegated power over enslaved persons. But, on closer examination, the example she cites of slavery in the pre–Civil War US shows the tensions that arise when slavery is instituted in a modern legal state, especially when it amounts to a constitutional democracy, which not only promises freedom to all but also is a federal state that contains several jurisdictions in which slavery is abolished.

These tensions reached their peak with 'Fugitive Slaves' who fled from slavery in the South to what they hoped would be freedom in the North. They were required to be returned to their owners by the constitutional compromise on slavery, which also permitted the enactment of a succession of federal Fugitive Slave Acts, designed to overcome the resistance by abolitionists in the North to the return of fugitives, a resistance often fought out by legal means in the courts. Such tensions played a significant part in precipitating the Civil War since they forced to the fore of the country's political imagination the question of the resolution of the 'dilatory compromise' the founders had built into the constitution.[24] The US had to come to terms, that is, with the legal experience of injustice of persons who faced a legal process

21 Ernest Fraenkel, *The Dual State: A Contribution to the Theory of Dictatorship* (first published 1941, 2nd edn, OUP 2017). I reserve capitalization in the text for the types of state, and so will have 'normative state' and 'prerogative state' since these are not, on my account, types of states, but the way Fraenkel described the spaces within the Dual State.

22 Ernest Fraenkel, *The Dual State: A Contribution to the Theory of Dictatorship* (first published 1941, 2nd edn, OUP 2017) 156. Fraenkel found his model in AV Dicey's influential work on the English constitution—see AV Dicey, *Introduction to the Study of the Law of the Constitution* (8th edn, Macmillan 1915)—which articulated a conception of the rule of law roughly akin to Fuller's inner morality.

23 Fraenkel (n 21) 70–71.

24 See Carl Schmitt, *Constitutional Theory* (first published 1928, Jeffrey Seitzer ed and tr, Duke University Press 2008) 84–88.

in which they could be relegated to a space of prerogative power, and, moreover, with an attempt to strip that process of any force in order to undermine access to substantive legal rights.

That the tensions could be resolved—to the extent there was a resolution—only by the most extreme sort of politics is significant. It shows that, ultimately, existential problems about who is in the political community cannot be decided by courts. However, such tensions were contingent on there being legal order at all, since that made the experience of injustice a legal one. It also made what would be recognizable to us today as human rights lawyering possible, although with enslaved persons it was difficult precisely because their experience was only in part legal. Within the space of private prerogative, they were ruled by a gunman writ small, albeit one backed by a gunman writ large, by that part of the US state committed to enforcing slavery even as other parts were committed to combating it. But that the former took place within an operative legal order meant that the issue that faced the US prior to the war was not only the moral question of slavery. It was also the legal question that arose because in some respects enslaved persons were legal subjects and in some respects not; in the US context, as we saw Shklar put it, 'three-fifths of a human being and two-fifths of a thing'.

In the Dual State in contrast, because its two spaces were held together by prudential factors and not by law, the jural community within the normative state was entirely precarious. One could be moved across the boundary between the two spaces at the will of a Nazi official. Moreover, once moved across that boundary, one was no longer a legal subject. Rather, one was an object of discretion, to be used as some official thought fit, which in the case of millions in Germany and in Germany's Occupied Territories meant fit for extermination. The significance of the construction of the legal space by prudential considerations rather than by law can be appreciated by contrasting the Dual State with the two other ideal types of state in which law is used to reduce the status of groups of subjects, though not to the extent of reducing them to things.

b. *The Apartheid State and the Parallel State*

The Apartheid State, exemplified of course by South Africa, is a perverse variant of a Rule-of-Law State. All inhabitants of apartheid South Africa were subject to the same general law. The racial laws of apartheid carved out vast exceptions to the rule of general law by creating the legal regimes that dominated the lives of black South Africans, subjecting them to severe discrimination. These regimes relegated black South Africans—the majority of the population—to an inferior status in almost all aspects of life. Nevertheless, the ideal that all South Africans were equal before the law—the specifically legal ideal of human dignity[25]—was maintained as an abstract ideal of the legal order throughout the apartheid era, even as particular laws made it ever clearer that the animating political ideology of the ruling party was one of White supremacy.

To be both within the jural community in some respects and without for others is to occupy a highly problematic legal status, that of second-class citizen. Second-class status is much more *legally* problematic than the status of slavery, provided the enslaved persons are relentlessly consigned to the status of objects or things. For if one is legally recognized as having status as a responsible agent in some respects but not others, the parts of the law that seem to relegate one to inferior status are thrown into question by those that do not in any case in which a challenge is brought to the former. Of course, the parts of the law that seem to relegate one to inferior status can be used to throw into doubt those parts that do not, to the point where inferior status for a group is so entrenched that individuals in the group are no longer second-class citizens because they are governed by an entirely different regime of law.[26]

In that case, the order would change into one in which there are two separate spaces of legality, albeit held together by law. It would become a 'Parallel State', and my example here is Israel and the Occupied Territories. The Israeli legal order (ILO) and the Occupied Territories legal order (OTLO) were unified during the initial period of occupation after the 1967 war when the Israeli Supreme Court became the apex court for both in that it started to take jurisdiction over appeals from the military courts operating in the OTLO. Within this unified legal order, a fairly clear distinction is maintained between the two sub-orders, except for the fact that the Court regards the military as governed by Israeli administrative law, on the basis that as an arm of the executive it is subject to the same administrative law norms as any arm of the state.[27] In this light, we can see that for an Apartheid State to rid itself of the internal tensions created by the legal relegation of the majority of its subjects to second-class status, it would have to choose between two options.

It could turn itself into a Parallel State, and indeed statutes implementing apartheid policy made over time an attempt to set up not just one parallel legal order but many, in the form of self-governing 'Bantustans', later called 'homelands'. In this way, the South African state tried unsuccessfully to escape the legal tensions that will exist in any operative system of law in which law is used to impose a rigid and racialized caste grid on a society

25 See Jeremy Waldron, 'How Law Protects Dignity' (2012) 71 CLJ 200.

26 See David Dyzenhaus, *Hard Cases in Wicked Legal Systems: Pathologies of Legality* (2nd edn, OUP 2010).

27 See David Kretzmer and Yaël Ronen, *The Occupation of Justice: The Supreme Court of Israel and the Occupied Territories* (2nd edn, OUP 2022) ch 3.

while maintaining the groups in one jurisdiction, which requires that the groups are in some respects subject to the same general norms.

The other option was to become a Dual State, and here we can note that the South African state's security legislation became ever more draconian, to the point where it permitted indefinite detention without trial on the basis of the entirely subjective opinion of the detaining officer about a person's risk to national security. These statutes were equipped with privative clauses that explicitly and considerably narrowed the procedural rights to contest their implementation by depriving detainees of the right to see a lawyer and ousting the jurisdiction of the courts. The situation of the targets of such legislation was thus perilously close to pockets of lawlessness, akin to the individuals who found themselves at the mercy of the officials of the Nazi prerogative state.

Still, there was a difference in that the Nazi normative state was contiguous with the prerogative state, which was not an exception to the order of the normative state in the sense that apartheid laws created exceptions—often vast—to the fundamental legal principles of the Apartheid State. Rather, as Fraenkel pointed out, the prerogative state was exceptional in that it was Carl Schmitt's 'state of exception' writ large,[28] a space unbounded by law in which those who wielded power were like the bounty hunters and federal commissioners who, in the antebellum US, rendered people into a space of lawlessness, although the prerogative state was unlike the prerogative space of slavery in that it had no legal boundaries.

Thus, while the governments that ruled South Africa for more than 40 years had a clear aim—the complete separation of the racialized groups considered inferior to the White population—so long as the state maintained its commitment to governing by law, the attempt to implement that policy created tensions within the legal order such that human rights lawyers could find legal resources to resist the attempt. Moreover, because the majority black population and members of other racialized groups remained subject to the legal order's general norms, they and the political organizations that represented them, including those that had resorted to armed struggle, retained a stake in the legal and political order.

In contrast, in my example of a Parallel State, there is an unresolved conflict between two ideologies. The official ideology is that there will be a 'two-state solution' to the political conflicts—that the Parallel State that now exists will become two fully independent states. On this view, the fundamental law of the OTLO consists of the public international law norms that govern belligerent and temporary occupation as refracted by the Israeli

28 Carl Schmitt, *Political Theology: Four Chapters on the Concept of Sovereignty* (first published 1922, George Schwab tr, MIT Press 1988). Fraenkel's many references to Schmitt in *The Dual State* show that he regarded Schmitt as the main theorist of the Dual State.

Supreme Court through the prism of administrative law. For this reason, the Court cannot accept that the normative regime that governs the West Bank is part of the Israeli constitutional order, and in fact does not assume that it has jurisdiction over the OTLO. Rather, it takes jurisdiction in the cases it decides on the basis that both the state and the lawyers for the Palestinian litigants consent to jurisdiction.[29]

The other ideology is the policy of greater Israel with 'creeping annexation' as the way to achieve its goal. On this view, there is no problem of belligerent occupation, since the territories were 'liberated' not occupied; the only problem the state encounters is dealing with Palestinian resistance and the international community. But while the logical terminus of this policy is a 'one-state solution', it seems politically unacceptable, since it would require one of two options.

First, a move to a Rule-of-Law State in which there are no second-class citizens and in which the Palestinian population would outnumber the Jewish population. Second, a move to a fully fledged Apartheid State, one riven with even worse tensions than the South African example, because those who are currently Palestinian citizens of Israel would either have greater rights than Palestinians from the OTLO or be stripped of their rights under current Israeli constitutional law.[30]

In deciding matters that come out of the OTLO, the Court thus must walk two tightropes at once, one strung between the competing political ideologies, and the other between Israeli public law and public international law. It stays on these tightropes by filtering constitutional norms from both its own law and from public international law through Israeli administrative law. The unfortunate effect for Palestinians in the OTLO is that, in their legal conflicts with settlers, their rights weigh less because they are counted as protected interests in administrative law, while settlers' rights are fully fledged constitutional rights, since their enclaves are treated as part of the ILO for these purposes. Moreover, the Court tends to defer to what it considers to be military expertise when it comes to matters of policy, especially any matter that involves security considerations.

However, the OTLO is not a prerogative state in which individuals are subject to the arbitrary will of those with power over them. The officials of the system may not disobey the standing commands or orders of the military authorities, and there is even less arbitrariness because the Court's oversight has resulted in more procedural safeguards than the military authorities thought appropriate. Further, there have been some decisions, especially those

29 See Kretzmer and Ronen (n 27) ch 2.

30 I do not assume that Palestinian citizens of Israel are first-class citizens. For discussion, see Hassan Jabareen, 'Hobbesian Citizenship: How the Palestinians Became a Minority in Israel' in Will Kymlicka and Eva Pföstl (eds), *Multiculturalism and Minority Rights in the Arab World* (OUP 2014) 189.

brokered between lawyers in 'the shadow of the Court', which have made a substantive difference.[31] Here, and in contrast to the Dual State, officials in the OTLO make decisions that are more rule-of-law compliant in order to avoid a situation in which the Court might give a judgment that definitively and publicly declares that they are acting lawlessly.

The tensions in issue arise because that Court presides at the same time over the ILO state, a Rule-of-Law State, which it has had a prominent role in designing. Within the OTLO, Palestinians are neither quite second- nor quite first-class citizens. To be a second-class citizen, there must be a group of first-class citizens in whose status the second-class citizens to some extent partake; and the Palestinian inhabitants of the OTLO are not subject to the fundamental principles at the basis of the ILO.

They are also not quite first-class citizens for two independent reasons. First, they live in areas contiguous with the enclaves in which settlers are deemed first-class citizens of the ILO, which puts them into a legal relationship on highly unequal terms. Palestinians in the Occupied Territories are virtual second-class citizens because they live under an occupation that provides full status for settlers and an inferior status for them while the Court's jurisdiction over them gives them a toehold, not a foothold, in the first-class space. But even that toehold is at best precarious since the Court both offers and withdraws the protections of legality. It gives them procedural rights to contest official action, but at the same time narrows dramatically the substantive resources available for that contest.

Second, even abstracting from that fact, while all the subjects of the OTLO are equally subject to the law, the law to which they are subject is the commands of those who occupy their land by force. The occupation authority may seem more in that respect like what Hart described as the gunman writ large of Austin's command theory of law than like a legislature which legislates by enacting the general laws which together could be said to make up a public order of law.[32]

To be a first-class citizen is to be treated with what we saw Fuller describe as dignity as a responsible agent. Within the OTLO, that ideal is reduced to what Joseph Raz describes as the 'guidance function' of law—the law just tells people what they must do. This is not nothing. To the extent that the law is not arbitrarily enforced, Palestinians can plan their lives, which, as Raz suggests, in a deliberate echo of Fuller, does provide for some measure of freedom and dignity and, indeed, without it there can be neither freedom nor dignity.[33] That there is some measure of freedom and dignity shows that,

31 See Kretzmer and Ronen (n 27) 507–10. They note, at 510, the suggestion that government lawyers may also play a restraining role through the advice they give to the military about the legality of proposed activities.

32 Hart, 'Positivism and the Separation of Law and Morals' (n 5) 603.

33 Joseph Raz, 'The Rule of Law and Its Virtue' in *The Authority of Law: Essays on Law and Morality* (OUP 1983) 213–14, 219–23.

even as law oppresses, it must enable something of moral worth, which is what makes human rights lawyering possible, though fraught and morally complex. That complexity is the foundation for the bridge that reaches from human rights lawyering to political legal theory, as I now explain.

c. *Human rights lawyering in unjust regimes*

In his book on his practice of human rights law in the OTLO, Michael Sfard argues that regime change cannot be an aim of human rights lawyers because they accept the limits the law imposes on their practice.[34] Not only do their losses in court help to shore up the legitimacy of the regime, but also their occasional victories, because the latter support the authorities' claim to be ruling in accordance with the rule of law. That fact has made Sfard and others wonder whether they should discontinue their practice because overall they do more harm than good, but they are unable to give up in part because the oppressed turn to them for help.

There is another reason for continuing. The experience of human rights lawyers during apartheid looms large in Sfard's argument.[35] On the last page of his book, he asserts that 'one day the occupation will end, like apartheid in South Africa' and, when it does, 'we'll find that we are not entirely bereft of a culture of good government, that we do have moral foundations to draw on'. That provides the reason why 'human rights lawyers must hold their heads high and know that they have a role in the appearance of cracks in the occupation'.[36]

On the way to this conclusion, Sfard sketches the heated debate that took place in South Africa in the 1980s when Raymond Wacks, in an inaugural lecture as a professor of public law, called on the few liberal judges on the bench to resign.[37] As Sfard notes, Wacks's challenge rested on three claims. First, Wacks suggested that the principles of apartheid ideology were so strongly embedded in the law that they had largely displaced the principles of freedom and equality that had at one point been part of the legal tradition of 'Roman-Dutch common law'. Second, and as a result, judges could in most cases give liberal or rights-protecting judgments only by lying about what the law required. Third, to the extent that South African law still offered a limited basis for such judgments, these would be overruled by legislative fiat and would in any case serve to bolster the regime's claim to legitimacy. Judges

34 Michael Sfard, *The Wall and the Gate: Israel, Palestine, and the Legal Battle for Human Rights* (Metropolitan Press 2018).

35 Michael Sfard, *The Wall and the Gate: Israel, Palestine, and the Legal Battle for Human Rights* (Metropolitan Press 2018) 443–44, 447–48.

36 Michael Sfard, *The Wall and the Gate: Israel, Palestine, and the Legal Battle for Human Rights* (Metropolitan Press 2018) 455.

37 The debate started in the national press and then continued in the South African Law Journal. See Raymond Wacks, 'Judges and Injustice' (1984) 101 SALJ 266; John Dugard, 'Should Judges Resign? A Reply to Professor Wacks' (1984) 101 SALJ 286.

should thus resign because they 'inevitably enhanced the regime's legitimacy without any real ability to make changes for the better'.[38]

The main response came from South Africa's leading human rights scholar, John Dugard. He conceded both that the room for judicial manoeuvre within the law had diminished and that judges' service on the bench lent legitimacy to the regime. But, on the first point, he suggested there was more room than Wacks supposed and, on the second, he argued that human rights lawyers participating in court and even law professors criticizing the courts and educating students in the basis for such criticism served to legitimate. There was, that is, 'no clear line of moral responsibility between a judge and a lawyer, a practitioner and an academic'. In answer to Wacks's third point, he argued that the 'price of legitimacy' was worth paying because the cost of resignation would be abandonment of the victims of injustice who sought representation and 'hoped that the courts would rule in their favour'. Dugard added that the human rights lawyers of his day also had to keep an eye on the future, on the benefit of keeping alive what we saw Sfard describe as the 'culture of good government'.[39]

Sfard does not note that Wacks based his claim about judicial duty on his understanding of Ronald Dworkin's 'interpretivist' theory of law, according to which judges must strive to show the law in its 'best moral light' by deciding 'hard cases' on the basis of the principles implicit in the relevant law. Wacks, that is, claimed that South African judges were under a duty to decide cases on the interpretation of apartheid statutes in light of the principles of the racist ideology implicit in the law.[40] Just as I said earlier that the Apartheid State is a perverse variant of a Rule-of-Law State, his intervention raises starkly the question whether in such a variant perverse Dworkinianism prevails, such that, as Raz once put it, Dworkin's position would seem to 'require a South African judge to use his power to extend Apartheid'.[41] Indeed, the Dworkinian dimension of Wacks's argument led Dugard to point out that the

> statutes comprising the law of apartheid do not provide a complete system of law within themselves. These statutes must still be interpreted in light of the common law, administrative powers exercised under these laws must still be reviewed in accordance with common-law principles of natural justice, and subordinate legislation must still be tested by the common law standards of reasonableness.[42]

38 Sfard (n 34) 447–48.
39 Sfard (n 34) 448–49.
40 Wacks (n 37) 270–78.
41 Joseph Raz, 'Authority, Law, and Morality' in *Ethics in the Public Domain: Essays in the Morality of Law and Politics* (OUP 1994) 208.
42 Dugard (n 37) 289–90.

That, he said, is 'the nature of South African law', since there was 'no statutory or common law directive to judges to adjudicate the laws of apartheid in accordance with the principles' of apartheid ideology.[43] He thus raised a doubt about whether the apartheid legal order could ever be made a system of unremitting injustice such that perverse Dworkinianism would prevail, though he left it unclear whether this was a contingent fact about this legal order or a claim about legal order in general.[44]

I suspect Sfard omits these details because he asserts that he can 'sidestep' the 'fervent debate between legal positivists and other schools of philosophy of law over the nature and characteristics of a legal norm'.[45] But he also asserts that a 'legal norm . . . does not have the power just to *dictate* but also to *justify*' and that

> [w]e obey laws not just because they come with mechanisms for enforcement but because we accept that following them is the right thing to do. We accept, for the most part, that a norm established through the prevailing constitutional order is justified.[46]

And with these assertions, he may seem to adopt a view of law that takes sides in the debate, if, as Hart understood it, it is about the 'Separation Thesis' that there is no necessary connection between law and morality.[47]

Hart's principal concern in this debate was to equip legal subjects to answer the question of obedience posed by unjust laws by helping them avoid the trap of 'obsequious quietism'—the view that, because X is the law, it will have a moral quality such that it should be obeyed.[48] But human rights lawyers like Sfard know not only that the particular laws they contest are unjust but also that the regime as a whole is unjust. Moreover, they are keenly aware that their participation in the OTLO bolsters the legitimacy claim of the Israeli state. Indeed, his co-authored book *The ABC of the OPT: A Legal Lexicon of the Israeli Control over the Occupied Palestinian Territory* observes the OTLO exclusively from what Hart described as the 'external point of view', the perspective of an observer who regards law as an order of coercion.[49] From this perspective, when reckoned in the currency of legitimation,

43 Dugard (n 37) 289–90.

44 See David Dyzenhaus, 'Dugardian Legal Theory' in Tiyanjana Malawah, Max Du Plessis, and Dire Tladi (eds), *The Pursuit of International Law in a Brave New World: Essays in Honour of John Dugard* (Brill 2017) 1.

45 Sfard (n 34) 435.

46 Sfard (n 34) 435 (his emphasis).

47 Hart, 'Positivism and the Separation of Law and Morals' (n 5) 52.

48 Hart, 'Positivism and the Separation of Law and Morals' (n 5) 53–54. Hart takes the term 'obsequious quietism' from Bentham.

49 Orna Ben-Naftali, Michael Sfard, and Hedi Viterbo, *The ABC of the OPT: A Legal Lexicon of the Israeli Control Over the Occupied Palestinian Territory* (CUP 2018). On the 'external point of view', see HLA Hart, *The Concept of Law* (3rd edn, OUP 2012) 88–91.

the cost of participation involved in taking the 'internal point of view' of a participant in the system is prohibitively high. The contrast between these two modes of scholarship highlights the topic of my next section on the consequences of the choice to take the internal point of view, whether it is the philosopher's choice to understand a legal order as more than a gunman situation writ large or the lawyer's choice to practice human rights law.

2. Legitimation in the normative sense?

Hart might well have agreed with Sfard that legal norms justify, as well as with his analysis of the dilemmas human rights lawyers working in an oppressive regime face, since he emphasized that legal officials (including judges) 'accept' the authority of law. Law, he argued, must be understood in the register of authority since at least the officials of the order do not obey its rules because they fear coercion. Rather, they enforce, implement, and interpret the rules because they accept their legal order as authoritative; they take, that is, the internal point of view. '[A] necessary condition of the existence of coercive power is that some at least must voluntarily co-operate in the system and accept its rules' so that '[i]n this sense it is true that the coercive power of law presupposes its accepted authority'.[50]

In later work, Hart accepted Raz's distinction between the 'committed' point of view of a participant in legal order who accepts its authority and the 'detached' or 'uncommitted' point of view of individuals who recognize that the legal order depends on the existence of at least a minority of committed sorts, but do not themselves accept its authority.[51] For Hart and Raz, the distinction allows philosophy of law to elucidate the nature of legal order as an authoritative system, without regard to questions about the actual legitimacy of legal order in general or of any particular legal order. As Hart explained, it identifies a 'type of detached statement made from the point of view of those who accept the law by those who do not in fact accept it'.[52]

Armed with this distinction, legal positivists may seem able to take on board Sfard's observations about legal norms. They can say that participants in legal order share the committed point of view of those who suppose that acting as they do is the right thing because legal norms do justify. In addition, they can accept that such participation amounts to what we can think of as 'legitimation work' in contrast to 'legitimacy work'. The former bolsters a regime's claim to legitimacy without making it actually legitimate—a concept more at home in

50 Hart, *The Concept of Law* (n 49) 203.

51 HLA Hart, *Essays on Bentham: Jurisprudence and Political Theory* (OUP 1982) 127, 153–61, referring mainly to Joseph Raz, *The Authority of Law: Essays on Law and Morality* (OUP 1983) 153–59.

52 Hart, *Essays on Bentham* (n 51) 157.

sociology than in political philosophy, where it is associated with Max Weber's pioneering inquiry into the legitimacy of the modern legal state.[53]

Recall here Hart's suggestion in the Preface to *The Concept of Law* that the book 'may also be regarded as an essay in descriptive sociology'.[54] Dworkin deemed this suggestion 'famously baffling',[55] but it is not so baffling when connected to Hart's remark in the previous paragraph that a 'central theme of the book' is that law cannot be understood without an appreciation of the 'crucial distinctions between two different kinds of statements', that is, those from the internal and those from the external points of view.[56] As Hart's biographer Nicola Lacey has pointed out, Hart's copy of Weber's *On Law in Economy and Society* is heavily annotated at the point where Weber set out his view of legitimation work and the necessity to understand it from his equivalent of the internal point of view.[57]

Hart, that is, wanted a theory of legal order in which the orientation of the actors or its participants towards the rightness of the order is fully accounted for observationally. As one might say, the observer accounts for the actors' orientation without making any judgment about rightness. Such observation is not from the external point of view since acceptance of rightness is irrelevant to a point of view that focuses exclusively on facts about conduct. Nor is it the 'fully committed' or 'full blooded' 'internal point' of view of the participant, which is why the 'detached point of view' seemed appropriate.[58]

However, Hart and Raz differed in that Hart has a sociological theory of the authority of law and Raz a moral theory. Hart argued that law as a matter of fact *has* authority, not merely that it *claims* authority, whereas a moral theory argues that law has the authority it claims only when its content lives up to the demands of a set of moral criteria independent of law. For Raz, law has authority only when it vindicates his 'Normal Justification Thesis', which requires that the reasons the law transmits to subjects in fact serve their interests better than if they were to judge for themselves. If a legal order lacks legitimate authority, it will, Raz suggests, have *de facto* authority—authority in fact—in that, while it does not have the authority it claims, it is 'capable of possessing the requisite moral properties of authority'.[59]

53 I owe this important distinction to Kieran McEvoy, Louise Mallinder, and Anna Bryson, *Lawyers in Conflict and Transition* (CUP 2022). See my review: David Dyzenhaus, 'Book Review' (2023) 50 J Law Soc 139.

54 Hart, *The Concept of Law* (n 49) v.

55 Ronald Dworkin, *Justice in Robes* (Harvard University Press 2006) 165.

56 Hart, *The Concept of Law* (n 49) v.

57 Nicola Lacey, 'Analytical Jurisprudence versus Descriptive Sociology Revisited' (2006) 84 Tex Law Rev 945, 951.

58 See Hart, *Essays on Bentham* (n 51) 154–61 and Raz, *The Authority of Law* (n 51) 153–59 for this array of terms.

59 Raz, 'Authority, Law, and Morality' (n 41) 199.

Hart rejected what he called the 'moral component' in Raz's theory of law's claim to legitimate authority, but he did confess to a large problem that rejection raised for his own account. The virtue of Raz's account, he suggested, is that it responds to the idea that when a subject is stated to have a duty to act contrary to his own sense of his interests, it is assumed that there exist reasons that are objective in that they 'exist independently of his subjective motivation'.[60] On this assumption, 'it would be difficult to deny that legal duty is a form of moral duty' because that denial would seem to entail that there were 'two independent "worlds" or sets of objective reasons, one legal and the other moral'. Hart thus conceded that his own 'non-cognitive' account of legal reasons seems committed to the 'paradoxical' and even 'confused' conclusion that 'judicial statements of a subject's legal duties need have nothing directly to do with the subject's reasons for action'.[61]

Hart therefore detected a problem for his positivist tradition. If one of the features of law that requires explanation is law's authority, the philosopher of law needs to explain how law provides reasons of a special kind to subjects—'authoritative legal reasons'.[62] But since Hart was not willing to countenance that such reasons have a moral quality to them, he confessed that he was at something of a loss. However, Raz may have a different version of the same problem since his distinction between legitimate and *de facto* authority invites questions which his theory does not help to answer.

First, does an illegitimate legal order have *de facto* authority? Second, if it is merely capable of having authority, is it a legal order at all, capable of producing valid laws? Third, if an illegitimate legal order has only *de facto* authority, what kinds of reasons do its laws supply to officials and subjects?

Because Hart's task is to explain the authority law has, not that which it merely claims, he can answer 'yes' to the first question. He may thus ignore the second question. But he is stuck with the answer to the third he found confused and paradoxical, one which, to borrow from philosophers who work in his tradition, understands the reasons that law supplies as 'normatively inert'[63] or as possessing only 'weightless normativity'[64]—as unauthoritative, authoritative legal reasons. Raz, in contrast, wavers between answering 'yes' and 'no' to the first question. 'Yes' permits him to ignore the second question, but 'no' squarely confronts his moral theory of authority, which then commits him with Hart to the paradoxical idea of unauthoritative, authoritative legal reasons.

60 Hart, *Essays on Bentham* (n 51) 266–68.
61 Hart, *Essays on Bentham* (n 51) 266–68.
62 Hart, *Essays on Bentham* (n 51) ch 10.
63 John Gardner, *Law as a Leap of Faith* (OUP 2012) 23.
64 Developed by Jeffrey Kaplan in his 2018 PhD thesis, 'Weightless Normativity: A Theory of Law, Language, and More' <https://escholarship.org/uc/item/8gb35173> accessed 17 June 2024. See also his unpublished paper, 'The Internal Point of View', on file.

The exchange between Hart and Raz does, however, help to illuminate the path forward. When Hart talked of 'official acceptance', he tended to think of the relationship of acceptance as one between the officials, on the one hand, and the fundamental rules of the legal order, on the other. Acceptance refers to the voluntary cooperation of each official with every other in upholding the fundamental rules of their operative system of law. But since their acceptance suffices for a legal order to exist, the acceptance of subjects is not an existence condition of legal order. The path forward has to do with the issue of the scope of the authority relationship, with acknowledging, adapting Hart's response to Raz, that 'judicial statements of a subject's legal duties need have [something] . . . directly to do with the subject's reasons for action'.[65]

This path brings legal subjects into the picture so that we can understand why legal officials are able to make decisions responsive to the subjects. Their activity is understood as part of the dynamic patterns of voluntary cooperation, 'creating *authority*' without which 'the coercive power of law and government cannot be established'.[66] But that path opens only when one sees how, in light of the argument so far, sociological legitimation shades into normative legitimation because of the participation of different actors in it, participation which is only possible if there is a basis inherent in legal order that makes human rights lawyering possible. And with this shift, legitimation work becomes unambiguously, though complicatedly, legitimacy work.[67]

3. The political sociology of obedience

In this section, I unpack Shklar's Hobbesian insight that '[w]ithout juridical institutions and the beliefs that support them, there can be no decent, just, or stable social relations, but only anxiety, mutual mistrust, and insecurity'[68] to get a better grip on her main insight that '[m]ost injustices occur continuously within the framework of an established polity with an operative system of law in normal times'.[69] I do so through a metaphor Hobbes himself deploys to understand law. Hobbes calls the civil law of the sovereign 'Artificiall Chains' that his subjects have 'fastened at one end to the lips of the Man or Assembly to whom they have given the Soveraigne Power, and at the other end to their own Ears'. He adds that these chains are in 'their own nature but weak' but may 'be made to hold, by the danger, though not by the difficulty of breaking them'.[70]

65 Hart, *Essays on Bentham* (n 51) 266–68.
66 Hart, *The Concept of Law* (n 49) 201 (his emphasis).
67 For instructive work on this kind of theme, see Amanda R Greene, 'Legitimacy without Liberalism: A Defense of Max Weber's Standard of Political Legitimacy' (2017) 39 Anal Krit 295.
68 Shklar, *Legalism* (n 7) 18.
69 Shklar, *Legalism* (n 7) 19.
70 Thomas Hobbes, *Leviathan* (Richard Tuck ed, rev student edn, CUP 1996) 147.

This exercise may seem doomed since Hobbes set out an extreme version of the 'normal model of justice'. Far from viewing injustice as an abnormality, he excluded its occurrence altogether in insisting that there is no more to justice than the content of enacted law. On his view, subjects should understand that they must regard that content as just because they have consented to be bound by the sovereign's commands, whatever their content. But I will show that the chain metaphor, properly unpacked, indicates the resources that make a legal order inherently resistant to certain kinds of injustice because, to remain operative, its law must be made, implemented, interpreted, enforced, and generally obeyed; and obedience in place not only because the law happens as a matter of fact to be accepted by subjects but also because it is in fact acceptable by them.

The metaphor of the law as chain is pervasive in political and legal philosophy. When Rousseau opens *The Social Contract* with 'Man is born free; and everywhere he is in chains', he has the civil law in mind, and the whole of the book can be understood as an argument about how to make such enchainment 'legitimate'.[71] In his 1934 *The Pure Theory of Law*, Hans Kelsen describes the legal system as a 'chain of creation'.[72] And in *The Morality of Law*, Fuller claims that the fact that there is an 'inner morality' to legal order establishes a 'bond of reciprocity' between lawgiver and citizen, which, if 'finally and completely ruptured by government', leaves 'nothing . . . on which to ground the citizen's duty to observe the rules'.[73]

Fuller's 'inner morality' and 'bond of reciprocity' may seem a far cry from the authoritarian top-down image of chains maintained by the force of the sovereign's sword associated with Hobbes. But recall that, on Hobbes's account, the subjects themselves fasten the chains. Moreover, at the end of *Leviathan*, he says that the point of the book is to set 'before men's eyes' the 'mutuall relationship between protection and obedience'.[74] He also therefore claims a reciprocal relationship. Of course, that claim may seem like an attempt to make palatable the truth in the chain metaphor: that the threat of the sword of the sovereign—the 'danger' of punishment by overwhelming force—is what makes the law into chains, just as in Rousseau the idea of a general will that binds citizens because they have themselves willed it, whatever its content, has at times earned him a place in the pantheon of authoritarian thinkers.[75]

71 Jean-Jacques Rousseau, 'The Social Contract' in *The Social Contract and Other Later Political Writings* (Victor Gourevitch ed and tr, CUP 2004) 41.

72 Hans Kelsen, *Introduction to the Problems of Legal Theory* (Bonnie Litschewski Paulson and Stanley L Paulson trs, OUP 1992) 56.

73 Fuller, *The Morality of Law* (n 14) 40.

74 Hobbes (n 70) 491.

75 See Jacob L Talmon, *The Origins of Totalitarian Democracy* (Secker & Warburg 1952).

Precisely this aspect troubled Hart, who acknowledged the metaphor as capturing the way in which the 'pressure' to obey 'appears as a chain binding those who have obligations so they are not free to do as they want' and commented that '[t]he other end of the chain is sometimes held by the group or their official representatives, who insist on performance or exact the penalty'.[76] But he complained that the metaphor 'haunts much legal thought':

> Natural and perhaps illuminating though these figures or metaphors are, we must not allow them to trap us into a misleading conception of obligation as essentially consisting in some feeling of pressure or compulsion experienced by those who have obligations.[77]

As he explained, 'if a system of rules is to be imposed by force on any, there must be a sufficient number who accept it voluntarily' since '[w]ithout their voluntary co-operation, thus creating *authority*, the coercive power of law and government cannot be established'.[78]

In addition, Hart agreed with Shklar that Fuller's inner morality is 'perfectly compatible with governments of a most repressive and irrational sort'. In fact, the agreement goes even deeper. Shklar's view of law is for the most part as an instrument of politics, a view that lends itself to absorbing, as Raz following Hart attempted to do, Fuller's principles of legality into legal theory by making them principles which, if followed, shape law into a more effective instrument of extra-legal politics.[79] The image of law that animates this view was well described by Fuller as a 'one-way projection of authority originating with government and imposing itself on the citizen'.[80]

Hart was not all that consistent in this regard since he assented to the following propositions: that law works in the register of authority; that the making of law is conditioned by fundamental legal rules; that law must conform to some degree to principles of legality;[81] that officials must abide by principles of procedural justice; that judges must try to decide their cases according to law in accordance with criteria that bring his account of

76 Hart, *The Concept of Law* (n 49) 87.

77 Hart, *The Concept of Law* (n 49) 88.

78 Hart, *The Concept of Law* (n 49) 201 (his emphasis).

79 Raz, 'The Rule of Law and Its Virtue' (n 33); HLA Hart, 'Lon L. Fuller, *The Morality of Law*' in *Essays in Jurisprudence and Philosophy* (OUP 1983) 342. Fuller has a list of 'Defects of book' at the end of his copy of *Legalism*; among them is that Shklar '*ignores* problem of *interpretation*' (his emphasis). And he remarked that she seemed to view law as the mere outcome of politics and politics itself as power struggle, referring to *Legalism* at 143 and 149.

80 Fuller, *The Morality of Law* (n 14) 207. In *The Long Arc of Legality*, I explain that such legal theories are 'static' in that they suppose that the content of the law is fully formulated outside of law so that the job of law is to transmit that content to subjects.

81 Hart, 'Positivism and the Separation of Law and Morals' (n 5) 81.

interpretation quite close to Dworkin's;[82] and that, substantively, the law of any legal order must offer protections to at least some proportion of subjects lest it become 'meaningless taboos'.[83]

In addition, while Hart retained from Austin the idea that for the existence of legal order when it comes to subjects the only necessary condition is that they have a habit of obedience, however induced, he did also say that an 'extreme case' arises if 'the internal point of view with its characteristic use of normative legal language (This is a valid rule) . . . [is] confined to the official world'. Such a society would be 'deplorably sheeplike; the sheep might end in the slaughter-house'. But, he added, 'there is little reason for thinking that it could not exist or for denying it the title of legal system'.[84]

Moreover, Hart was deeply troubled by the possibility of a 'breakdown in the complex congruent practice' of both officials and subjects that sustains a legal order.[85] Such a breakdown will occur when the 'solid gains' brought by the invention of the form of rule of the modern legal state are outweighed because its 'centrally organized power' is used for 'the oppression of numbers with whose support it can dispense'.[86] He remarked that if a system 'is fair and caters genuinely for the vital interests of all those from whom it demands obedience, it may gain and retain the allegiance of most for most of the time, and will accordingly be stable'. Most will 'look upon its rules from the internal point of view as accepted standards of behaviour' and thus not from the external point of view of 'malefactors or mere helpless victims' upon whom 'these legal standards have to be imposed by force or threat of force'. In contrast, the system 'may be

82 See Hart, *The Concept of Law* (n 49) 205, on the 'characteristic judicial virtues': 'impartiality and neutrality in surveying the alternatives; consideration for the interest of all who will be affected; and a concern to deploy some acceptable principle as a reasoned basis for decision'.

83 Hart, 'Positivism and the Separation of Law and Morals' (n 5) 82. At 81–82, he conceded that in any legal order there will 'justice in the administration of law', the 'natural procedural justice' which 'prevents us from treating [law] . . . as if morally it is utterly neutral, without any contact with moral principles'. This kind of justice he distinguished from 'justice of the law' to point out that law clearly unjust in the second sense could be applied in perfect conformity with justice in the first sense:

> [A] legal system that satisfied these minimum requirements might apply, with the most pedantic impartiality as between the persons affected, laws which were hideously oppressive, and might deny to a vast rightless slave population the minimum benefits of protection from violence and theft.

What he failed to see is the implications of the connection between procedural justice and the substantive protections and of what happens when a state deprives subjects of either resource.

84 Hart, *The Concept of Law* (n 49) 117.

85 Hart, *The Concept of Law* (n 49) 118.

86 Hart, *The Concept of Law* (n 49) 202.

narrow and exclusive', 'run in the interests of the dominant group, and it may be made more repressive and unstable with the latent threat of upheaval'.[87]

This picture presents a stark distinction between who is within the jural community and who without, between an in-group and an out-group. But Hart usefully blurred this distinction when he continued: 'Between these two extremes various combinations of these attitudes are to be found, often in the same individual'.[88] The combination is not, however, as Hart seemed to indicate, of attitudes alone, because one must factor in the reasons for attitudes.

My account of the politics of legal space shows that this kind of pathology arises when a significant part of the jural community is relegated to the status of second-class citizenship. Challenges to this status will usually be made on behalf of an individual subject, but when the stakes raised by the challenge pertain to the contours of legal space, its basis will be the status of equality before the law of the group to which the individual belongs. The trigger for a change in the configuration of legal space is a legal norm that negatively affects the equality before the law of a group of subjects.

In any state on the continuum of legality, subjects will be able to challenge such a law on the basis that it conflicts with norms that protect their status as members of one jural community in which all are equal before the law. To make such a challenge is to participate voluntarily in the process of creating authority, but the challenge merely makes explicit the tensions in the passive habit of obedience, itself a kind of voluntary participation. The challenge requires the officials to answer the question that I have summarized elsewhere as 'But, how can that be law for me?'[89]

In this regard, Sfard notes that his clients 'start out as nobodies, weightless entities in space':

> The authorities ignore them, sometimes not even responding to their communications, batting them away like bothersome flies. Until they file a petition. As soon as the clients hire legal representation and enter the legal process, they gain heft and volume and visibility.[90]

I want to go even further. It may seem startling, even offensive, to suggest that Palestinians who have been subject to more than 50 years of belligerent occupation are legal subjects, part of a jural community in which they participate in fastening the legal chains that bind them to the lips of their effective sovereign, the Israeli military. But, at least when they litigate on the basis of their

87 Hart, *The Concept of Law* (n 49) 201–02.
88 Hart, *The Concept of Law* (n 49) 202. He did not mention that Austin grappled with the same problem: Austin (n 10) 243–45.
89 Dyzenhaus, *The Long Arc of Legality* (n 1).
90 Sfard (n 34) 439. See also McEvoy, Mallinder, and Bryson (n 53) 78–79, quoting from Waldron, 'How Law Protects Dignity' (n 25) 201.

legal rights, they are asserting their subjecthood; and such an assertion is not merely about their subjection to law. It is also an assertion of a kind of legal citizenship, which is at the same time political. It is, one might say, 'citizenship though participation' in a 'negotiated practice'.[91]

On my account, Palestinian citizenship in the OTLO is not determined by the legal order since the tensions sketched earlier are exploited by lawyers like Sfard as part of a political struggle in which the lawyers make starkly visible the question of what kind of citizenship their clients have and could have. They do so through making wholly explicit the peculiarly legal experience of injustice.[92] While the facts on the ground suggest something permanent, the Israeli state for the most part and its Supreme Court maintain the legal fiction of temporary belligerent occupation, governed by the relevant norms of public international law. Not only the judges but also both the lawyers like Sfard and the clients they represent participate in sustaining that fiction, but that it is a fiction does not make it either unreal or lacking effects. It remains a basis for arguments to which judges must respond and so presents a continual challenge to the Israeli state in regard to its fundamental legal commitments, to what kind of jural community it governs, and thus to its fundamental constitutional and political commitments as well. Because the Palestinians are subject to law, the question is to which law: to public international law or Israeli public law or both? The Court's workaround, as I suggested, is to filter the norms of both through administrative law, which makes the legal contest uneven but still one that allows for human rights lawyering.

It is a pathological situation, but one on the continuum of legality. For that reason, what makes the system of law operative provides resources—both procedural and substantive—that human rights lawyers can exploit, as did the system of the Apartheid State, though the way legal space was configured there made a rather different kind of lawyering possible. Indeed, I suggested that, while an Apartheid State relegates whole groups of subjects to second-class status, because they remain subject to the constitutional norms of their legal order, the implementation of their second-class status is vulnerable to legal challenges on the basis of these norms. A kind of Dworkinian interpretivism is possible, and not the perverse kind which Wacks suggests. Rather, judges can make a stand on legal principle in a way that tempers unjust policy.

Moreover, the last point is not undermined by noting that, in an unjust regime, the activity of Dworkinian judges and of human rights lawyers may

91 See James Tully, *Public Philosophy in a New Key: Volume 2: Imperialism and Civic Freedom* (CUP 2008) 248.

92 See Eyal Weizman, *Forensic Architecture: Violence at the Threshold of Detectability* (Zone Books 2017) for an exploration of other ways of making injustice visible, often in the service of human rights lawyers, prominently Sfard. In this respect, Austin's own account of his habit of obedience is quite helpful. See Austin (n 10) 169–72.

do more harm than good because their victories not only can't get at the fundamental injustice of the regime but also may serve overall to legitimize it. We still need an explanation of why the law still offers, as Dworkin once argued, reasons that are 'weak' yet strong enough to morally complicate the situation of those who confront unjust laws. He denied that such reasons arise from the potential for judges to adopt his interpretive model. Rather, they come from the existence of a 'general political situation', such that 'the central power of the community has been administered through an articulate constitutional structure the citizens have been encouraged to obey and treat as a source of rights and duties, and that the citizens have in fact done so'.[93] But he did not explain why this is so.

Fraenkel offers the key to the explanation. His analysis of the Dual State supports at least a negative hypothesis that the kind of arbitrary rule that we associate with tyranny is not possible within a Rule-of-Law State, even a perverse one. Recall a distinction central to Dworkin's legal theory between 'legislative rights'—'rights that the community's lawmaking powers be exercised in a certain way'—and 'legal rights'— 'political rights, but a special branch because they are properly enforceable on demand through adjudicative and coercive institutions without need for further legislation or lawmaking activity'.[94]

Since such enforceability requires officials to interpret the law, the only way to preclude something like Dworkin's interpretive model of law is to make the space of law subject to the decisions of officials in a prerogative state. In a Rule-of-Law State, human rights lawyers can use the procedural rights required to ensure congruence to contest those parts of the law that treat groups as inferior based on those parts of the law that give the groups equal status. If the procedural rights are abolished or rendered vacuous, the order will become a Dual State in which whether subjects have legal rights at all will increasingly come into question. If the groups are deprived, largely verging on altogether, of access to the protections afforded in the space of first-class citizenship, the legal order will begin to change into a Parallel State in which the tensions sketched earlier come to the fore.

The 'general political situation' of the Rule-of-Law State thus excludes the prerogative state. That shows that Fuller is right insofar as the general political situation is much as he describes legal order—authority, plus formal principles of legality, plus the procedural principles that are required for subjects to have the assurance that official decisions are congruent with the law. The state and its officials may act only within the limits of the authority they have from law.

93 Ronald Dworkin, 'A Reply' in Marshall Cohen (ed), *Ronald Dworkin & Contemporary Jurisprudence* (Duckworth 1984) 257.

94 Ronald Dworkin, *Justice for Hedgehogs* (Harvard University Press 2011) 407.

That does not by itself support the positive hypothesis that in a Rule-of-Law State, the discipline of legality to which the ruler is subject will produce reciprocity for all in the jural community such that the individual subjects is treated with 'dignity as a responsible agent'.[95] It does show, though, that to the extent that subjects are treated in a way that does not respect their dignity, they will be able to contest the law that negatively affects their subject status by resort to legal resources which lawyers can help them to exploit. Such human rights lawyering builds legitimacy from within, a highly problematic exercise within an unjust legal order since it legitimates the very injustice they struggle against.

On my account, Shklar's two insights tell us that even in states that we consider to be the best candidates for decency in our ever-troubled world, the practice of human rights lawyering will be morally fraught. Such lawyers will be legitimating injustice in the full knowledge that they cannot through court work alone change the regime against which they struggle. But as Sfard so eloquently tells, the lawyers can open cracks in the regime which force the society to confront the question of its most fundamental legal and political commitments. As long as those legal commitments are maintained, the space of law affords a kind of politics in which even the 'nobodies, weightless entities' may 'gain heft and volume and visibility'. And that may bring us close enough to the positive hypothesis.

For as long as a legal system is operative, Sfard's 'moral foundation' of 'a culture of good government' will be present, however shaky. While that foundation does not suffice to change the regime, it does provide a basis for human rights lawyers to contest aspects of it, which opens the cracks that can be contested by political movements with which the lawyers may be allied. In putting the challenge to the state on behalf of their clients, the lawyers are asking the state to articulate the nature of the bond between it and those subject to the law, the individuals in the jural community—all those over whom the state claims authority.

95 Fuller, *The Morality of Law* (n 14) 162. See Kristen Rundle, 'Form and Agency in Raz's Legal Positivism' (2013) 32 L & Phil 767.

Chapter 2

A taxonomy of injustice

Duncan Ivison

1.

John Rawls famously claimed that justice was the 'first virtue of social institutions, as truth is of systems of thought'.[1] Judith Shklar, on the other hand, when ranking the vices that posed the greatest threat to liberal democracy, said that we should put cruelty first. She defined cruelty as 'the deliberate infliction of physical, and secondarily emotional, pain upon a weaker person or group by stronger ones in order to achieve some end, tangible or intangible'.[2] For her, the best understanding of liberalism starts from the premise that the basic elements of political life are 'not discursive and reflective persons, nor friends and enemies, nor patriotic citizen-soldiers, nor energetic litigants, but the weak and the powerful'. The experience of injustice was also far broader and more diverse than how liberal theorists of justice tend to see it. Thus, what liberalism should focus on, above all, is securing 'freedom from the abuse of power and the intimidation of the defenceless that this difference invites'.[3] She called this the 'liberalism of fear'.

The relationship between Shklar's conception of the liberalism of fear and her analysis of injustice is not straightforward.[4] She thought cruelty was first

1 John Rawls, *A Theory of Justice* (rev edn, Harvard University Press 1999) 3.

2 Judith N Shklar, *Ordinary Vices* (Harvard University Press 1984) 7–9. This includes the fear of cruelty as well: see 8–9; Judith N Shklar, 'The Liberalism of Fear' in Nancy Rosenblum (ed), *Liberalism and the Moral Life* (Harvard University Press 1989) 21–22. Shklar isn't claiming that 'putting cruelty first' is a *sufficient* basis for political liberalism, as we'll see, but she does think it is a 'first principle, an act of moral intuition based on ample observation, from which liberalism can be built' ('The Liberalism of Fear' 29–30). See also Sally Haslanger, 'Systematic and Structural Injustice: Is There a Difference?' (2023) 98 Philosophy 1, 2.

3 Shklar, 'The Liberalism of Fear' (n 2) 27–28; Judith N Shklar, 'Rights in the Liberal Tradition' (2023) 71 PSR 279. As we'll see, this is a more demanding ideal than many critics assume, as she argues that the avoidance of not just cruelty but all forms of 'avoidable fear' ('Rights in the Liberal Tradition' 286) should be the aim of the liberalism of fear.

4 For a helpful analysis, see Robin Douglass, 'Cruelty, Injustice, and the Liberalism of Fear' (2023) 51 PT 790.

DOI: 10.4324/9781032676159-3

among the vices liberals should worry about, given the nature of politics.[5] However, although cruelty was often a source of injustice, it didn't exhaust it. Injustice is a broader and more complex phenomenon than most people think, she argued, and stems from feelings of anger, betrayal, disappointment, and resentment, as much as from cruelty.[6] Interestingly, as we'll see, she was somewhat leery of putting injustice first—at least in terms of its political importance.

But is the general claim true? Do we perceive or intuit injustice more directly than justice (and perhaps, more broadly, what is bad or wrong as compared to what is good)? Are the wrongs of hunger, torture, humiliation, or arbitrary power more vivid and accessible to us than being treated fairly or impartially? Theodor Adorno claimed that 'we may not know what the absolute good is or the absolute norm, we may not even know what man is or the human or humanity—but what the inhuman is we know very well indeed'.[7] In a recent book, Andrea Sangiovanni argues that we should not look for the basis of moral equality in general conceptions of dignity or equal moral worth, but rather in more fine-grained analyses of paradigmatic instances of dehumanization and objectification.[8] And Shklar thought so too; she claimed that a sense of injustice packed more of an emotional punch than justice did.

There are two claims, then, that I want to explore in this chapter. First, that a sense of injustice is more immediate and tangible than a sense of justice. And second, that cruelty and injustice, rather than justice, should be our starting point for legal and political theorizing about liberalism. Call these two claims, combined, the *asymmetry thesis*. Adopting this perspective has become an increasingly influential way of thinking about the nature of justice and liberalism, as we'll see. But what kind of injustice? Whose injustice?

Part of its appeal lies, I believe, in an increasing dissatisfaction with the 'high liberalism' of the Rawlsian era.[9] The ideal theory characteristic of his approach (and those influenced by him), so the argument goes, has failed to provide appropriately action-guiding theories for reshaping the world we live

5 Shklar isn't claiming that 'putting cruelty first' is a *sufficient* basis for political liberalism, as we'll see. But she does think it is a 'first principle, an act of moral intuition based on ample observation, from which liberalism can be built' (Shklar, 'The Liberalism of Fear' (n 2) 29–30).

6 Shklar, *Ordinary Vices* (n 2) 7, 18; Judith N Shklar, *The Faces of Injustice* (Yale University Press 1990) 83, 11, 52, 57.

7 Theodore Adorno, *The Problems of Moral Philosophy* (Stanford University Press 1999) 175.

8 Andrea Sangiovanni, *Humanity without Dignity: Moral Equality, Respect, and Human Rights* (Harvard University Press 2017). See also Ian Shapiro, *Democratic Justice* (Yale University Press 1999).

9 Interestingly, Shklar did not aim her critique of the standard model of justice at Rawls. As Katrina Forrester points out, she defended his approach against various critics, despite her more general concerns about formalism in moral and legal theory ('Judith Shklar, Bernard Williams and Political Realism' (2012) 11 Eur J Political Theory 247, 260–63).

in today. For some, this is because Rawlsians have the wrong social theory underpinning their account of which injustices matter and why. Thus, the Rawlsian story has become a ghost story: although the social and economic conditions required for the realization of justice as fairness no longer obtain, the theory still lingers, like a bad dream, clouding our political imagination.[10] For others, the extent to which highly moralized conceptions still structure much of Rawls's argument (even in the avowedly 'political' version of his theory) misconstrues the distinctive task of political philosophy, which is not, as Bernard Williams puts is, simply applied moral philosophy.[11]

Alongside this methodological dissatisfaction with high liberalism has been an increasing demand for greater attention to be paid to political theory forged on the ground, or to what Deva Woodly calls, after Dewey, the 'social intelligence' of social movements. According to her, writing about Black Lives Matter:

> while the vision for the movement arises from imagination, its end goal is neither fixed nor utopian, but is instead guided by an ethic of care and habit of inquiry that is embedded in an intelligent and iterative political process aimed at both changing the subject and ushering in new world possibilities.[12]

In this chapter, I want to assess the claims at the heart of the asymmetry thesis. To begin with, I will explore Shklar's argument in more detail, as well as two other approaches that start from injustice—Amartya Sen's and Philip Pettit's. This will give us a sense of the diversity of ways of making sense of injustice. I then want to step back and offer a taxonomy of the kinds of injustice we find in contemporary political theory, informed by these different approaches, as a way of testing the plausibility of the asymmetry thesis.

The upshot of my argument will be that although aspects of the thesis might be empirically true—it might well be that our sense of injustice is more vivid and immediate than that of justice—it is normatively problematic. Our

10 Katrina Forrester, *In the Shadow of Justice: Postwar Liberalism and the Remaking of Political Philosophy* (Princeton University Press 2019). I don't evaluate Forrester's argument here. However, it's clear that Rawls's positive theory was informed by a social critique of American society, especially what he saw as its underlying meritocratic ideal. Rawls thought that, left unaddressed, the inequalities of American society would lead inevitably to a politics of resentment, envy, and bitterness on the part of the worst-off (Rawls, *A Theory of Justice* (n 1) 91, 197–98, 468–69).

11 Bernard Williams, *In the Beginning Was the Deed: Realism and Moralism in Political Argument* (Princeton University Press 2008) 2–3. See also Raymond Geuss, *Philosophy and Real Politics* (Princeton University Press 2008).

12 Deva Woodly, *Reckoning: Black Lives Matter and the Democratic Necessity of Social Movements* (Princeton University Press 2022) 57. See also Erin Pineda, *Seeing Like an Activist: Civil Disobedience and the Civil Rights Movement* (OUP 2021).

sense of injustice can be just as limited and prone to distortion from ideology, resentment, and moral blindness as that of justice.[13] Thus, injustice should not take conceptual priority over justice. Rather, we need to grasp the complex relation between them. Ideal justice is often radically indeterminate, but it isn't useless. Our theories of justice need to be sensitive to the location specificness—the particularity—of claims of injustice.[14] Interestingly, Shklar helps us see this.

2.

For Shklar, as I have already mentioned, a sense of injustice is more palpable than a sense of justice: 'even when justice and fairness do prevail', Shklar writes, 'they are undramatic and forgettable, while injustice is always keenly felt and memorable'.[15] This is because our claims about injustice are usually anchored in feelings of anger, betrayal, humiliation, and being dissed, especially by those who exercise power over us.[16] They are also often borne of frustration, of not being able to find the right words to describe our feelings, or of not being heard when we do. Shklar turns to literary examples to make this point. The characters of Nora in Ibsen's *A Doll's House*, or Coalhouse in EL Doctorow's *Ragtime*, among others, provide vivid examples of people struggling to articulate their sense of wrongness and injustice within the existing linguistic and social registers of justice.[17]

Injustice is also not mainly about the violation of rules or principles. It is more pluralistic and complex than that. However, for Shklar, betrayal is at the heart of it.[18] And in a liberal democracy, a sense of betrayal and being let down is inevitable—by our fellow citizens, our governments, the legal system, and other institutions—which means disappointment is never far

13 As Shklar herself points out: see *The Faces of Injustice* (n 6) 4, 58, 27–28, 60–65.

14 See Eric Beerbohm, 'The Conceptual Priority of Injustice' (2014) 5 Jurisprud 329, 342–43, and the following text.

15 Shklar, *The Faces of Injustice* (n 6) 105. There is evidence from the psychological literature that 'negative emotions' (fear, anger, disgust, rage) and negative information tend to weigh more heavily on the brain than do positive emotions and information: see Stuart Soroka, Patrick Fournier, and Lilach Nir, 'Cross-national Evidence of Negativity Bias in Psychophysiological Reactions to News' (2019) 116(38) Proc Natl Acad Sci U S A 18888.

16 Shklar, *Ordinary Vices* (n 2) 184–85, 220; Shklar, *The Faces of Injustice* (n 6) 11, 52, 57, 83.

17 *The Faces of Injustice* (n 6) 95–98; but see the entire chapter ('The Sense of Injustice'). See also the discussion about the uses of fiction and literature in political theory in *Ordinary Vices* (n 2) 230; and Forrester, 'Judith Shklar, Bernard Williams and Political Realism' (n 9) 257. Ibsen's *A Doll's House* is discussed in a similar vein by Stanley Cavell, *Conditions Handsome and Unhandsome: The Constitution of Emersonian Perfectionism* (Open Court 1990). See also Philip Pettit, *Just Freedom: A Moral Compass for a Complex World* (W.W. Norton & Company 2014); Rainer Forst, *Justification and Critique: Towards a Critical Theory of Politics* (Polity 2014).

18 Shklar, *The Faces of Injustice* (n 6) 52.

behind.[19] Democracy is thus a delicate balancing act between trust and distrust.[20] There can even be injustice *in* justice, given that any set of political and legal institutions will inevitably end up disrupting the expectations of some citizens more than others. Shklar is sceptical that more formalist theories of justice can account for the diversity of our experiences of injustice.[21]

As I mentioned previously, the relationship between cruelty and injustice in Shklar's work is complex. However, her account of liberalism draws on both the ubiquity of injustice and the threat that cruelty poses to liberal societies. This led her to offer what seems like an austere account of liberalism as focused mainly on minimizing the damage we can do to each other. However, in her first book, *After Utopia* (1957), she lacerated 'conservative liberalism', and especially libertarianism, for turning its back on the Enlightenment ideals of individual and collective emancipation and embracing instead a parched fatalism about the limits of politics. 'The Enlightenment has no heirs', she declared, and thus 'the belief that people can control and improve themselves and, collectively, their social environment'.[22] This included what must be one of the earliest critiques of neoliberalism, which she saw as falsely equating Enlightenment hopes of social and political freedom with the evils of 'rationalism' and 'planning' that led to twentieth-century totalitarianism. According to Samuel Moyn, this was a devastating critique of the very 'cold war liberalism' she would eventually embrace herself.[23]

Whatever the ultimate trajectory of Shklar's liberalism, there is no question that in her later work, and especially in *Ordinary Vices*, *The Faces of Injustice*, and *American Citizenship*, she focused increasingly on the conflicts between the individual and her social and political environment, as well as the repeated failures of the state to treat its citizens respectfully.[24] As she put

19 Shklar, *Ordinary Vices* (n 2) 72, 162; Shklar, *The Faces of Injustice* (n 6) especially chs 1–2.

20 I have tried to say more about this balancing act in Duncan Ivison, 'Democratic Trust and Injustice' (2023) 2 JSPP 78.

21 Shklar, *Ordinary Vices* (n 2) 7–8. See the discussions by Bernard Yack, 'Putting Injustice First: An Alternative Approach to Liberal Pluralism' (1999) 66 Soc Res 1103; and Forrester, 'Judith Shklar, Bernard Williams and Political Realism' (n 9) 247–72. Forrester argues that this scepticism didn't extend to Rawls's theory, for reasons that aren't entirely clear.

22 Judith N Shklar, *After Utopia: The Decline of Political Faith* (Princeton University Press 1957) 219.

23 Samuel Moyn, 'Before—and Beyond—the Liberalism of Fear' in Samantha Ashenden and Andreas Hess (eds), *Between Utopia and Realism: The Political Thought of Judith N Shklar* (University of Pennsylvania Press 2019) 24–30; and Samuel Moyn, *Liberalism Against Itself: Cold War Intellectuals and the Making of Our Times* (Yale University Press 2023).

24 For a perceptive discussion of Shklar's psychological framing of politics and the way it moves between exposing the psychic costs of transformative politics on the one hand, and the value of individuality and freedom on the other, see Katrina Forrester, 'Experience, Ideology, and the Politics of Psychology' in Samantha Ashenden and Andreas Hess (eds), *Between Utopia and Realism: The Political Thought of Judith N Shklar* (University of Pennsylvania Press 2019) 136.

it in a letter to Quentin Skinner in 1991, commenting on his then-emerging conception of 'neo-republican' liberty:

> You want to see a more engaged and a more active citizenry ready to take part in day-to-day politics, and to find in collective action a recognisable form of freedom. As long as this does not mask the awful irrationality and sheer violence that are the characteristic mark of politics here and now, and especially the function of xenophobia in providing the normal social glue, I don't see why anyone should object to this project.[25]

Two aspects of the liberalism of fear can be glimpsed in this passage. First, the unblinking recognition of the persistence of both cruelty and injustice in political life. Liberalism is a fragile achievement, and the equal rights and legal protections provided through liberal citizenship are neither inevitable nor immune from being undermined (in fact, Shklar understood the origins of liberal rights as, in part, stemming from expressions of 'outrage' at instances of injustice and cruelty).[26] The history of American political thought and political institutions reflects this struggle: 'America embarked on two experiments simultaneously', Shklar argued in her 1990 presidential address to the American Political Science Association, 'one in democracy, the other in tyranny'.[27] Putting cruelty and the fear of cruelty first also means addressing inequality, which creates the conditions for cruelty to emerge in the first place.[28] So, liberalism needs to be tough on cruelty but also on the causes of cruelty.

This leads to the second and perhaps less commented-on aspect of the liberalism of fear: that democracy is a necessary condition for liberal freedom, just because of the ubiquity of injustice.[29] Liberal societies need to find ways to ensure that the voices of victims receive their due. It's fatal to the sustainability of liberal institutions if they don't. Although Shklar's vision of democratic liberalism is tempered by a 'grim realism' about political power,

25 Quentin Skinner, 'The Last Academic Project' in Samantha Ashenden and Andreas Hess (eds), *Between Utopia and Realism: The Political Thought of Judith N Shklar* (University of Pennsylvania Press 2019) 261. Is there a better example of a project being damned with faint praise?

26 Judith N Shklar, 'Injustice, Injury, and Equality' in Frank S Lucash (ed), *Justice and Equality Here and Now* (Cornell University Press 1986) 24–27.

27 Judith N Shklar, 'Redeeming American Political Theory' (1991) 85 APSR 3. Slavery is also at the heart of her analysis of citizenship in Judith N Shklar, *American Citizenship: The Quest for Inclusion* (Harvard University Press 1991).

28 Shklar, *Ordinary Vices* (n 2) 28–29; Shklar, 'Liberalism of Fear' (n 2) 29–31; Shklar, 'Rights in the Liberal Tradition' (n 3) 285–88.

29 But see Douglass, 'Cruelty, Injustice, and the Liberalism of Fear' (n 4); and Samantha Ashenden and Andreas Hess, 'Republican Elements in the Liberalism of Fear' (2018) 9 ZPTh 209.

the institutions of representative democracy and procedural justice are not merely formal.[30] They provide citizens access to political forms of 'rectification' for expressing their sense of injustice and having their social standing affirmed in the process.[31] Moreover, they impose a duty of public deliberation not only on public officials, but on all of us. At the very least, they provide a voice to the victims of injustice, without being able to fully satisfy their unquenchable desire for redress.[32] Almost every law and instance of social and political change will be experienced by someone as unjust. That doesn't mean change can never be justified. But, as Bernard Williams argued, there can still be 'reasonable resentment' felt by those whose liberty is justifiably constrained.[33] The promise of liberal democratic institutions is that they provide a way of striking a balance between the importance of settled expectations, on the one hand, and the need for social and political change, on the other.

As a result, the liberalism of fear places considerable demands on citizens. It also creates what Shklar refers to as 'extraordinary ethical difficulties' for them, including being willing to live with deep diversity, unresolvable conflicts, and a constant balancing between public and private imperatives. It seeks to promote

> at every turn, policies, practices, and beliefs that will diminish the sources of fear and fortify us sufficiently to enable us to respect ourselves and others and to enable us to argue with rather than to destroy those who differ from us.[34]

And even once 'primary justice' is secured—always imperfectly and contingently—new forms of power will emerge, which in turn will generate new demands for social and political change, and thus new demands on citizens. Although ruthlessly pragmatic, it's a less austere vision of liberalism than many suggest.

3.

Shklar never had the opportunity to extend her argument about the liberalism of fear beyond a relatively high-level sketch (although, as I have suggested, there are hints of a richer account spread across her work). How else might our thinking about justice be shaped by taking injustice and cruelty, as Shklar insisted, as distinctive phenomena in their own right?

30 Shklar, *Ordinary Vices* (n 2) 42–43.
31 Shklar, *The Faces of Injustice* (n 6) 124; Shklar, 'Rights in the Liberal Tradition' (n 3) 287.
32 Shklar, *The Faces of Injustice* (n 6) 125–26.
33 Williams (n 11) 122–24; see also Yack, 'Putting Cruelty First' (n 21).
34 Shklar, 'Rights in the Liberal Tradition' (n 3) 287. See also Shklar, 'Liberalism of Fear' (n 2) 33–34.

I want to consider two recent approaches that claim to start, to a certain extent, from the experience of injustice: Amartya Sen's conception of 'anti-transcendentalist' justice and Philip Pettit's conception of 'republican freedom'.

In *The Idea of Justice*, Sen argues that we should abandon what he calls Rawls's 'transcendental institutionalism' and adopt a more practically oriented 'realization-focused comparison'.[35] Drawing on something like the asymmetry thesis, he claims that we don't need a fully worked-out theory of justice to identify which injustices matter or what to do about them. Indeed, even more strongly, he claims that focusing on *ideal* theories of justice is a mistake, because it obscures important aspects of injustice that the Rawlsian approach, for example, is incapable of addressing.

I won't reconstruct the entire argument here, but rather focus on Sen's critique of ideal theory and the development of his more comparative approach. By 'transcendental', Sen means the attempt to develop an ideal or perfectly just society as a means of social critique. By 'institutionalism', he means the attempt to specify the necessary institutions required for realizing justice, as opposed to focusing on the behaviour of individuals. Rawls focuses his principles of justice on what he calls the 'basic structure' of society, as opposed to individual behaviour (although there are 'very great' virtues associated with being a citizen of a well-ordered society, and individuals are responsible for their behaviour within generally just institutions). The problem, Sen thinks, is that this fails to deliver a theory of justice for the 'real world'. There are at least three reasons why.

First, grasping the injustice of the 'iniquities of hunger, illiteracy, torture, arbitrary incarceration, or medical exclusion', or the 'grotesque subjugation of women', does not require an account of the perfectly just society.[36] We can compare societies as more or less just based on these criteria without an ideal theory; indeed, he argues that it is neither necessary nor sufficient for enabling us to make the kind of judgments that help us understand how close or far away arrangements are from justice. Ideals of perfect justice help us understand 'absolute justice' but not relative justice in imperfect circumstances. A society in which people are regularly tortured is clearly more unjust than one in which they aren't. We don't need a theory of perfect justice to tell us that. But more importantly, an approach that is focused on a set of constraints to which society should conform (in Rawls's case, the two principles), rather than a goal or target it should promote, fails to offer sufficient guidance as to what happens when there is less than full compliance with those constraints.

Second, ideal theories of justice are inevitably parochial. For Rawls, justice is realized mainly through the state. This 'institutionalist' character of perfect

35 Amartya Sen, *The Idea of Justice* (Harvard University Press 2009).
36 Amartya Sen, *The Idea of Justice* (Harvard University Press 2009) 96.

justice tends to ignore or downplay global forms of injustice, and thus the need for transnational conceptions of distributive justice. Despite Rawls's attempt at developing the international dimensions of his argument in his *Law of Peoples*,[37] as well as various attempts by others at extending his theory in a more cosmopolitan direction, Sen thinks the Rawlsian approach inevitably entails a form of nationally constrained transcendental institutionalism.

Finally, Sen thinks the Rawlsian approach is inflexible, and insufficiently pluralistic, since it's unrealistic to think a theory of justice for the real world can be grounded in such a narrow set of principles.[38] Indeed, the expectation that we will converge on a narrow set of principles precludes a wider dialogue about justice that is required given the deeply pluralistic world we live in today. We should expect our principles to change and adapt as we encounter unexpected challenges and learn to appreciate new forms of domination and injustice. Starting from an ideal of perfect justice militates against this kind of dialogic and social learning approach to public reasoning more generally.

There is much that is problematic with Sen's account of Rawls's approach, but I won't try to defend Rawls here. Instead, my point is simply to demonstrate one way in which theorizing about justice might go, starting from premises akin to the asymmetry thesis. For Sen, our thinking about justice should start from our sense of injustices today and work up from there, as opposed to starting from ideal principles and working down.[39]

Consider a second possibility, this time Philip Pettit's neo-republican account of 'just freedom'. Freedom, for Pettit, requires not just the absence of interference but of actual and potential subjection to another. Freedom as non-domination is to be free of subjection to the will of others.[40] However, for our purposes, what is interesting is the way Pettit frames his approach. First, he sets it against what he calls the standard approach to justice. These

37 John Rawls, *The Law of Peoples; with the Idea of Public Reason Revisited* (Harvard University Press 1999).

38 Sen (n 35) 106–07.

39 It's interesting to contemplate whether 'justice as capabilities' meets these criteria, at least as developed by Nussbaum, which draws on Aristotelian and Indian sources, as well as developmental economics, for its claims about those central human capabilities and functioning required for well-being: see Martha C Nussbaum, *Creating Capabilities: The Human Development Approach* (Harvard University Press 2011). On the face of it, it doesn't, given that Nussbaum is trying to establish an independent benchmark against which to assess existing social and political arrangements. She also embraces Rawls's political turn in his later work—and especially the 'fact of reasonable pluralism' about the good—as a critical part of the overall justification of the capabilities approach. See John Rawls, *Political Liberalism* (Columbia University Press 1993).

40 There are different ways of making sense of both domination and non-domination. I will come back to this below. Three notable alternatives that inform my approach, in addition to Pettit's, are Iris Marion Young, *Responsibility for Justice* (OUP 2011); Charles W Mills, 'I—Racial Justice' (2018) 92 Aristot Soc Suppl 69; and Sally Haslanger, *Ideology in Practice: What Does Ideology Do?* (Marquette University Press 2021).

approaches invoke our intuitions about what justice means and demands in a particular society. But our intuitions are often vague and conflicting, and they are capable of being extended to support diametrically opposed conceptions. Moreover, why trust our intuitions? Aren't they often the product of deeply unjust arrangements and forms of ideology themselves? The freedom ideal, on the other hand, offers a 'more sharply focused approach'.[41] The requirements for social justice should be determined by which social arrangements 'best promote people's enjoyment of freedom of non-domination'. Freedom, in this sense, is a 'gateway good'—a good whose realization promises to bring the realization of other goods in its train.[42] We don't need to fall back on vague intuitions about justice to determine which social arrangements are required, but rather should focus on what is required for people to be non-dominated by those in power. Thus, for example, to be poor is unjust because it places you at the mercy of others who have more resources, to live in fear of how the rich and powerful will treat you, and to lack the ability to exercise your choices according to your own preferences.[43]

Second, the focus on domination is itself meant to be realistic, in the sense of being anti-moralistic and indeed 'anti-transcendental'—of 'guiding people's judgements of their actual society and their actions within it'.[44] Republicans start from the 'domination complaint', which is ubiquitous in the world we inhabit. Most of us have had the experience, Pettit claims, of being under the whim of another, even when we don't necessarily experience ill treatment, whether in our personal or collective lives. Most of us understand what it might feel like to have no legal or social recourse against such arbitrary power over our choices. The ideal of freedom of non-domination—although still an *ideal*—emerges from these experiences and emotions. It is resolutely 'anti-transcendental', according to Pettit, because it offers a target to be realized and then a set of practical heuristics for measuring how well one set of arrangements might do in meeting the ideal as compared to another, and thus the kind of political interventions required to realize it.[45] The extent to which

41 Philip Pettit, *Just Freedom: A Moral Compass for a Complex World* (W.W. Norton & Company 2014) xviii.

42 Philip Pettit, *Just Freedom: A Moral Compass for a Complex World* (W.W. Norton & Company 2014) xix.

43 Philip Pettit, *Just Freedom: A Moral Compass for a Complex World* (W.W. Norton & Company 2014) xviii–xix. Critics argue that Pettit's agent-centred focus on choice and individual freedom, as well as the intentional nature of domination (even in refraining from interfering) misses the structural aspects of domination and especially those impersonal and unintended actions of a multitude of actors. See Amy Allen, 'Domination in Global Politics: A Critique of Pettit's Neo-Republican Model' in Barabara Buckinx, Timothy Waligore, and Jonathan Trejo-Mathys (eds), *Domination and Global Political Justice: Conceptual, Historical and Institutional Perspectives* (Routledge 2015); Haslanger, 'Systemic and Structural Injustice' (n 2). Structural injustice sits within what I call 'political injustice' below.

44 Philip Pettit, 'Political Realism Meets Civic Republicanism' (2017) 20 CRISPP 331, 333–35.

45 Philip Pettit, 'Political Realism Meets Civic Republicanism' (2017) 20 CRISPP 337–38.

any regime fails these tests is 'likely to be perceptible to people within the society, notwithstanding the power of ideology'.[46]

Although there are important differences between the two approaches, both Sen and Pettit aim to start our thinking about justice from a more realistic place. Sen wants to link justice more closely with the realization of a rich set of human capabilities—the kinds of lives that people can lead—as opposed to a minimal set of basic capabilities (Rawls's 'primary goods') secured through pure procedural justice. Pettit wants to ground social justice in the experience of domination and to secure the means to ensure citizens can enjoy the greatest extent of freedom as non-domination possible, given the world as it is.

The sense of injustice looms large, then, in each of these accounts. For Pettit, we need to put domination first. Citizens need to be able to look each other in the eye, without fear or deference, and in doing so, enjoy a communal form of recognition that they are 'each more or less proof against the interference of others'.[47] From this 'eye-ball test', we can then get a sense of the adequacy of various institutional and distributional requirements required for securing freedom as non-domination. It gives us a rough-and-ready guide as to how much is required for protecting our freedom, and it grounds this protection in both relational and substantive equality.

For Sen, we need to put realizable forms of human flourishing at the heart of our politics. More specifically, we need to focus on the development of a rich array of human capabilities, combinable in different modes of human 'functionings', that have material and structural conditions required for their fulfilment. We get there by starting with injustice. We should forsake our dreams of perfect justice and concentrate, instead, on what we can realize in the here and now.

4.

Thus, in starting from injustice, we can end up in different places. For Shklar, we get to the liberalism of fear. For Sen, it's the capabilities approach to justice. For Pettit, it's the conception of freedom as non-domination. In each case, injustice isn't basic in the sense that it is fully independent of our thinking about justice, but rather, that it shouldn't be reduced to the violation of rules and principles.

There are powerful criticisms of this focus on the primacy of injustice and the rejection of ideal theory. One is the Kantian counter-argument that in rejecting a regulative ideal of justice, we either obscure the extent to which we

46 Philip Pettit, 'Political Realism Meets Civic Republicanism' (2017) 20 CRISPP 339. But on the power of ideology that focuses on its structural aspects to a greater extent than Pettit does, see Charles W Mills, ' "Ideal Theory" as Ideology' (2005) 20 Hypatia 165ff.

47 Pettit, *Just Freedom* (n 41) 99.

Table 2.1 Spheres of injustice

Moral	Distributive
Discursive	Political

are actually relying on one or risk arbitrariness in justifying what follows from our claims for social and political change.[48] And it's clear that Shklar, Sen, and Pettit all appeal to *some* kind of independent standard in assessing what is just or unjust, or which injustices are worse. However, I won't be assessing these critiques here. Instead, I want to step back and try to provide a rough taxonomy of contemporary conceptions of injustices, building on Shklar's insight that they are inherently diverse. I am not claiming that this exhausts every possible instance of injustice we can imagine. Human beings are endlessly creative in behaving badly towards each other. The categories I propose are general, within which there will be multiple variations and complexities. Nevertheless, I hope they capture some of the most important senses of injustice at play—at least for the moment—in contemporary political theory.

There are four broad categories of injustice—moral, political, discursive, and distributive. Any politically salient injustice will be a complex assemblage of these different aspects. I will return to this point below. However, for analytical purposes, I want to try and separate them out. I use a simple two-by-two table to visualize the broad spheres, but the action will be in the layering and cross-over between them as we come to understand the complexities on the ground.

A caveat: although the four spheres of injustice might seem to map onto corresponding spheres of justice, it's not my intention to defend a strict alignment between them here. There will always be remainders of injustice that resist easy conversion from one sphere to the next.

Moral injustice

By moral injustice, I mean the sense of being denied one's status as a moral agent, as someone who is entitled to be treated with equal respect and consideration by others. More specifically, it means being denied the ability both to raise certain kinds of claims against others and to be seen as owed certain things by others. This form of injustice is part of Shklar's argument for the prioritization of cruelty as the *summum malum* of political life, given the seemingly inescapable urge of the powerful to dominate the weak. The primary sense of injustice here is not a lack of resources or primary goods, but a sense of not being treated in a respectful way.

48 Rainer Forst, *Justice, Democracy and the Right to Justification: Rainer Forst in Dialogue* (Bloomsbury 2014) 194–200.

Now, there are different ways of cashing out the nature of this form of disrespect. For Pettit, as we saw, arbitrariness has to do with the ability of others to interfere with my *choices* as a citizen in substantial ways. You're only truly free if you have a certain 'depth' of freedom in relation to those choices that matter, which are the basic liberties.[49] Neo-Kantians like Rainer Forst, on the other hand, link this sense of injustice to being denied the respect owed as a 'subject of justification': that is, to be respected 'in one's dignity as a being who offers and demands justifications' for exercises of rule over them, and more specifically, to eliminate those that involve domination and exploitation.[50] To demand and offer justifications is part of what it means to be a moral agent and to be treated as a participatory equal in social and political life. Another variation of this idea can be found in Lon Fuller's account of the 'inner morality of law', departures from which are, as he put it, an 'affront to man's dignity as a responsible agent'.[51]

Whether the focus is on securing my ability to make choices that matter or that I am owed reasonable justifications for exercises of power over me, moral injustice involves the denial or violation of the moral agency that underpins such conceptions. I am diminished, as Jean Hampton put it, in the sense that my moral worth is taken to be of less value than others.[52] Slavery is the most egregious example of such injustice, but the idea can be extended in a range of ways, including, for example, to the situation of many migrant workers, asylum seekers, and refugees today. It can also be extended to the category of the non-human. One way of making sense of the idea of ecological injustice is the lack of due consideration being given to the moral standing of non-human animals, as well as to that of the value of nature itself.[53]

Discursive injustice

The site of discursive injustice lies, broadly, at the intersection of how knowledge is formed and deployed in social and political life. It sits within a broader set of questions to do with how language and interpretive schemes shape social and political outcomes and, in so doing, benefit some more than

49 Pettit, *Just Freedom* (n 41) 28–73.

50 Forst, *Justice, Democracy and the Right to Justification* (n 48) 7–10.

51 Lon Fuller, *The Morality of Law* (rev edn, Yale University Press 1969) 162. See also Darwell's conception of 'moral recognition respect' and the broader debate about recognition in contemporary political theory: Stephen L Darwall, 'Two Kinds of Respect' (1977) 88 Ethics 36.

52 Jean Hampton, 'Correcting Harms versus Righting Wrongs: The Goal of Retribution' (1992) 39 UCLA Law Rev 1659.

53 For this argument, see Dany Celermajer, Darren Chang, David Schlosberg, and Christine Winter, 'Liberalism and the More-Than-Human' in Duncan Ivison (ed), *The Elgar Research Handbook on Liberalism* (Edward Elgar Publishing 2024) 324–25.

others (even if we all benefit in coordinating around language and interpretive schemes more generally).[54] Our use of categories and interpretive schemes—packages of interrelated categories and concepts—is unavoidable and helps us make sense of and act on the world, but they can also distort our understanding when they are incomplete or inappropriate. We overlook or underestimate things we don't code for. And our discursive resources are inevitably shaped by unequal power relations that are structural in nature (see following discussion).[55] The powerful are almost never lost for words: the powerless frequently are.[56] There are two senses of discursive injustice here. First, when the voices of particular individuals and groups are literally suppressed—for example, through a denial of their basic political rights (the right to free speech, to vote, to assemble, to practice their religion, and so on).[57] The second is the way people are constructed as members of certain social kinds—as 'wives', 'mothers', 'citizens', 'migrants'—and which can result in them being subject to certain social constraints (or enablers), some of which might be harmful, including the extent to which they are genuinely 'heard' in various contexts.[58]

The wrongs of discursive and ontic injustice have to do with the way in which a society's epistemic systems embody inequalities, prejudices, and biases that disadvantage some groups more than others (or help perpetuate the advantage of a few). This can result in claims not being heard and/or discredited in various ways. There are hints of this form of injustice in Shklar's analysis of victimhood in *The Faces of Injustice*. No democrat, she argues, can accept an account of 'primary justice' that systematically silences expressions of injustice, however distorted they might be. Indeed, one of her arguments against minimalist forms of neoliberalism is that they are often impotent in the face of citizens' claims about their 'suffering'.[59]

But important recent work goes further in identifying the mechanisms at play. As Miranda Fricker (who takes inspiration, interestingly, from Shklar[60]) argues, a person's claim to recognition as a conveyor of knowledge is critical

54 Robert E Goodin, *Perpetuating Advantage: On the Mechanisms of Structural Injustice* (OUP 2023) 76–88.

55 Elizabeth Anderson, 'Epistemic Justice as a Virtue of Social Institutions' (2012) 26 Soc Epistemol 163.

56 Miranda Fricker, *Epistemic Injustice: Power and the Ethics of Knowing* (OUP 2007) 148, 161.

57 Here, the 'discursive' and 'political' quadrants of my table intersect and layer on top of each other.

58 See Katherine Jenkins, 'Ontic Injustice', (2020) 6 J Am Philos Assoc 188, 191.

59 Shklar, *The Faces of Injustice* (n 6) 117, 124–26.

60 Shklar provides the epigraph for Fricker's book (from *The Faces of Injustice*), as well as the inspiration for looking at an area of epistemic activity where injustice is the norm, rather than an aberration, and that the only way to see what is involved in epistemic justice is to start with that 'negative space' (Fricker (n 56) vii).

to her creating and achieving value. To be denied acknowledgement as a subject of knowledge harms one's self-development, just as much as it prevents society from seeing an injustice. To be silenced given the available public conceptual resources, and thus to be unable to interpret one's experience appropriately, or claim a hearing for that experience—what Fricker refers to as 'hermeneutical injustice'—can prevent people from becoming 'who they are'.[61] And as Elizabeth Anderson points out, as much as we can't avoid relying on stereotypes of various kinds in making credibility assessments—for example, education as a marker of credibility in situations where expertise is called for—these become problematic when educational resources are unequally distributed in ways that perpetuate advantages for some at the expense of others.[62] What seems like a reasonable set of assumptions about the credibility of a speaker can overlap with structural disadvantage faced by members of groups that are denied access to a decent education.

Thus, discursive injustice can distort or block socially and culturally disadvantaged groups' experience of injustice from being expressed and recognized. This prevents their claims from making their way into what William Connolly calls the 'register of justice'.[63] Our interpretive schemes can lock in and perpetuate disadvantage over time, unavoidable as they are.[64] They can operate both implicitly and explicitly as 'frames', or what Sally Haslanger calls 'cultural technē': clusters of social meanings upon which social practices and structures depend and which provide a 'stage-setting' for practical action in any social and political context.[65]

Ideology is cultural technē gone wrong. It blocks certain individuals and groups from recognizing or creating forms of value and/or distributes them in unjust ways. To make it even more complicated, most of us don't even know how ideology shapes us and how we reinforce its deleterious effects, given how we are interpellated into it through various means of socialization and subjectivation (the processes through which we become a social subject capable of recognizable agency). Racism, for example, is not merely a set of beliefs or attitudes, but also a set of material social practices—including, for example, segregation, police practices, educational policies, wage and employment patterns, and cultural norms. These all work to create and sustain distorted

61 Fricker (n 56) 5–8.

62 Anderson, 'Epistemic Justice as a Virtue of Social Institutions' (n 55) 169.

63 William E Connolly, *The Ethos of Pluralization* (University of Minnesota Press 1995).

64 Goodin, *Perpetuating Advantage* (n 54) 89–90.

65 Haslanger, *Ideology in Practice: What Does Ideology Do?* (n 40) 67. More specifically, a cultural technē is 'a cluster of concepts, background assumptions, norms, heuristics, scripts, metaphors, (and so on) that enable us to interpret and organize information and coordinate action, thought and affect' (62–63). Goodin pithily refers to this as the 'mental component' of structures (Goodin, *Perpetuating Advantage* (n 54) 89).

social meanings of race and shape social and political life—and thus people's opportunities—in profound ways.

What are the best means of criticizing those structures, practices, systems, and ideologies that perpetuate disadvantage, given how insidious they are and the way they shape both people's preferences and options? Interestingly, several of the approaches cited draw on something like the asymmetry thesis. Haslanger argues for 'collective, practice-directed, embedded' forms of social critique that resist postulating a normatively binding ideal (like Rawls's), but rather start from an embedded standpoint.[66] Charles Mills, on the other hand, despite a withering critique of Rawlsian ideal theory as a form of ideology itself, still believes Rawls's approach can be repurposed to support 'black radical liberalism'.[67] However, this requires taking the racist aspects of the 'basic structure' of society seriously. Drawing on Rawls's device of the veil of ignorance, Mills argues that we need to re-imagine it in non-ideal circumstances, now as members of groups (but not knowing which) in 'a racially oppressive, ill-ordered [White]-supremacist society, in which [Whites] dominate [non-Whites], as modelled by the racial domination contract'.[68] The kinds of principles that will emerge from this starting point, as opposed to Rawls's original one, will be dramatically different. Instead of distributive principles for a society envisaged as a fair system of cooperation, we get principles of corrective justice envisaged for a structurally oppressive society. Mills is clear that racial justice is not equivalent to social justice. A racially just society will continue to be unjust in other ways. However, it now forms part of a wider, more inclusive project of multidimensional social justice.

Distributive injustice

By distributive injustice, I mean the lack of access to the resources and opportunities required to live a decent life or to realize certain essential human functionings. This is perhaps the most familiar conception of injustice linked to egalitarian liberalism, but it stretches back to the ancient maxim of 'to each (or from each) his own'.

66 Sally Haslanger, 'Methods of Social Critique' in Anne Siegetsleitner, Andreas Oberprantacher, Marie-Luisa Frick, and Ulrich Metschl (eds), *Crisis and Critique: Philosophical Analysis and Current Events* (De Guyter 2021). No system is airtight. As individuals and groups move between different social contexts, they gain critical distance on different aspects of the cultural technē within which they are enmeshed. The idea that there is always slack in a system of relations of power is also central to Michel Foucault's conceptions of power and freedom. See Michel Foucault, 'Afterword: The Subject and Power' in Hubert L Dreyfus and Paul Rabinow (eds), *Michel Foucault: Beyond Structuralism and Hermeneutics* (Routledge 1982).

67 Charles Mills, *Black Rights/White Wrongs: The Critique of Racial Liberalism* (OUP 2017) 161–80, 201–16; Charles Mills, 'Theorizing Racial Justice' <https://tannerlectures.utah.edu/_resources/documents/a-to-z/m/MILLSTANNERLECTURE.pdf< accessed 5 June 2024.

68 Mills, 'Theorizing Racial Justice' (n 67) 47.

In contemporary political theory, this way of thinking about injustice has been shaped by two kinds of questions about inequality. First, 'equality of what'? Is it resources, welfare, liberty, or capabilities that people lack and are entitled to? And second, the question of how inequality emerges in the first place. Why are people in a situation where they lack basic liberties, resources, or capabilities? The former question has dominated egalitarian liberal theorizing, the latter its critics.

Rawls's theory presents a complex case for this quadrant, as he is concerned *both* with the equal distribution of goods, as well as the equal standing of citizens able to claim them. The problem of distributive justice then is 'how are the institutions of the basic structure to be regulated as one unified scheme of institutions so that a fair, efficient, and productive system of social cooperation can be maintained over time?'.[69] A just society must enable its citizens—conceived of as 'free and equal' and having capacities for both a sense of justice and a conception of the good (the two 'moral powers')—to have the means to realize their higher-order interests in developing and exercising these moral powers (and not only their material and physical desires). What needs to be distributed equally then are the 'all-purpose means' required for developing and exercising the two moral powers, which include basic rights and liberties (covered by the first principle), fair equality of opportunity (the first part of the second principle), income and wealth (where inequalities can exist only for the benefit of the worst off), and the social bases of self-respect.[70] To lack these primary goods *and* to be denied the standing to claim them is to suffer injustice.

There is no question that distributive injustice constitutes a powerful form of injustice—recall Shklar's warning that inequality breeds the conditions for cruelty. But, as Elizabeth Anderson and others point out, it is also incomplete.[71] Just distributions might still leave unjust social relations

69 Rawls, *A Theory of Justice* (n 1) 458.
70 Rawls, *Political Liberalism* (n 39) 75–76, 180–81.
71 Elizabeth Anderson, 'What Is the Point of Equality?' (1999) 109 Ethics 287. See also Samuel Scheffler, 'Choice, Circumstance, and the Value of Equality' (2005) 4 PPE 5. Rawls's position is complex, however, as the stability of a society structured by the two principles of justice requires that citizens are able to maintain their sense of self-respect (the most important primary good), which is secured by 'the public affirmation of the status of equal citizenship for all', consistently, over time, in their engagements with each other and the state (Rawls, *A Theory of Justice* (n 1) 478). This is lacking in a meritocratic society, argues Rawls, which ends up as a status competition between citizens over positional goods (like money and power) and where 'social cooperation to increase the conditions of self-respect is impossible' due to the fact that the 'means to status are . . . fixed and each man's gain is another's loss' (478). This leads ultimately to the emergence of a politics of resentment and 'hostile breakouts of envy' (469). For an interesting development of this theme, see Leif Wenar, 'A Society of Self-Respect' in Paul Weithman (ed), *Rawls's a Theory of Justice at 50* (CUP 2023) 336–55.

and institutions intact. 'Luck' egalitarians see the aim of justice as the undoing of unchosen inequality. But once we have equalized the circumstances of citizens' choices, they must bear the consequences of them, even if it leaves them worse off in other respects, including in ways that might undercut their ability to participate on equal terms in democratic society (both socially and politically). The heart of the critique is that these kinds of egalitarians miss what really matters about equality: not the equal distribution of primary goods, or welfare, but equality in social and political relations—what Anderson and others call democratic equality. Shklar anticipates this critique:

> the realm of injustice . . . does not stand outside of the gates of even the best of known states. Most injustices occur continuously within the frameworks of an established polity with an operative system of law in normal times.[72]

Thus, theories of distributive justice need mechanisms that allow their 'registers' of justice and injustice to be challenged and reshaped given new articulations of harm or wrongness.[73] This leads to my final sphere of injustice.

Political injustice

Political injustice stems from the lack of an equal opportunity to participate politically. To be treated unjustly is thus not only to lack certain goods, or to be discounted as a knower, or a speaker, or to lack a certain moral standing, but also to lack the effective means to exercise control over those institutions and practices that affect your most important interests, both directly and indirectly, in significant ways.[74] In other words, to have the right to participate

72 Shklar, *The Faces of Injustice* (n 6) 19. There are a range of experiences of injustice within an operative legal and political system: a Palestinian's experience of the legal regime of the Israeli occupation of the West Bank is very different from that of a welfare recipient in Australia, even if both involve forms of disrespect. I am indebted to conversations with David Dyzenhaus on this point and his chapter in this volume.

73 Rawls's delineation between the background culture, the public political culture, the public political forum, and public reason provides one account of how conceptions of justice (and injustice) can change over time: 'new variations may be proposed from time to time and older ones may cease to be represented. It is important that this be so; otherwise, the claims of groups or interests arising from social change might be repressed and fail to gain their appropriate political voice': John Rawls, *Political Liberalism* (expanded edn, Columbia University Press 2005) 452. For a discussion of how public reason can change, see Paul Patton, 'The Historicity of Public Reason' in Duncan Ivison (ed), *The Elgar Handbook to Liberalism* (Edward Elgar Publishing 2024).

74 There can be stronger and weaker senses of 'control' here. At a minimum, it means something like the ability to contest those forces acting on your most important interests, even if it's never possible to fully control for them.

on equal terms in the political process, as well as to enjoy social relationships that are, in Scheffler's phrase, 'unstructured by differences in rank, power and status endemic to human social life'.[75]

Although often overlapping, moral and political injustices are distinct and can come apart. Duties of civic reciprocity required to help sustain just institutions might not apply in circumstances of persistent, deep inequality—or where the burdens of unavoidable injustice become concentrated in one part of the community. But that doesn't necessarily void our moral duties towards others. We still have obligations to respect others' basic rights and not to treat them cruelly, even when forms of political disobedience or resistance might be justified.[76] Political injustice is one of the outcomes of what people mean, I think, when they talk about structural injustice. And this is what makes it both ubiquitous and so difficult to address. In Iris Young's classic formulation, structural injustice is produced when many people interact in complex ways—and according to normally accepted rules and practices—to produce outcomes that are unjust over time.[77] 'Social structures' are the accumulated outcomes of the actions of masses of individuals, the combination of which 'affects the conditions of the actions of others, often producing outcomes not intended by any of the participating agents'.[78] It's not just the exercise of brute power by the few, but the way advantage (and disadvantage) becomes embedded in impersonal structures that shape the subsequent exercises of agency by others over time. Structures, whether physical or social, channel the exercise of agency in a myriad of ways through various mechanisms that become entrenched in our social and political institutions.[79]

Racism is a particularly egregious example of a constraining feature of social structures, as are the ongoing legacies of colonial dispossession.[80] Sometimes this involves brute power exercised by individuals or groups over others, or the threat of doing so, but often it doesn't. Power can be exercised in ways other than through interference or even the threat of interference. The challenge is thus how to reshape these social practices and the structures they hold in place so that they enable members of disadvantaged groups to be on a more equal footing with others. And this is hard, just because the

75 Scheffler (n 69) 17.

76 Tommie Shelby, *Dark Ghettos: Injustice, Dissent, Reform* (Harvard University Press 2018) 217–22.

77 Iris Marion Young, *Justice and the Politics of Difference* (Princeton University Press 1990); Iris Marion Young, *Responsibility for Justice* (OUP 2011).

78 Young, *Responsibility for Justice* (n 77) 62–63.

79 For a helpful taxonomy of the mechanisms through which structural injustice is perpetuated, see Goodin, *Perpetuating Advantage* (n 54).

80 For a detailed discussion of the latter, see Duncan Ivison, *Can Liberal States Accommodate Indigenous Peoples?* (Polity Press 2020).

roots of these disadvantages run deep.[81] Distributive justice still matters, but now derivatively, as part of a broader project of overcoming the underlying distortions in relational power between differentially situated individuals and groups. This broader project is best characterized, I think, as creating the conditions for the realization of genuine democratic equality. Hence why I am calling it *political* injustice. To address it effectively requires not only 'head-on' attacks on the mechanisms that perpetuate advantage, but also more indirect and nuanced approaches. This might include, for example, in addition to ensuring the 'fair value' of people's liberty, in Rawls's phrase, also pluralizing the dominant modes of public reason in a political community, as a means of disrupting social biases by enabling minority groups to contribute to public debates and policy-making. But this requires democratic innovation.[82]

5.

The asymmetry thesis combines a claim about the apparent immediacy of our sense of injustice with a view that starting with injustice is a better way of proceeding when it comes to conceptualizing justice, as well as liberalism. Shklar argued that a sense of injustice was ineradicable from politics, but that there are better and worse ways of ensuring the voices of victims can be heard. Democratic institutions, the rule of law, a deep wariness of state power, and a kind of chastened citizenship—a willingness to 'argue with rather than to destroy those who differ from us'—form the outlines of a liberalism of fear. The only reliable test for identifying which injustices matter the most is 'to ask the likeliest victim'.[83]

It is no small irony that despite being seen as one of the most powerful exponents of starting with injustice, Shklar expresses some ambivalence about doing so.[84] Although liberal democratic institutions provide the best means of venting the emotions that drive claims of injustice, they are limited in being able to reconcile them. So, although there might be grounds to put

81 It's also hard, as Goodin and Young point out, because structural injustice acts through multiple channels and mechanisms—including through language, social norms, expectations, organizational structures, and networks—and therefore interventions must be designed to address the different channels through which advantage (and disadvantage) flow (see Goodin, *Perpetuating Advantage* (n 54) 18–9, 197–98).

82 See Goodin, *Perpetuating Advantage* (n 54) 174–98. A recent example of democratic innovation—and the challenges it can face—is the call for a constitutionally recognized Indigenous 'Voice to parliament' in Australia (see Ivison, *Can Liberal States Accommodate Indigenous Peoples?* (n 80)). Compare also recent work on introducing more 'popular' accountability into liberal constitutional regimes: eg, Camila Vergara, *Systematic Corruption: Constitutional Ideas for an Anti-Oligarchic Republic* (Princeton University Press 2020).

83 Shklar, 'Liberalism of Fear' (n 2) 17.

84 Shklar, *Ordinary Vices* (n 2) 3, 4, 221; Shklar, *The Faces of Injustice* (n 6) 39, 107, 109.

cruelty first, it's not clear that we should always put injustice first. (*The Faces of Injustice*, unlike *Ordinary Vices*, is not a rankings exercise.) She warned that the demands these claims generated might prove to be unquenchable. Prioritizing cruelty thus means learning to live with injustice.

Taking inspiration from Shklar's approach, but resisting her narrowing of focus for liberalism, I have tried to show that claims of injustice in contemporary politics usually involve a complex compound of the four spheres outlined above. Instead of putting cruelty or injustice first, we need to find ways of democratizing our conceptualizations of both justice and injustice to ensure we don't reify either. And for that, we need a rich account of democratic liberalism, rather than a minimalist one.

Chapter 3

Political contempt, divided societies, and transitional justice

Colleen Murphy[1]

This chapter explores one face of injustice: political contempt. Although Judith Shklar does not directly address contempt, it can be one way the sense of injustice is expressed. As I discuss in greater detail in the next section, to hold another in contempt is to regard them as responsible for failing to meet an interpersonal ideal. *Political* contempt takes as its object the character of individuals qua fellow legal subjects/members of a political community, and/or qua officials as measured against some ideal for those roles. Such character can, but need not necessarily, be revealed by the commission of specific acts of injustice.

More specifically, I concentrate upon political contempt within deeply divided political contexts where transitional justice is required, being proposed, or pursued. Transitional justice processes, such as trials, truth commissions, or reparations, are established within profoundly imperfect, non-ideal communities and are charged with responding to widespread human rights violations. The contexts in which such processes are adopted are ones in which injustice is deeply rooted, contempt is pervasive, and the structure of political relationships is in need of transformation.[2]

My aim in this chapter is to challenge the claim that political contempt is a permissible response to injustice, *especially* in contexts where injustice

1 Earlier versions of this chapter were presented at the Julius Stone Institute of Jurisprudence at the University of Sydney, the Department of Political Science at LUISS University, the UNAM Philosophy Institute at the Universidad Nacional Autónoma de México, the Centre for International Criminal Justice at the Vrije University Amsterdam, the North American Society for Social Philosophy Annual Conference, and the Department of Political Science and International Relations and the Thumos Center at the Department of Philosophy in the University of Geneva. I am grateful for the very helpful feedback I received from participants. Special thanks to Juan Espindola, Emanuela Ceva, Beatriz Mayans, Barbora Hola, Kevin Walton, and Valentina Gentile for the invitations to present and to Kristen Rundle for extremely detailed and insightful comments. Finally, I thank an anonymous reviewer for comments on an earlier draft and Kevin Walton, Wojciech Sadurski, and Coel Kirby for editorial guidance.

2 On this understanding, see Colleen Murphy, *The Conceptual Foundations of Transitional Justice* (CUP 2017).

DOI: 10.4324/9781032676159-4

runs deep and transitional justice is needed. Analytic philosopher Michelle Mason articulates the account of contempt with which I begin. Mason argues that contempt, properly focused, can be morally justified.[3] In making this case, she draws on intuitive reactions to Nazis such as Franz Stangl. Her line of argument resonates with philosophers such as Macalester Bell writing about oppression and the importance of political contempt for victims of oppression.[4]

I argue that the ability to judge an individual's character in the manner political contempt expresses depends on conditions that are missing in deeply divided societies. In making my case, I adapt theoretical starting points and draw upon central insights of Shklar. Like Shklar, my analysis is rooted not in the context of the nearly just societies of ideal theory, but rather in the non-ideal contexts of deeply divided societies grappling with how to address and redress widespread wrongdoing. As if heeding Shklar's injunction to avoid injustice by taking 'the victim's view into full account and give her voice its full weight',[5] transitional justice is increasingly 'victim-centred', prioritizing the needs and voices of victims. This prioritization developed out of recognition that the experience of victims during periods of conflict or repression are often neither understood nor acknowledged, either officially or by many segments of the community. The view of victims is needed for processes of justice or repair to be effective. Finally, Shklar famously recognized that the line drawn between bad luck and injustice is deeply political and drawn differently by various individuals and communities.[6] The divide between bad luck and injustice institutionally recognized often fundamentally changes through transitional justice. Massive legal confiscation of land by the South African apartheid government during the implementation of the Group Areas Act left the Black South Africans whose land was taken 'out of luck'. Yet such confiscation became the grounds for calls for redress and land redistribution following the transition to a multiracial democracy. In the new South Africa, the lines between luck and injustice officially changed.

However, despite these close affinities, my argument against contempt is in part an argument against Shklar's conception of the sense of injustice. Shklar correctly recognizes that the subject's experience or sense of injustice is not infallible, and that judgments of the line between luck and justice can be in conflict. She also discusses forms of group-based injustice and oppression sanctioned and enforced by the state, such as slavery in the context of the United States. Yet, at its core, the experience of the sense of injustice is, for Shklar, an individual one, which is directly experienced unmediated by the

3 Michelle Mason, 'Contempt as a Moral Attitude' (2003) 113 Ethics 234.

4 Macalester Bell, 'A Woman's Scorn: Toward a Feminist Defense of Contempt as a Moral Emotion' (2005) 20 Hypatia 80; Macalester Bell, *Hard Feelings: The Moral Psychology of Contempt* (OUP 2013).

5 Judith N Shklar, *The Faces of Injustice* (Yale University Press 1990) 126.

6 Judith N Shklar, *The Faces of Injustice* (Yale University Press 1990) 126.

prevailing ideologies underpinning and justifying institutional orders or by the groups of which they are members.[7] As Katrina Forrester puts it:

> [t]here was, Shklar seemed to assume, a realm of experience uncontaminated by ideology, and a psychological subject that existed apart from politics, even if molded by it. This realm provided the ground for criticism when it came to explaining what was wrong with an ideology. It was not only an ideology's objective features that mattered, but the gap between it and this experience.[8]

In explaining why political contempt is problematic, I explain why and how the sense of injustice in deeply divided political contexts is mediated by group identities in a way that Shklar does not adequately recognize. Constitutive of deeply divided societies are incommensurable narratives of who is a victim and who the perpetrator, of who has been betrayed, and of what constitutes wrongdoing or injustice.[9] *How* these incommensurable perspectives develop among individuals is, contra Shklar, deeply tied to the background political institutional context and the structure of group-based identities, both of which influence the judgments and experiences of injustice.

In my view, political contempt in divided societies does not express an evaluation of the character of its object because there is no judgment of the *individual* and their character that is made. Nor is there the basis present to make such individualized judgments. The normative upshot is that inferences about or judgments of character taken to be revealed by parties implicated in human rights violations should be eschewed. Rather than taking the sense of injustice expressed through contempt as the starting point for political action, this sense of injustice should be set aside. Instead of reacting to who someone is, reactive attitudes should focus (exclusively) on what someone did.

The first section of this chapter explains what contempt is and why it is morally permissible, according to Mason and Bell. The second section draws out the implications of their analysis. In societies in which transitional justice is being pursued or is needed, the permission for political contempt will be expansive. However, I argue, the permission entailed by political contempt to refuse to engage carries significant moral costs in impeding the possibility of transitional justice. The third section illustrates what pervasive contempt looks like, drawing on the example of the contemporary United States, and explains why it is appropriate to include some examples of consolidated democracies in discussions of deeply divided societies in need of transitional justice. The fourth turns to the

7 On this point, see Katrina Forrester, 'Experience, Ideology, and the Politics of Psychology' in Samantha Ashenden and Andreas Hess (eds), *Between Utopia and Realism* (University of Pennsylvania Press 2019).

8 On this point, see Katrina Forrester, 'Experience, Ideology, and the Politics of Psychology' in Samantha Ashenden and Andreas Hess (eds), *Between Utopia and Realism* (University of Pennsylvania Press 2019) 144.

9 Robin Douglass, 'Cruelty, Injustice, and the Liberalism of Fear' (2023) 51 PT 790, 800.

structure of group identities in deeply divided communities and how that structure undermines the epistemic grounds needed for there to be properly focused political contempt, grounds that Bell and Mason too easily assume are present.

1. Contempt as a face of injustice

Philosopher Michelle Mason has argued that contempt, properly focused, can be morally justified.[10] Contempt, Mason argues, is a reactive attitude that is responsive to the will of another, where the will is taken to reflect the other's basic character. Contempt reacts to *who someone is*, which is often revealed by how someone acts.

Contempt, Mason writes, is an attitude in which the object is viewed 'as low in the sense of ranking low in worth as a person in virtue of falling short of some legitimate interpersonal ideal of the person, one the contemner endorses if not one that she herself succeeds in meeting'.[11] The object of contempt is seen as inferior. She has less value in virtue of failing as a person along a particular dimension. In revealing who they are, the contemptible show themselves to be the kind of people who do not merit our respect.

Phenomenologically, contempt is experienced as repulsion or aversion to the object of our contempt. Our aversion to someone 'permeates' our interactions. At its limit, Mason writes, 'contempt can so contaminate one person's view of another that there is a point beyond which forgiveness and reconciliation might no longer be forthcoming'.[12]

Under certain conditions, Mason argues, contempt can be properly focused and morally appropriate.[13] Specifically, contempt is fitting when it is (1) a response to a person because they have in fact violated an interpersonal ideal (2) that it is legitimate to expect them to meet, and (3) this violation is a product of a character trait for which an individual is responsible. Mason also notes that justifications of contempt require the contemner to be non-hypocritical. Should it turn out that the contemner herself fails to meet the ideal to which she is holding the contemptible to account, she would regard herself as contemptible as well.

Mason distinguishes contempt from bigotry. While bigotry is based on a judgment that someone fails to meet an ideal, this failure is not predicated on the violation of a legitimate interpersonal ideal for which an individual is responsible. Instead, bigotry is predicated on a judgment of failure 'to meet a certain ideal of ethnicity, sex, or color of skin'.[14] Bigotry, Mason argues, thus fails condition

10 Mason (n 3).
11 Mason (n 3) 241.
12 Mason (n 3) 249.
13 Mason (n 3) 250.
14 Mason (n 3) 257.

(2) above, by focusing on aspects of a person that are beyond their control, and bigotry fails condition (3) by appealing to an ideal that is not legitimate.

Mason also argues that contempt is compatible with recognizing the dignity of persons. Contempt is a reactive attitude directed towards moral agents. To be incapable of feeling contempt towards someone is, Mason suggests, to fail to see or treat someone as a moral agent. The contemptible does not merit *appraisal respect*, which is earned when an individual achieves a certain interpersonal ideal.[15] Though they lose appraisal respect, Mason is careful to note that the contemptible still merits *recognition respect*. This respect is grounded in our status as moral persons and is not earned. Recognition respect places negative constraints on the kind of treatment to which we can properly be subject. Torture, even for the contemptible, is never permissible.

Mason's explanation of the compatibility of respect and contempt is not without controversy. Thomas Hill, Jr, for example, argues that contempt is incompatible with recognition respect.[16] Drawing on a broadly Kantian framework, Hill argues that our moral concepts and principles presume an ideal of deliberation with fellow moral agents in determining what moral principles will govern us. For such deliberation to occur, however, we must regard all persons as potential co-legislators of such principles. To regard a person in this way is to listen to and consider the claims they advance. However, especially when permanent, contempt entails a 'a deep dismissal, a denial of the prospect of reconciliation, a signal that conversation is over'; for Hill, contempt thus precludes the consideration that recognition respect requires.[17]

When pressed, Mason admits this point, insisting that under certain conditions you can in fact forfeit the prospect of engagement. Nazis such as Franz Stangl (Nazi commandant of Treblinka), she argues, forfeited this prospect. Mason argues that victims and survivors enjoyed a moral permission to permanently forgo any interaction with him. Stangl seems to have come later in his life to recognize his guilt for and implication in the Holocaust through conversations with journalist Gita Sereny, who spoke with Stangl while he was imprisoned. However, while achieving a good outcome, nobody was required to engage in the conversation that produced it. As Mason writes:

> From Sereny's description, it is plausible to believe that Stangl finally did experience genuine remorse and a change of heart. . . . Ought such a person's victims, or rather the survivors . . . feel morally pressured to stifle their contempt? I suggest there is no such moral claim on them. . . . It is

15 Mason (n 3) 269. On appraisal versus recognition respect, see Stephen Darwall, 'Two Kinds of Respect' (1977) 88 Ethics 36.

16 Mason (n 3) 265–69.

17 Mason (n 3) 268.

> an admirable thing, perhaps, that Sereny, in being willing to carry on the conversation in his case apparently was instrumental in bringing about his change of heart. But I suggest that no one morally owed this to him, least of all his victims.[18]

Engagement is not a demand of recognition respect, Mason insists.

Though I will not defend this claim at length, I note briefly that I believe Mason is wrong about the scope of obligation that recognition respect generates and, specifically, she is wrong that recognition respect places negative constraints on action only. Animals, even those without cognitive capacities, can merit recognition respect, as Mason defines it, insofar as we are required to refrain from inflicting unnecessary suffering. To show recognition respect for persons seems intuitively to entail more demanding requirements, such as the robust and collective shaping and identification of shared moral rules that Hill proposes.

Macalester Bell adds to the line of argumentation advanced by Mason.[19] Bell insists on the importance of contempt specifically for victims of oppression and injustice. Contempt motivates the kind of refusal to engage and continue interaction that may be morally required in contexts of oppression, given the interpersonal and social costs of engagement for the oppressed and given the morally unjustifiable structure of interaction. Contempt asserts the comparative superior value of the contemner, which is especially critical in countering a broader social context in which the relative inferior status of the contemner is institutionally and interpersonally circumscribed. Contempt is a way of expressing self-respect and demanding respect from others. Contempt can properly draw attention to the fact that injustice implicates not just actions but people. Individuals fail as individuals when they commit or are implicated in injustice, and contempt properly expresses this fact. Finally, Bell argues, contempt has important epistemic value. Through the failure by oppressors to properly respond to contempt expressed by the oppressed, we learn about precisely the morally problematic status of marginalized and oppressed communities. The refusal by men to accept or understand women's anger provides knowledge to women about the structure of sexism that continues to exist.

In the next section, I challenge the analysis of Mason and Bell. It is important to emphasize that contempt towards Nazis and contempt by the oppressed are instances of *political* contempt. It is contempt focused on the character of individuals as members of a political community. For Mason, the focus is on participation in a political organization such as the Nazi party. For Bell, the focus is on participation in the institutions of what Rawls calls

18 Mason (n 3) 256, 269 (emphasis added).
19 Bell, 'A Woman's Scorn' (n 4); Bell, *Hard Feelings* (n 4).

the 'basic structure of society' and the injustice of such institutions.[20] Political contempt is the object of my analysis in the next section. My scepticism is specifically with respect to the possibility of political contempt's proper focus. For my purposes, I set aside the question of interpersonal contempt.

2. Contempt and transitional justice

Mason and Bell suggest there is no moral obligation to engage with fascists or Nazis, especially on the part of victims. The appropriate response can be permanent isolation and silence. My argument in this chapter is that this view is incorrect. Engagement is morally necessary, even for victims and even with Nazis and fascists.

Before beginning my argument, I want to underscore that to call for engagement is *not* to call for agreement or acquiescence. Forms of engagement cover a wide range, including, importantly, critique and calling others to account for their roles in wrongdoing. What I am rejecting is the thought that under certain conditions it is morally permissible to permanently exclude certain people from any form of engagement whatsoever by virtue of who they are.

If Mason and Bell are right that political contempt can be properly focused, and if permanent refusal to engage is the correct response to Nazis or perpetrators of injustice, then the implications of their analysis for contexts where transitional justice is pursued are significant. In such contexts, the scope of individuals eligible as potential targets of permanent contempt is quite expansive. Transitional justice involves processes designed to respond to widespread forms of wrongdoing, characteristically human rights violations that in many cases constitute international crimes (for example, crimes against humanity, war crimes, and/or genocide). Mason focuses on the Holocaust and Nazi Germany, one case study of significance in the literature on transitional justice. Other such cases include apartheid South Africa, in which the oppressive system of institutionalized racial segregation and discrimination was recognized to constitute an international criminal order; and contexts of war such as the recent roughly ten-year conflict in Syria, during which both an estimated 500,000 people have been killed and torture by the regime of Bassar al-Assad has been systematic. On the analysis of Mason and Bell, victims of such wrongs owe no duty of engagement to perpetrators of such wrongs—permanent contempt is warranted. Consequently, victims of injustice enjoy a permission to permanently refuse to engage with significant portions of their political community grounded in properly focused contempt.

The moral permissibility of permanent non-engagement for large segments of societies pursuing transitional justice is not simply a theoretical possibility. Contempt is a prominent feature of paradigmatic transitional societies. As

20 John Rawls, *Theory of Justice* (Harvard University Press 1972).

I discuss in greater detail in the next section, the societal cleavages and divisions that exist in the aftermath of widespread wrongdoing are cleavages in part around who are the 'decent' members of a community and who are the real 'victims' and 'perpetrators' of conflict. Contempt that is subjectively perceived to be justified towards members of the group or community in conflict underpins the refusal of many to engage with individuals across such divides.

However, refusal to engage with 'the devil' is profoundly morally problematic in transitional contexts.[21] Engagement with the devil is a functional prerequisite for human rights violations to end in virtually every context where human rights violations are widespread. Refusing to engage with the devil may allow individuals to maintain a sense of moral integrity and to keep their hands clean, but peace of mind and purity come at the expense of the continuance of bloodshed and further destruction. Ending apartheid required the African National Congress and Nelson Mandela to engage with the National Party and FW de Klerk. The Troubles in Northern Ireland only ended because of the multiparty talks facilitated by United States Senator George Mitchell that brought 'terrorists' into conversation with 'oppressors'. Restoring the devolved government in Stormont after a political impasse in 2007 required Gerry Adams of Sinn Fein to shake hands with Ian Paisley of the Democratic Unionist Party. Adams is widely recognized to have been the head of the Irish Republican Army (IRA) and directly implicated in multiple political bombings during the Troubles. Paisley led the only major Unionist political party to reject the negotiations leading up to the Good Friday Agreement (GFA) in 1998, and part of his party's rejection stemmed from a categorical rejection of Catholics as political equals in Northern Ireland. Ending 50 years of bloodshed with eight million victims necessitated the government of Colombia to engage with leaders of the Revolutionary Armed Forces of Colombia-People's Army (FARC). Without such engagement with 'the devil', there would not have been a formal end to violence in Colombia, the Troubles in Northern Ireland, or apartheid in South Africa. Even with such engagement, violence did not completely cease, a reflection of the fragility of contexts of transition; but engagement created a context in which violence and oppression could be reduced and their end imagined, even if not completely realized.

It is not only in contexts where negotiated compromise is the only path to the end of conflict that engagement is critical. Even where victory is decisive, as in the case of the Rwandan Patriotic Front in Rwanda (RPF), engagement with the devil is a moral necessity. Arguably hundreds of thousands of Hutus were implicated as direct perpetrators, collaborators, accomplices, or supporters of the Rwandan genocide against the Tutsi. The RPF fought successfully to end the genocide and subsequently acquired political power, but once

21 The phrase references the memoir Roméo Dallaire, *Shake Hands with the Devil* (Da Cap Press 2004), in which Dallaire discusses the Rwandan genocide.

in power, they faced the moral necessity of engaging with and including the Hutu population. Engagement politically of some form is necessary because the alternatives are morally untenable. Excluding permanently the Hutu citizenry, in part or whole, would have been incompatible with the pursuit of democratic governance and would have set the stage for additional conflict down the line.

In addition to these instrumental reasons grounding a requirement to engage, I suggest, the refusal to engage can reflect a failure of epistemic humility in contexts of deep division and profound injustice. As I explain in the next sections, parallel and often in respects incommensurable narratives of politics, conflict, and history mediate judgments of character in deeply divided societies. The conditions required to be able to accurately judge individuals as individuals—let alone to judge their character—are not in place in a way that would allow for confident assessments that contempt is properly focused.

3. Contempt in deeply divided societies

Political contempt of the kind Mason and Bell defend is an increasingly prominent feature of democratic societies that are deeply divided and at risk of or engaged in backsliding. In this section, I illustrate using the dynamics of pervasive contempt in the United States. I use that example as representative of dynamics found in other deeply divided societies that are often categorized as paradigm 'stable democracies' and contrasted with 'transitional societies'.

Contempt is a prominent feature of deeply divided societies that are not often considered in discussions of transitional justice. Consider the United States:[22] increasingly, political disagreement does not simply track differing conclusions as to the best or more effective policy to address a recognized social problem. Political disagreement and political affiliation are taken to signal the relative worth or value of the individual with whom one is in disagreement. Political disagreement can itself be a signal of moral failing in who someone is, not simply what someone believes.

Consider the increasingly common appeal to 'fascist' to describe Republicans. Following the coup on 6 January 2022, Dana Millbank from *The Washington Post* wrote of Republicans in the aftermath: '[t]o call a person who endorses violence against the duly elected government a "Republican" is itself Orwellian. More accurate words exist for such a person. One of them is "fascist."'[23] The refusal to disavow the Republican Party or the label of

22 Some scholars do explicitly recognize the relevance of transitional justice for contexts like the United States. See Yuvraj Joshi, 'Weaponizing Peace' (2023) 123 Columbia Law Rev 1141; Yuvraj Joshi, 'Racial Justice and Peace' (2022) 110 Geo L J 1325; Yuvraj Joshi, 'Affirmative Action as Transitional Justice' (2020) Wis L Rev 1.

23 Dana Milbank, 'There's a Name for Someone Who Calls Violence "Legitimate." It Isn't "Republican"' *Washington Post* (Washington, 7 February 2022) <www.washingtonpost.com/

oneself as a Republican is taken by Millbank to entail a conclusion about who someone is. Only fascists would continue to affiliate with the Republican Party after 6 January.

In turn, Republicans increasingly view Democrats as Nazis. The COVID era provides the resources for this claim, which analogizes government efforts to control the pandemic with Nazi-era repression. Consider Republican Representative Marjorie Taylor Greene, who stated following President Joseph Biden's commitment to send medical personnel into communities to provide the COVID vaccine: 'People have a choice. They don't need your medical brown shirts showing up at their door ordering vaccinations. You can't force people to be part of the human experiment'.[24]

The perception of political differences as grounded in fundamentally different moral characters (and moral failings) is not limited to individuals with prominent public platforms. According to a study by psychologist Justin Landy, 'Democrats perceive faces labeled as Republicans as physically disgusting and vice versa'.[25] In explaining what undergirds this physical reaction of disgust, Landy writes that it 'probably has very little to do with judgments of people's actions, but other researchers have suggested that it might be involved in judgments of the people themselves—*their moral character*'.[26] What Landy is picking out is arguably mutual contempt. The aversion and repulsion accompanying the perception of another as a member of a different political party carries with it a judgment about the morally flawed character of the other, generating repulsion. Both the phenomenological experience of contempt and contempt's constitutive judgment are present.

In the United States, individuals claiming the moral high ground in the face of opponents who are seen as fascists call for a refusal to engage with democratically elected representatives who promote the Big Lie or challenge the legitimacy of democratic elections. Increasingly, public voices from the Republican side question the standing to vote of citizens who endorse critical race theory. The refusal to engage is laying the foundation for the continual—and not simply rhetorical—erosion of democratic governance in the United States.

One might simply respond to the pervasiveness of mutual contempt in the United States by arguing that some of these examples are cases of unjustified

---

opinions/2022/02/07/rnc-legitimate-political-discourse-insurrection/> accessed 18 June 2024.

24 Noah Berlatsky, 'Rep. Majorie Taylor Greene Can't Stop Making Covid-Nazi Comparisons' *Think* (8 July 2021) <www.nbcnews.com/think/opinion/rep-marjorie-taylor-greene-can-t-stop-making-covid-nazi-ncna1273312> accessed 18 June 2024.

25 Eric W Dolan, 'Republicans and Democrats Feel "Grossed Out" and "Nauseated" by Each Other' *Psychpost* (9 February 2022) <www.psypost.org/republicans-and-democrats-feel-grossed-out-and-nauseated-by-each-other/> accessed 18 June 2024.

26 Eric W Dolan, 'Republicans and Democrats Feel "Grossed Out" and "Nauseated" by Each Other' *Psychpost* (9 February 2022) <www.psypost.org/republicans-and-democrats-feel-grossed-out-and-nauseated-by-each-other/> accessed 18 June 2024 (emphasis added).

contempt. For example, Representative Greene is simply incorrect to equate public health responses to COVID with Nazi-era atrocities and to characterize Democratic President Biden's administration as comprised of Nazis. But this response is too quick. Part of the point of the next section is to explain why the basis for making correct judgments about the character of others is profoundly diminished in deeply divided communities. Asserting or denying the truth of the judgment that Republicans are fascists or Democrats are Nazis presupposes the presence of conditions needed for the ability to assess character accurately. Such conditions are precisely what is missing in contexts of divided polities in which grave wrongdoing is or has occurred.

It might also be objected that by focusing in this section on contemporary political discourse in the United States and the prevalence of contempt, I am conflating two very different kinds of cases: transitional societies (for example, post-WWII Nazi Germany) and consolidated democracies (for example, the United States). While the conditions for justified contempt may well be absent in transitional contexts, the objection goes, there is no reason to think they are absent in the same way in consolidated democracies like the United States.

In response, I reject the claim that the cases are as radically different as the objection imagines. The issue raised by this objection concerns the basis for grouping societies as falling in the same category. The categories of interest may vary depending on why categorization is sought; for example, the World Bank categorizes countries as 'low income', 'middle income', or 'high income' for purposes of comparing the relative gross national income per capita.

Here the question raised by the objection concerns whether it makes sense to group countries widely considered to be consolidated democracies with societies widely classified as transitional in virtue of the presence of similar epistemic obstacles to accurate assessments of character by fellow members of a political community.

Transitional justice is pursued in contexts where deep and profound societal divisions exist. Colombia, South Africa, and Northern Ireland are contexts in which the depth of divisions across communities is well-known and where the pursuit of transitional justice was prominent. The three examples underscore the ways in which the fault lines of division can vary across ethno-national, ethnic, regional, and/or racial lines. What generates and reinforces these fault lines is the presence of what I have called in other work *pervasive structural inequality* and *normalized collective and political wrongdoing*.[27]

Structural inequality refers to the institutionally defined norms and rules for interaction among members of a society. Such norms and rules are codified by laws and reflected in more informal social and cultural norms for interaction. They specify what sorts of actions members of a specified group (for example,

27 *Murphy, Conceptual Foundations (n 2).*

all legal subjects, individuals over 18 years old, women) are required, permitted, and prohibited to engage in when interacting with members of a specified group (for example, all legal officials, children under 18, men). Such norms are maintained in part through formal and informal penalties for infraction. Criminal punishment is a penalty risked by violators of the criminal law. Shunning or shaming can be the response to violators of social and cultural norms. The structure of interaction matters because it shapes 'life prospects', what various members of a community can do and become of value (for example, being educated or employed). The structure of interaction is not static but can change over time through formal processes such as acts of Congress or by the gradual evolution of social norms embraced within a community.

Structural *inequality* exists when there are differential restrictions on the institutionally defined opportunities open to various groups within a society to do and become things of value (for example, being educated or employed) and on the ability of members of different groups to influence the content of the rules for interaction themselves. Such restrictions can be formally codified, such as in apartheid South Africa, but they need not be so codified. Restrictions can also be a product of informal discrimination in hiring or pay, de facto residential segregation, or practices of political gerrymandering to dilute the political influence of certain groups; all such examples are problems that Catholics in Northern Ireland have faced since partition, grounding the initially non-violent Civil Rights movement in the 1960s that led to the onset of the 30-year period of violence known as The Troubles.[28]

Underpinning structural inequality are animating schemas and ideologies that attempt to explain why differential opportunities or rights are defensible. Tommie Shelby, for example, defines racism as 'a set of misleading beliefs and implicit attitudes about "races" or race relations whose wide currency serves a hegemonic social function'.[29] To use one of Shelby's examples, stereotypes represent Blacks as inferior with respect to Whites in terms of intelligence, moral integrity, and work ethic; such stereotypes can be and are used to justify and explain inequality in outcomes, such as inequality in income. More specifically, structural inequality and the ideologies that underpin it can facilitate and justify the commission of human rights violations by, for example, providing resources to deny or diminish the rights claims of members of targeted or marginalized communities.[30] The result can be *normalized wrongdoing*—violations of human rights that become empirically a matter of fact for members of targeted groups who must shape their conduct around the anticipation of potentially being a victim of human rights violations.

28 For a brief history of Northern Ireland, see John McGarry and Brendan O'Leary, *Explaining Northern Ireland: Broken Images* (Wiley-Blackwell 1995).

29 Tommie Shelby, 'Racism, Moralism, and Social Criticism' (2014) 11 DBR 57, 66.

30 Tommie Shelby, 'Racism, Moralism, and Social Criticism' (2014) 11 DBR 57, 66.

With respect to consolidated democracies like the United States, deep divisions and cleavages are increasingly acknowledged and discussed; the partisan political divide between Republicans and Democrats reflects deepening political polarization throughout the United States. Underpinning such divisions are the same problems of structural inequality and normalized wrongdoing that are found in paradigm transitional societies. Race has, since the inception of the United States, shaped law and politics. Written into the founding Constitution itself was a three-fifths compromise—that (Black) people who were subjected to chattel slavery would count as three-fifths of a free (White) person for purposes of determining congressional representation—and the continuance of slavery was the wedge that drove the country to civil war in the 1860s. The post-Civil War Jim Crow era of racialized apartheid sparked the non-violent civil rights movement and eventual passage of the Civil Rights Act of 1964. However, 60 years after that act, sharp inequalities along racial lines continue to be present in educational attainment, wealth, and health. Gerrymandering efforts to eliminate the political influence of African Americans continues to be employed in Southern states and continues to be the subject of court litigation. Accompanying such inequality has been various forms of normalized wrongdoing disproportionately affecting Black and Brown people in the United States, from the vigilante violence of lynching utilized in the Jim Crow era to the excessive use of force by police, which became the subject of the Black Lives Matter-led racial justice protests that began in summer 2020 following the police murder of George Floyd. Because of how race informs politics and the racial demographics of the Republican and Democratic parties, the partisan divide reflects racial divides that continue to exist.[31]

In previous work, I have argued that judgments about where transitional justice is needed should be based on the relative presence or absence of what I have called the circumstances of transitional justice. These circumstances make the just pursuit of societal transformation necessary and possible. Pervasive structural inequality and normalized wrongdoing are two of the circumstances I identify.[32] When we examine the conditions or circumstances

31 APSA Presidential Task Force on Political Parties, *More Than Red and Blue: Political Parties and American Democracy* (July 2023); Dan Balz, 'What Divides Political Parties? More Than Ever, It's Race and Ethnicity' *The Washington Post* (9 September 2023) <www.washingtonpost.com/politics/2023/09/09/race-divides-political-parties/> accessed 18 June 2024.

32 See *Conceptual Foundations* (n 2). The other two circumstances I discuss are *serious existential uncertainty*—fragility and uncertainty regarding the political future of a community—and *fundamental uncertainty about authority*, stemming from the ways in which government actors and institutions are implicated in past human rights violations and the absence of stable consensus over the source of the right to rule. While I don't for purposes of this chapter explain why these two conditions are salient as well in the United States, I have made that case elsewhere. See, eg, Colleen Murphy, 'How Nations Heal' *Boston Review* (21 January 2021) <www.bostonreview.net/articles/colleen-murphy-transitional-justice/>

that generate the need for transitional justice, I have suggested, we find that the circumstances are found not only in more paradigmatic contexts such as Colombia and Northern Ireland but also in the United States. Viewed through the lens of the circumstances of transitional justice, which create and maintain the divides in deeply fractured political communities, the United States is not radically different from societies that are widely taken to be paradigmatic transitional contexts.[33]

4. Deeply divided societies, the erosion of respect for agency, and transitional justice

Within deeply divided societies, mutual respect for moral agency gets eroded and undermined, both institutionally and interpersonally. In this section, I focus on the erosion of interpersonal respect for agency. I explain how the erosion of respect for agency is tied to the structure of group identities in deeply divided contexts. I then discuss how this structure of group identities in turn makes accurate assessments of character epistemically challenging. Judgments of character of the kind contempt expresses are fraught because of how such divisions impede the accurate assessment of individual character.

By respect for agency, I refer to the respect shown to another when they are seen and treated as possessing the capacity to choose courses of action to attain their goals and the capacity to formulate and endorse certain goals for themselves. Exercising agency depends on a predictable context for action, in which we can reliably anticipate what the consequences of different courses of action will be, and so the relative ability of different choices to further our ends and goals. Respect for the agency of others thus can also entail the responsibility to help create and maintain a context in which it is possible to exercise agency and respond to others based on their agential choices.[34]

Three foundational capacities for interacting as moral agents are diminished in deeply divided political communities.[35] As philosopher David Shoemaker argues, our ability to interact with others as moral agents depends on three capacities: (1) the capacity to recognize and apply the second-person

accessed 18 June 2024; Colleen Murphy and Kelebogile Zvobgo, 'Not a Moment But a Movement: The Case for Transitional Justice in the U.S.' *Ms. Magazine* (16 December 2020) <https://msmagazine.com/2020/12/16/movement-transitional-justice-united-states/> accessed 18 June 2024.

33 Colleen Murphy, 'Transitional Justice and Redress for Racial Injustice' in Melissa Schwartzberg and Eric Beerbohm (eds), *NOMOS LXV: Reconciliation and Repair* (NYU Press 2023); Colleen Murphy, 'The Movement for Black Lives and Transitional Justice' in Brandon Hogan, Michael Cholbi, Alex Nadva, and Benjamin Yost (eds), *The Movement for Black Lives: Philosophical Perspectives* (OUP 2021).

34 On this point, see Lon Fuller, *The Morality of Law* (rev edn, Yale University Press 1969).

35 David Shoemaker, 'Moral Address, Moral Responsibility, and the Boundaries of the Moral Community' (2007) 118 Ethics 70, 71–75.

moral reasons of others; (2) the capacity to be susceptible to the emotional address of others, which in turn depends upon an identifying empathy; and (3) the capacity to be motivated to act on second-person moral reasons that others provide. I first summarize each capacity and its role in making possible interaction predicated on respect for moral agency. I then illustrate the absence of each capacity in contexts of deep divisions.

Relationships predicated on mutual respect for moral agency depend on a mutual ability to recognize the second-person moral reasons of others. Second-person moral reasons derive their normative force or authority from the normative significance and authority of the individual offering the reason. The demand expressed in a second-person reason is therefore important insofar as the demander is important.[36] If we do not view an individual as having any claim on us, we are unable to recognize the second-person demands they make on us.

Contexts of conflict and repression are ones in which human rights of members of certain groups are formally unrecognized or de facto ignored. There is no broad public recognition of the normative authority of members of marginalized or targeted groups to demand and claim a certain level of treatment. The dismissal of complaints about treatment by security forces or the police is one manifestation of the denial or dismissal of the second-person authority of members of marginalized or targeted groups.

Relationships among moral agents are relationships characterized by reactive attitudes, such as anger and contempt, which are forms of second-personal moral address. In expressing resentment or anger, for example, we are calling on the target of our attitude to feel and understand the wrong they have done to us and to respond appropriately in light of our judgment about their action. Our ability to understand accurately the emotional address of others depends on our capacity for identifying empathy, Shoemaker claims. We need to be able to imagine caring about what the other cares about and imagine how we would be affected, if we so cared, by the action to which the other was subject.

The absence of identifying empathy is reflected in the profound ignorance, especially on the part of members of privileged groups, of how those with whom one is in conflict live. Antjie Krog, a White South African journalist who reported on the South African Truth and Reconciliation Commission (TRC), had a nervous breakdown during the course of covering the TRC proceedings. This breakdown was in part caused by how overwhelmed she became when hearing the testimonies of suffering during apartheid; she had little knowledge or understanding of the lives being lived by Black South Africans and opponents of apartheid.[37]

36 David Shoemaker, 'Moral Address, Moral Responsibility, and the Boundaries of the Moral Community' (2007) 118 Ethics 86.

37 Antjie Krog, *Country of My Skull: Guilt, Suffering and the Limits of Forgiveness in the New South Africa* (Three Rivers Press 2000). See also Myisha Cherry, 'Black People Look Up

The inability to understand what political opponents care about is illustrated powerfully in a 2018 poll in the United States.[38] The aim of the survey was to capture how citizens viewed fellow citizens who voted differently from how they did. Republican respondents were asked: 'In your opinion, how many citizens voting for the Democrats did so because they sincerely believe that the Democratic party is best for the country?' Only 25% of Republican respondents believed that this was the case:

> Rather, many Republicans told us that Democratic voters were 'brainwashed by the propaganda of the mainstream media', or voting solely in their self-interest to preserve undeserved welfare and food stamp benefits. . . . They see Democrats as voting in order to get 'free stuff' 'without having to work for it'.

One respondent stated, 'This is really hard for me to even try to think like a devilcrat! I am sorry but I in all honesty cannot answer this question. I cannot even wrap my mind around any reason they would be good for this country'. It was impossible for Republicans to imagine Democrats as motivated by the good of the country and caring about anything beyond themselves.

Though Democratic individuals surveyed expressed a greater willingness to consider Republicans as motivated by the good of the country (42%), many also exhibited a lack of identifying empathy. Rather than trying to empathetically imagine how someone could have voted Republican, some respondents used the survey 'to express their anger and outrage at the other side. Rather than really try to take the position of their opponents, they said things like, "I like a dictatorial system of Government, I'm a racist, I hate non-whites."'[39]

Finally, relationships predicated on mutual respect for agency are ones in which we respond appropriately to the emotional address of others. To be motivated to respond appropriately to the second-person moral address of others, we must at a certain level care about the others. To care for others is to be disposed to grieve at the ill fortune of another and delight in their success and good fortune. Care provides the necessary motivation to want to make amends for anger caused, instead of delighting in or being indifferent towards another who is upset.

---

and Down, White People Look Away: Charles Mills, James Baldwin, and White Ignorance' (2022) 25 Radic Philos Rev 219.

38 Eric Plutzer and Michael Berkman, 'Americans Not Only Divided, But Baffled by What Motivates Their Opponents' *The McCourtney Institute for Democracy* (November 2018) <https://democracy.psu.edu/poll-report-archive/americans-not-only-divided-but-baffled-by-what-motivates-their-opponents/> accessed 18 June 2024.

39 Eric Plutzer and Michael Berkman, 'Americans Not Only Divided, But Baffled by What Motivates Their Opponents' *The McCourtney Institute for Democracy* (November 2018) <https://democracy.psu.edu/poll-report-archive/americans-not-only-divided-but-baffled-by-what-motivates-their-opponents/> accessed 18 June 2024.

Unsurprisingly, divided contexts are ones characterized by an absence of care and the subsequent motivation to act on the second-person reasons offered by individuals from a group with which one's own group is in conflict. Krog summarizes a conversation with her colleague who was a Black South African in these words: ' "Whites," says Kondlo, throwing back the last of his drink with a grimace, "have no ubuntu . . . they choke on all their rights, but they have no human compassion." '[40]

Group identity

Group identity is at the core of how and why there is a blunting of the ability of individuals to recognize the second-person reasons, empathetically identify with emotions expressed, and care about other members of their political community. Group identity does not simply play the crude role that Mason suggests, reflecting indefensible pure bigotry. Group identity mediates our interpretation of who others are in terms of character traits for which they are properly held morally accountable for possessing or lacking.

Marc Howard Ross's *Cultural Contestation in Ethnic Conflict* provides the key resources for understanding the mediating role of group identity.[41] Group identities are constructed through psychocultural narratives. Such narratives are fundamentally historical and interpretive, providing an interpretation of the group's origin, history (including, importantly, the history of relationships with groups in conflict), values, and obligations. History is emotionally powerful, evoking both powerful images and powerful responses such as grief and pride to the collective triumphs and failures of a given group.

Furthermore, history is normative and prescriptive. As Ross writes,

> [w]e make sense of the present in relation to the past by interpreting it, by seeing what lessons we can derive from it or how it can shed light on the principles, practices, and institutions that constitute our shared life.[42]

Lessons learned can include how to understand and interpret the motivations and actions of members of groups with whom one's own group is in conflict. Against a background of historical recollections and normative lessons learned, groups develop a sense of common fate. This fate encompasses shared expectations of treatment by members of other groups, expectations which in turn can ground shared fears about the survival of the group itself, the risks of potential future humiliation members face, the loss of political

40 Krog, *Country of My Skull* (n 37).
41 Marc Howard Ross, *Cultural Contestation in Ethnic Conflict* (CUP 2007).
42 Marc Howard Ross, *Cultural Contestation in Ethnic Conflict* (CUP 2007) 32.

power to which a group is vulnerable, and vulnerability to physical safety individual members face.

Expectations and fears are often grounded on stereotypical characterizations of members of other groups, generalizations about what others whom we know very little about are like in virtue of the features they share with members of the groups to which we take them to belong. Stereotypes tend to homogenize members of groups other than those to which an individual belongs. Recognition of heterogeneity within one's own group(s) is coupled with homogenization of members of other groups.[43]

Psychocultural dramas arise in divided communities when there are intensely emotional conflicts over resources, social policy, and language. Parades in Northern Ireland produced such dramas, as did the question of whether professional athletes kneel for the national anthem in the United States before professional sporting events, such as American football.[44] From the outside, it can be baffling as to how or why a parade or kneeling could evoke violence, as parades have in Northern Ireland repeatedly, or permanent professional ostracism, as kneeling did for professional American football player Colin Kaepernick. However, Ross claims that such gestures or activities evoke powerful emotions in virtue of how they touch on the deepest fears that often drive conflict within communities.

Debates around parades in Northern Ireland are debates over equality and identity. Nationalists in Northern Ireland are largely Catholic and identify as Irish. Unionists are largely Protestant and identify as British. Parades, which are predominantly Unionist, commemorate Protestant victories, such as by William of Orange over Catholic James II. Such parades are viewed by Unionists as expressions of history and culture. To refuse to allow parades is from their perspective to suppress Unionist culture and identity. When parades occur through Catholic neighbourhoods, however, they are viewed by locals as reminders of historical dominance and expressions of desires for continuing superiority. They are reminders of the inferior standing that Catholics have historically had and continue to have within Northern Ireland. In these ways, parades touch the deepest fears driving conflict. Nationalists fear a return to a period of Unionist domination and discrimination. Unionists fear a loss of rights and recognition should Ireland be unified, and the inability to celebrate their culture through parades is seen as the first step in this process.[45]

43 Marc Howard Ross, *Cultural Contestation in Ethnic Conflict* (CUP 2007) 32.

44 See, eg, Tadd Haislop, 'Colin Kaepernick Kneeling Timeline: How Protests During the National Anthem Started a Movement in the NFL' *Sporting News* (13 September 2020) <www.sportingnews.com/us/nfl/news/colin-kaepernick-kneeling-protest-timeline/xktu6ka4diva1s5jxaylrcsse> accessed 18 June 2024.

45 Katy Hayward and Milena Komarova, *The Border into Brexit: Perspectives from Local Communities in the Central Border Region of Ireland/Northern Ireland* (Irish

These fears have been amplified since the Brexit referendum, in which the United Kingdom voted to leave the European Union (EU). Negotiations to end The Troubles led to the 1998 Belfast Good Friday Agreement (GFA), which enshrined the birthright of all Northern Irish citizens to identify as British citizens, or Irish citizens, or both.[46] It recognized the legal status of Northern Ireland in the UK and also enshrined a recognition that Northern Ireland could be united with Ireland should a majority in Northern Ireland desire this in the future. The GFA ended direct rule by the British and established a shared governance structure in which Nationalists and Unionists would split executive roles, and a Northern Irish Assembly would be structured in a way that included effective cross-community vetoes on foundational questions. The GFA set up processes for deepening ties between the Republic of Ireland and Northern Ireland and between the British and Irish Governments.

The governing structure of the GFA was possible because both the UK and Ireland were in the EU, which facilitated movement of people and goods across otherwise sovereign borders and provided an overarching EU framework within which passports for specific countries were acquired. Brexit reopened the identity questions at the core of the conflict between Nationalists and Unionists by requiring, from the British government's perspective, a 'hard' border between the United Kingdom and the EU and by making the acquisition of British or Irish passports suddenly differential because of the differential access to the EU they respectively provide. The Republic of Ireland remains part of the EU. In part, this contributed to the collapse of power-sharing institutions from 2017–2020 and subsequent suspension since 2022. The existential fears driving conflict remain.

Taking a different example, politics in the United States is profoundly racialized. It is no accident that respondents of the survey referenced earlier associate the Democratic party with immigration and immigration with 'illegal immigrants' largely characterized as Latinx. Against the background of racialized politics, a Black professional athlete kneeling during the national anthem evoked deep fears about the future of the United States among many White men and women, a demographic that is the predominant group in the Republican party. Colin Kaepernick's refusal to be silent in the face of ongoing racial injustice and acquiesce in rote displays of patriotism evoked deep fears regarding the future place of White men and women as the country quickly approaches a majority-minority demographic makeup. The core fear is that this will result in the loss of power and privilege among White Americans.

Central Border Area Network 2019) <https://ukandeu.ac.uk/wp-content/uploads/2019/12/The-Border-into-Brexit-perspectives-from-local-communities-in-the-central-border-region-of-Ireland-and-Northern-Ireland.pdf> accessed 18 June 2024.

46 The Secretary of State for Northern Ireland, *The Belfast Agreement: An Agreement Reached at the Multi-Party Talks on Northern Ireland* (Cmd 3883, 1998).

By contrast, the crushing punishment of National Football League (NFL) quarterback Colin Kaepernick by the owners of professional football teams, in ways publicly supported by then-President Trump, reminded members of the multiracial Democratic party of just how far White Americans will go to ensure that White supremacy remains the norm of the land. It evoked fears of a return to entrenched historical practices of physical, economic, social, and professional punishment of Black Americans who challenge racial injustice and White supremacy. The professional football league owners in Kaepernick's case blacklisted him as a player in the NFL (despite his performance as a player being among the very best quarterbacks in the NFL) and effectively ended his career as a football player. When members of historically marginalized groups are stereotyped and not viewed as full members of a community because of how membership in a political community is defined and conceptualized, it is unsurprising that the second-person authority of members of such groups to make demands goes unacknowledged by members of a historically dominant and privileged group.

5. Conclusion: properly focused contempt?

What then of contempt and its proper moral focus? Mason's analysis of the defensibility of permanent contempt presupposes the ability of individuals to accurately and unproblematically assess the traits and motivations of others. The character of someone like Stangl is evident to the reader of Mason's piece as easily as it was to contemporaries of Stangl's time. The analysis provided here, however, suggests that judging the character of individuals implicated in widespread wrongdoing and atrocity is anything but straightforward. Group-based identities mediate how actions and motivations are understood, simplifying and distorting the actions and motivations of members of 'the other side'. Empirical work on atrocity underscores just how varied the motivations of actors, even actors implicated in the most egregious of atrocities, are, defying any easy or simple normative characterization.

We can grant Bell's basic point that subjects of oppression have epistemic insight into the nature of oppression from their position that oppressors or privileged individuals lack. This insight might even entail that victims of oppression or injustice are in fact better epistemically situated to evaluate the character of perpetrators of injustice than perpetrators are to judge the characters of their victims. However, being comparatively better situated is not sufficient to establish that contempt can and will be properly focused by victims. The argument above suggests that even for victims of oppression there will be some, even if less, distortion in judgments of character.

Contra Mason and Bell, we should urge the eschewal of contempt. Contempt is properly viewed as presumptively unjustified, *especially* in the complicated contexts in which wrongdoing becomes widespread. Contempt is among the most difficult reactive attitudes to properly focus, because of the obstacles to accurately understanding the character that actions ultimately reveal.

Contempt may play important functional roles for victims of oppression that make it, all things considered, justified as a mechanism for maintaining self-respect in response to injustice. In such cases, what my argument suggests is that we recognize the costs involved in recourse to this tool. We should urge and prefer other routes for asserting self-respect and demanding proper treatment that avoid engaging in the epistemically fraught task of judging the character of others and avoid endorsing the morally fraught refusal to engage with the devil.

In response to worries that I am urging the condoning of Nazis, I want to underscore that I am not. Nothing I have said here entails a refusal to judge and condemn actions as wrongful and to hold individuals to account for their actions. Egregious wrongdoing merits forceful reactive attitudes in response, but the attitudes merited are ones that focus on and judge actions, not individuals. Humility, even among victims, should be the default with respect to our ability to judge accurately the character of others in divided polities.

Chapter 4

Finding justice between accommodation and refusal

Eddie Synot[1]

1. Approaching justice

Considerations of the position of Indigenous peoples within the political philosophy of liberalism too often fall into formalistic approaches to rights and justice that provide inadequate responses to Indigenous justice claims. Of course, liberalism is a broad church. I am not concerned with a particular account of liberalism but rather with approaches that often proceed from ideal or a priori standards of justice, which are usually focused on the universalized, free, and equal subject as a standard against which all other claims are judged.[2] I am concerned with these elements of liberalism when they are used as starting points for the assessment of Indigenous claims due to their ubiquitous presence in theorizing about how we should organize society. The nature of this kind of theorizing reflects too little of the material reality of Indigenous justice claims,[3] the inequalities of power and injustice within existing institutions, and the differences that make up the lives of those governed by

1 This chapter draws on my doctoral thesis, 'Laws of Recognition: Redemptive Liberalism and the Politics of Recognition', and my involvement as a member of the Uluru Dialogue working towards achieving a First Nations Voice in the Australian Constitution. Parts of this chapter have been published as Eddie Synot, 'Arresting the Tide of History: The Uluru Statement from the Heart' (*TWAILR*: *Reflections* #13/2020) <https://twailr.com/arresting-the-tide-of-history-the-uluru-statement-from-the-heart/> accessed 6 June 2024.

2 I am thinking here of John Rawls, but perhaps more importantly, Rawls as read and adapted by a great many more. The critiques I am drawing on are many but come from the likes of Iris Marion Young, *Justice and the Politics of Difference* (Princeton University Press 1990); William E Connolly, *Why I Am Not a Secularist* (University of Minnesota Press 1999); Raymond Geuss, *Philosophy and Real Politics* (Princeton University Press 2008); Raymond Geuss, *Not Thinking Like a Liberal* (Harvard University Press 2022).

3 Indigenous justice claims can be broadly understood according to two issues. The first is the comparative socioeconomic status of Indigenous people due to historical and contemporary forces of exclusion, racism, and dispossession. The second is the claims Indigenous people maintain, having not ceded sovereignty to their territories and political and cultural rights.

DOI: 10.4324/9781032676159-5

these institutions.[4] Some would consider this unfair criticism. As Peter Balint argues, these theories and claims, such as those to neutrality, should be understood as incomplete ideals we aspire to rather than representations of our real world.[5] Yet as Raymond Geuss notes, these ideals of liberalism are nonetheless prolific: 'they constitute the final framework within which our political thinking moves'.[6] The problem is that liberalism's ideals are so prolific yet offer such unsatisfactory responses to immediate demands for justice, especially when their focus is on future or ideal institutional designs that appear or are used to justify, either explicitly or implicitly, the exclusion of particular and immediate demands that do not fit the language of liberalism or the 'overlapping consensus' required for dialogue within those societies.[7] Restatement of these principles of liberalism in response to ongoing inequality and suffering render these approaches 'short-sighted, confused or mere cover for hegemonic designs', seemingly incapable or unwilling to produce change.[8] This means that, too often, explorations of the place of Indigenous peoples begin with questions of how Indigenous claims meet those ideals—demanding a justification in those terms, asking whether or not liberal systems can accommodate Indigenous peoples—and become fixated on extreme examples that come to represent the problem of accommodating Indigenous peoples.[9]

These approaches too easily collapse justice into a formalized, 'mechanical' equality that eschews fairness of outcomes, as well as differences and inequalities in status and opportunity.[10] This is, of course, despite many theoretical approaches, especially those influenced by John Rawls, being concerned with a just distribution of resources to address inequality. The problem, however, is that they are too often grounded in abstract ideals that fail to reflect the immediate and real nature of most justice claims, circumstances which from the outset inhibit the implementation of systematic and ideal solutions. This

4 For example, Charles Mills, in his sustained critique of the political philosophy of liberalism, and particularly of John Rawls, argues that liberalism is fundamentally unable to deliver racial justice and requires significant reform. See Charles W Mills, 'Race and the Social Contract Tradition' (2000) 6 Soc Ident 441.

5 Peter Balint, 'Identity Claims: Why Liberal Neutrality Is the Solution, Not the Problem' (2015) 63 PSR 495.

6 Raymond Geuss, 'Liberalism and Its Discontents' (2002) 30 PT 320, 320.

7 See, eg, Amartya Sen, 'What Do We Want from a Theory of Justice?' (2006) 103 J Philos 215.

8 Guess, 'Liberalism and Its Discontents' (n 6) 321.

9 See, eg, Duncan Ivison, 'The Logic of Aboriginal Rights' (2003) 3 Ethnicities 321; Duncan Ivison, Paul Patton, and Will Sanders (eds), *Political Theory and the Rights of Indigenous Peoples* (CUP 2008); Benjamin J Richardson, Shin Imai, and Ken McNeil (eds), *Indigenous Peoples and the Law: Comparative and Critical Perspectives* (Hart Publishing 2009); Sandra Irene Tomsons, Lorraine Mayer, and Don Mills (eds), *Philosophy and Aboriginal Rights: Critical Dialogues* (OUP 2013); Duncan Ivison, *Can Liberal States Accommodate Indigenous Peoples?* (Polity Press 2020).

10 Julius Stone, 'Equality and the Search for Justice' (1980) 12 AJFS 151, 161.

situation compounds the difficulty that Indigenous peoples face in overcoming dispossession, racism, and exclusion, along with making claims on a more fundamental basis to their *existence* as Indigenous peoples, when the constitutive parts of those claims are denied as being determinative of Indigenous recognition and rights claims. The argument from proponents of these types of liberalism is that it is precisely because of these inequalities and differences that something like Rawls's 'veil of ignorance' and principles of neutrality are preferred as a tool—an ideal to measure our society against—to think through the universal value of justice that should determine the obligations of fairness in assessing what we owe each other.[11] Brian Barry, in *Culture and Equality*, for example, in what is otherwise a broad polemic against group rights and cultural rights, claims that it is because egalitarians care about and understand these differences and inequalities that they are not elevated to a universal standard or provided with equal protection and status.[12] Instead, cultural claims are understood properly as an individual's right to choose and not as legitimate claims in their own right.

Those whom Barry has in his crosshairs for adapting liberalism to accommodate Indigenous and other cultural and religious claims have been concerned by, as Iris Marion Young put it, the liberal 'tendency to reduce political subjects to a unity and to value commonness or sameness over specificity and difference'.[13] It should be easy to understand how this 'tendency' provides unsatisfactory responses to Indigenous justice claims. More than this, Will Kymlicka, Charles Taylor, James Tully, and others, more recently including Duncan Ivison, have made admirable strides in opening space for Indigenous rights within liberalism. They discuss in different ways how embracing Indigenous claims can enhance democratic and egalitarian systems and thereby the lives of individuals within them that Barry claims are incapable of accepting special or unique rights claims. Yet the 'tendency to reduce', which Young diagnoses, is more than just a personal affront to individuals that have specific claims, whether based on their unique existence or the injustice that they have suffered. That tendency operates as a structural function of dominant cultures and institutions in liberal democracies that can obscure inequality and difference, only allowing them to have value in determining what has value and is worthy of recognition to the extent that they are the result of individual choice or misfortune. This process further serves to entrench injustice and subordinate Indigenous claims. The problem remains starting from a place that is

11 See, eg, Rawls's own explanation in John Rawls, 'The Sense of Justice' (1963) 72 Philos Rev 281 and John Rawls, *Justice as Fairness: A Restatement* (Harvard University Press 2001) 16–17.

12 Brian Barry, *Culture and Equality: An Egalitarian Critique of Multiculturalism* (Blackwell Publishers 2001). See also Brian Barry, *Liberty and Justice* (OUP 1991); Brian Barry, *The Liberal Theory of Justice* (OUP 1973).

13 Young (n 2) 3–4.

abstracted and universalized as the standard by which all are measured, as if that measure, the society within which it occurs, and the norms by which it is judged are neutral or objective and can deliver justice on that basis.

This, of course, raises the questions of what is meant by 'justice' and how it can be achieved, if at all, if we have such different demands, which leads us back to Barry's claim of intractable issues. We might think that these issues give us all the more reason to establish universal standards that guarantee a minimum by which all are measured, so as not to give preference to any one standard of justice, or one culture over another, including for the stability of society itself, where preference for majoritarian positions, such as for a standard language, may be required to ensure stability.[14] My argument, however, isn't that a universal standard of justice has no place. As Amartya Sen has claimed in his assessment of what we should want from a theory of justice, '[t]he world in which we live is not only unjust, it is arguably, extraordinarily unjust' and requires from us a more attentive commitment to justice *now*, not for us to turn away from its demands.[15] For Sen, in response to ideal or transcendental theories of justice, '[i]t is not frivolous to seek a framework for a theory of justice that concentrates on advancement, not transcendence, and also allows being globally interactive, rather than being intellectually sequestered'—that is, being open and responsive to different justice demands.[16] The universal here would be better considered a commitment to engagement and review between differing claims and people and not one that forces those claims to conform to a dominant and exclusive base or ideal, individual subject. Fundamentally, ideal claims of liberalism crash hard against reality; yet at the same time, these criticisms do little to change the prolific nature of liberalism or to intervene in favour of undervalued or unheard justice demands. I can't answer these demands here, as they require significant attention in their own right. I can, however, focus on how we should be thinking about and approaching these issues in order to break the hold that ideal theorizing has on assessing Indigenous justice claims. It is these realities to which a universal orientation of justice should be applied through a practice of continued engagement, informed by a commitment to the *real* of where people exist, especially when justice as formal equality or ideal fairness fails to provide adequate responses. This does not mean we should necessarily abandon liberalism and its institutions—as Geuss notes, despite his deep criticism of liberalism, how could we?[17] Rather, those institutions and their starting points should be continually revised to better reflect the kind of just outcomes that the reality of our differentiated community demands.

14 See Balint (n 5).
15 Sen (n 7) 237.
16 Sen (n 7) 237.
17 See Geuss, 'Liberalism and Its Discontents' (n 6).

Young claims that, for such a different orientation towards justice to exist and for it to be capable of doing justice, we 'should begin with the concepts of domination and oppression'.[18] This, for Young, lays bare occluded structural functions of power and decision-making 'that bear on social justice, but are often ignored in philosophical discussions'.[19] Again, achieving this in practice is another matter, but my aim is to highlight the need to approach our theorizing and understanding of these issues from different and diverse standpoints in order to provide more satisfactory answers to Indigenous justice claims. This orientation is shared by many who have spoken from the position of the oppressed by centring injustice or exclusion as key to understanding not only systems of justice but also how conceptually and materially important they are to shaping the positive rights and identity of those otherwise served well by those same systems. Judith Shklar too draws on the importance of understanding injustice in *The Faces of Injustice*, claiming that '[p]hilosophy has little to say' about 'the real victims of injustice'.[20] For Shklar, unless 'one takes full account of their experience, the picture of injustice is incomplete'.[21] The reality of law and injustice, for Shklar, is that 'injustice occurs continuously within the framework of an established polity with an operative system of law'.[22] The problem continues to be how we approach and understand that injustice, if we are even capable of seeing and understanding it, separately from how we ideally organize ourselves in liberal democracies. If we persist with ideals that occlude underlying structures of power and decision-making by remaining faithful to abstracted rights of the objective or neutral individual as the standard by which justice is measured, we simply persist with a 'normal model of justice' that 'limits itself to matching [a victim's] situation against the rules, which is inadequate as a way of recognizing victims'.[23] For Shklar, this means injustice persists because there exists an 'irreducibly subjective component that the normal model of justice cannot easily absorb'.[24]

Julius Stone addresses these same limitations of the normal modes of justice and their exclusion of the subjective. Stone identifies this problem as an 'intense and wide-ranging espousal of the ideal and goal of equality as the core of justice'.[25] Stone problematizes this automatic equation of justice with equality by exploring the facts of inequality and difference that are demanding of justice themselves and to which a mechanical or mathematical rules-based equality cannot deliver justice. Recognizing the increasing difficulty of being

18 Young (n 2) 3.
19 Young (n 2) 3.
20 Judith N Shklar, *The Faces of Injustice* (Yale University Press 1990) 35.
21 Judith N Shklar, *The Faces of Injustice* (Yale University Press 1990) 35.
22 Judith N Shklar, *The Faces of Injustice* (Yale University Press 1990) 19.
23 Judith N Shklar, *The Faces of Injustice* (Yale University Press 1990) 35.
24 Judith N Shklar, *The Faces of Injustice* (Yale University Press 1990) 37.
25 Stone (n 10) 151.

clear as to what justice means among ever-growing, competing claims, Stone does not dismiss this difficulty by referring to bare universals, which he otherwise understood as both appealing and not without merit and success;[26] rather, he claims that 'enclaves of justice' should be 'in constant change and travail'.[27] Stone's concerns with the minimal rule-based offerings of justice as equality are shared by Shklar, who notes the existence of a 'false intellectual self-assurance that positively encourages us to be unjust'[28] when we 'trust the rules' and, as a result, 'tend to become too sure of our competence and that makes us arrogant, cruel, and tyrannical'.[29] Certainly, when we claim that equality and justice are being done or that Indigenous peoples enjoy the same opportunities and rights and are subject to the same rules as everyone else, in the face of abject poverty and suffering and a history of exclusion and injustice, continuing to deny the recognition of Indigenous peoples, then how can the characterization of our society and faith in the rule of law be anything other than 'arrogant, cruel, and tyrannical'? The greater point Stone makes is that we exclude too much of who we are, who we are becoming or may become, including who we have been, by remaining wedded to justice as equality: 'there is no pot of justice at the end of the rainbow of equality'.[30] Illuminating Raymond Geuss's point that 'detached general statements' and concepts like 'equality' 'do not wear their meaning on their sleeves',[31] Stone notes that 'wider concepts of justice have to be invoked' to give equality meaning.[32] For Stone, 'the effect of simplifying justice to equality is to conceal, truncate, foreclose or disguise by fictional, arbitrary or ambiguous formulae, the range of values available to us when doing, rather than arbitrarily determining, justice'.[33]

This brief survey of the political philosophy of liberalism is applicable to Australia and its responses to Indigenous justice demands. I characterize the predominant Australian approach to Indigenous claims as 'redemptive liberalism'. Effectively, despite Australia's origins in colonial invasion, dispossession, and racism, the Australian state has developed away from its exclusionary and discriminatory past towards being a modern, social-democratic society, operating according to equality and the rule of law, with protections against further discrimination, and some programs to address historical and continuing disadvantage. To a certain extent, this is true. The infamous 'protection' regimes in Australia, instruments of socio-biological racism and genocide, are no longer in force; many Indigenous peoples now enjoy, to varying degrees,

26 Compare Brian Barry—see the references in n 12—and others.
27 Stone (n 10) 153.
28 Shklar (n 20) 20.
29 Shklar (n 20) 27.
30 Stone (n 10) 161.
31 Geuss, *Philosophy and Real Politics* (n 2) 14.
32 Stone (n 10) 160.
33 Stone (n 10) 162.

recognition and protection of their native title rights; we now have protections for cultural heritage and against racial discrimination that were largely introduced to improve the situation of Indigenous peoples; and we have many preferential programs aimed at addressing ongoing Indigenous disadvantage. Yet, these cursory highlights and individual successes deceive, achieving the same sort of occlusion of inequality and difference that faith in universal, rules-based approaches to justice as equality, and even justice as fairness in idealized forms, perform. It obfuscates the fact Indigenous peoples remain the most impoverished and vulnerable; it ignores the fact Indigenous children are being removed from their families in record numbers; it ignores the fact Indigenous peoples fill our prisons; it ignores the fact systems set up to recognize and protect Indigenous culture and heritage fail to protect them from being destroyed; it ignores the failure of the Australian state to reach any kind of meaningful settlement with Indigenous peoples; it ignores what justice is for Indigenous peoples by granting abstract rights and opportunities that do little to address Indigenous justice claims; it fails to address the power and decision-making issues at the core of these issues by refusing to allow Indigenous peoples, as Indigenous peoples, to meaningfully and adequality participate in the power and decision-making structures of democratic governance.

In what remains, I explore two responses to this situation that mirror the problems of the political philosophy of liberalism as applied to Indigenous justice claims. I argue this logic has informed two approaches from the Australian state and from Indigenous peoples—one focussed on a limited accommodation that does little to see greater justice done or understand inequality and difference and another that refuses to engage those with whom we, as a matter of unalterable fact, exist. I discuss both examples, emphasizing they exist because of our inability to organize ourselves differently and meaningfully address structural inequality, including in a way better accommodating of the range of difference claims that are determinative of our being and cannot simply be discarded as irrelevant categories of race, gender, and culture. I conclude by arguing for an always reforming approach to our system of democratic institutions and assessment of justice claims that if, following Shklar, are to mean 'anything morally', they must 'signify that the lives of all citizens matter, and that their sense of their rights must prevail'.[34]

2. Redemptive liberalism's accommodation of Indigenous peoples

Mythologized by many, *Mabo (No 2)* represents not just the achievement of Indigenous land rights but also modern Australia coming to terms with its colonial past.[35] Having overturned the doctrine of *terra nullius* that had

34 Shklar (n 20) 27.
35 *Mabo v Queensland (No 2)* (1992) 175 CLR 1.

justified over 200 years of Indigenous dispossession, *Mabo (No 2)* recognized a common law native title right to property that survived British invasion and continued to exist, where circumstance allowed.[36] The importance of *Mabo (No 2)* reaches beyond its limited recognition of native title: it offered recognition that had otherwise been denied. However, Australia's political history from the 1990s onward reveals such an idyllic reading of *Mabo (No 2)* to be a myth. The 1996 election of the Howard Government fundamentally shifted the Commonwealth's attitude towards Indigenous peoples within a charged political and cultural environment in which *Mabo (No 2)* was key. The consequences of this conservative social change, with a preference for 'practical measures' over self-determination, continues to impact Indigenous people today.[37] Prime Minister John Howard's politics echoed and cajoled a conservative backlash against Indigenous rights and the 'introspection and examination'[38] that resulted from successive national inquires such as the *Royal Commission into Aboriginal Deaths in Custody*, the *Bringing Them Home Report*, and the legislative enactment of *Mabo* under the *Native Title Act 1993* (Cth). This was a politics that well suited Barry's denial of group and cultural rights and instead focused on the equality of the individual, despite inequality and difference existing otherwise.

Myths about *Mabo (No 2)* originate from Indigenous and non-Indigenous sources. For some, *Mabo (No 2)* was an act of judicial overreach, a moralistic intervention in the legislative authority of parliament. For others, it was a progressive step that brought the Australian legal system in line with contemporary human rights standards.[39] For many Indigenous people, however, the overturning of *terra nullius* exposed the illegitimate foundations of the Australian state. *Mabo (No 2)* confirmed a violent dispossession that raised the question of the justification of the Australian state. Yet the narrow reality of *Mabo (No 2)* has always been more sombre. According to the High Court, at least, there is no residual sovereignty—of the law-making type that belongs to nations and states—that resides with Indigenous people. This is plainly

36 *Terra nullius*, meaning broadly a land belonging to no one, was the legal fiction used to justify the history of Indigenous dispossession. See Andrew Fitzmaurice, 'The Genealogy of *Terra Nullius*' (2008) 38(129) Aust Hist Stud 1.

37 Perhaps the best-known of these is the Northern Territory Intervention of 2007, which continues today in modified form. However, the impact of changes extends much further. They include the disbandment of the Aboriginal and Torres Strait Islander Commission (ATSIC) in 2005 (a legislatively enacted self-determining representative body) and the subsequent untold amount of lost progress towards self-determination.

38 John Howard, as quoted in Carol Johnson, 'John Howard's "Values" and Australian Identity' (2007) 42 AJPS 195, 205.

39 See generally Margaret Stephenson and Suri Ratnapala (eds), *Mabo: A Judicial Revolution: The Aboriginal Land Rights Decision and Its Impact on Australian Law* (University of Queensland Press 1993) and Peter Howard Russell, *Recognizing Aboriginal Title: The Mabo Case and Indigenous Resistance to English-Settler Colonialism* (University of Toronto Press 2005).

ridiculous to Indigenous people, who see this as one of the successive legal fictions that operate to deny Indigenous justice claims. Yet beyond the narrow legalism of *Mabo (No 2)* and its strict restatement of state sovereignty, which the High Court could not (or would not) question, is a reality with which Indigenous people must reckon. That reality, however unjust, is the subordinate position of Indigenous people in comparison to that of the Australian state when considering the enforcement and protection of Indigenous rights. Here, *Mabo (No 2)*'s greater symbolic weight has always been its inability to answer those foundational questions, those lasting questions that animate Indigenous claims.

One of the lasting legacies of *Mabo (No 2)*, besides its achievement of land rights and its perpetually unrealized, latent threat to non-Indigenous Australia, is its re-authorization of the Australian state by operation of the 'tide of history'.[40] Justice Brennan's reference to the 'tide of history' and its operation with the 'skeleton of principle which gives the body of our law its shape and internal consistency' set the limits of native title recognition by avoiding the undermining of Crown sovereignty—the mythical and unilateral act of discovery from which the High Court draws its authority.[41] Justice Brennan's insistence that 'when the tide of history has washed away any real acknowledgement of traditional law and any real observance of traditional customs, the foundation of native title has disappeared' echoes in the persistent failure of the Australian state to address these foundational questions.[42] Justice Brennan's 'tide of history' operates as a structural mechanism of the Australian state, much in the same way that the obfuscation of inequality and difference occurs by way of justice as equality. It is an affective concept bloodied with what Maurice Blanchot described as the 'excessive theoretical freight' of its own (re)production and affect.[43] It becomes a convenient description for Justice Brennan to operationalize in place of what his Honour is unable or unwilling to address and, having corrected the application of justice as equality, to look forward from, by moving beyond past exclusionary actions that now have no connection to the cleansed and re-affirmed state. It is the *tabula rasa* achieved by erasing all difference and inequality to instantiate a veil of ignorance from which to determine the future governance of supposed equals. It further represents the paradigmatic operation of the Australian state to redeem itself and the law at the expense of others. Redemption is achieved by the law having shed its exclusionary and oppressive histories and by offering limited accommodations to Indigenous people without having addressed the structures of the relationship that are at the

40 *Mabo (No 2)* (n 35) 60.
41 *Mabo (No 2)* (n 35) 45.
42 *Mabo (No 2)* (n 35) 60.
43 Maurice Blanchot, *Writing of the Disaster* (University of Nebraska Press 1995) 87.

core of injustice, both original and ongoing. Ultimately, Australia and the common law are cleansed and renewed by the 'tide of history' and the promised 'civilized standards' of a modern society are authorized by the common law's correction, lest it be 'frozen in an age of racial discrimination', yet all the while not having to account for the inequality and difference it occludes.[44]

The 'excessive theoretical freight' of the 'tide of history' works to scaffold further the Australian state's 'skeleton of principle', disavowing culpability for Indigenous dispossession while performing re-authorization. The 'tide of history' is a vehicle for the Australian state to survive the stain and insinuation of accusations of illegitimacy. By producing redemption and legitimacy, it completes the law's and the Australian state's authorizing circle without the question of their origin, which rests at the core of Indigenous justice claims, having been seriously and justly faced. Yet the origin question and its contemporary relevance remains core to the original grievance of both the current inequality of Indigenous people and the lack of respect, dignity, and recognition afforded to them. Those questions erased by the 'tide of history' did not go entirely unanswered following *Mabo (No 2)*. The then Keating Government promised a social justice package to address the broader position of Indigenous people. This included funds to purchase land for those—the majority—that would not benefit from native title and asking the then Aboriginal and Torres Strait Islander Commission (ATSIC), a legislatively enacted self-determining representative body, to suggest measures to 'address the dispossession of Aboriginal and Torres Strait Islander people'. ATSIC's report, *Recognition, Rights and Reform*, was extensive. Chaired by Charles Perkins, a renowned Indigenous activist, leader, and bureaucrat, the report focused 'on institutional, structural, collaborative, cooperative reform', emphasizing the need for improved relationships between Indigenous and non-Indigenous peoples. Importantly, the report insisted on constitutional reform as being key to facilitating substantive and lasting reforms.[45] The social justice package, however, was only minimally implemented. While some have benefited, most Indigenous peoples still face ever-growing levels of abject poverty and inequality. Had John Howard not won the 1996 federal election by a landslide and had ATSIC been supported rather than disbanded in 2005, the current state of Indigenous affairs would be very different. This history suggests, in the absence of meaningful reform and given retrograde decisions in Indigenous affairs, Indigenous people have been restricted by an enlarged application of the 'tide of history' that refuses

44 *Mabo (No 2)* (n 35) 42.

45 Aboriginal and Torres Strait Islander Commission, *Recognition, Rights and Reform: A Report to Government on Native Title Social Justice Measures* (Commonwealth of Australia 1995) ix–xiii.

to address foundational questions or to recognize the continued impact of the 'dispossession which underwrote the development of the nation'.[46]

3. Refusal of the irredeemably colonial

In contrast to the inability of accommodation to achieve justice for Indigenous people, many have drawn on international examples of Indigenous refusal and resurgence to overcome the 'tide of history' and progressive liberalism's confinement of Indigenous peoples by the politics of recognition. For example, in *Red Skins, White Masks*, Glen Coulthard argues for refusal and resurgence as alternatives to recognition and the rights offered by the politics of recognition.[47] Coulthard maintains the politics of recognition is problematic because it confines Indigenous people to limited and symbolic incorporations within the settler-state while being unable to deliver justice to them.[48] Rather than empower them, the politics of recognition fails to engage with Indigenous people as equal sovereigns and forces them, through limited options backed by the material and ideological force of the state, into subordinate positions.[49] The politics of recognition not only fails in this regard, but Coulthard argues that it is a distraction from the fact that illegitimate societal structures are incapable of reform.[50] For Coulthard, rather than empowering them, recognition ends up subjectifying Indigenous people as they invest in settler-colonial ways of being and are further assimilated and dispossessed.[51]

Tony Birch, an Indigenous author and activist, has adopted this critique in his argument against constitutional reform in Australia. Birch, also drawing on Audra Simpson's *Mohawk Interruptus*,[52] insists that symbolic recognition granted by the colonizer to the colonized fails Indigenous people for the very reasons Coulthard identifies.[53] Birch argues that, by rejecting symbolic recognition, 'direct activist campaigns'[54] have enabled a 'bypassing [of] symbolic gestures' that will force the Australian state to negotiate 'fresh and meaningful approaches to Indigenous/non-Indigenous relationships'.[55] How this will force the Australian state to negotiate is hard to understand, but refusal

46 *Mabo (No 2)* (n 35) 69.
47 Glen Coulthard, *Red Skins, White Masks* (University of Minnesota Press 2014).
48 Glen Coulthard, *Red Skins, White Masks* (University of Minnesota Press 2014) 3–4.
49 Glen Coulthard, *Red Skins, White Masks* (University of Minnesota Press 2014) 42, 140.
50 Glen Coulthard, *Red Skins, White Masks* (University of Minnesota Press 2014) 151–79.
51 Glen Coulthard, *Red Skins, White Masks* (University of Minnesota Press 2014) 42.
52 Audra Simpson, *Mohawk Interruptus* (Duke University Press 2014).
53 Tony Birch, 'On What Terms Can We Speak? Refusal, Resurgence and Climate Justice' (2018) 24 & 25 Coolabah 2.
54 Tony Birch, 'On What Terms Can We Speak? Refusal, Resurgence and Climate Justice' (2018) 24 & 25 Coolabah 6.
55 Tony Birch, 'On What Terms Can We Speak? Refusal, Resurgence and Climate Justice' (2018) 24 & 25 Coolabah 9.

has, for Birch, 'raised the political conscience of young Aboriginal people who have decided that Australian governments are unable to move beyond the mentality of the colonial master'.[56] Like Coulthard drawing on Taiaiaike Alfred,[57] Birch argues that the Australian state is incapable of change and, therefore, Indigenous people must turn away to realize an Indigenous future.[58] Birch is explicit about the inability of the Australian state to change. This is clear when Birch asks 'why any group or individual would seek formal recognition in such a document. The Australian constitution should be torn up and rewritten as a bill of universal human rights'.[59] For Birch, '[a]s Aboriginal people, we must refuse the invitation to sit at the big table where, ultimately, we are made fools of'.[60] Birch is right about the failure of symbolic recognition; that failure also informed the development of the Uluru Statement from the Heart, which sits at the centre of the most recent demand for change in the relationship between Indigenous and non-Indigenous people in Australia and which calls for a constitutionally enshrined Voice to Parliament as a way to directly speak to the structural issues of power and decision-making within Australia's democratic institutions and move beyond limits of formalized justice as equality or idealized fairness.[61] Birch is right about the failure of recognition, but his adoption of refusal misconceives our challenge, Indigenous agency, and opportunities for reform. Birch is mistaken about the origin and symbolic nature of the Uluru Statement from the Heart and the meaning of any government engagement. This is evident in Birch's conflation of the Referendum Council that facilitated the regional dialogues which led to the Uluru Statement from the Heart with the prior 'Recognise' campaign that ended once it was clear that the Uluru Statement from the Heart had marked a change in direction for constitutional reform.[62] 'Recognise' *was* purely symbolic, and an overwhelming majority of Indigenous people came to reject it because it didn't offer substantive structural reforms and was aimed simply at including recognition of the unique place of Indigenous people in the preamble to the Constitution. It provided no substantive, structural reform to address the constitutional place of Indigenous people.

Birch rejects any engagement *whatsoever* with the settler-state, which is believed to be unchangeable, assimilationist, and makes fools of Indigenous peoples. This is a sentiment informed by the only-too-real experience of Indigenous people. Yet, rallying against symbolism, Birch himself relies on

56 Tony Birch, 'On Sovereignty' (2017) 229 Overland 88, 89.
57 Coulthard (n 47) 158–59.
58 Birch, 'On What Terms Can We Speak?' (n 53) 10.
59 Tony Birch, 'On Recognition' (2017) 227 Overland 43, 44.
60 Birch, 'On Sovereignty' (n 56) 89.
61 See generally Megan Davis and George Williams, *Everything You Need to Know About the Uluru Statement from the Heart* (UNSW Press 2021).
62 Birch, 'On What Terms Can We Speak?' (n 53) 5.

the symbolic power of myth to undermine the claim of the Uluru Statement from the Heart to be representative by suggesting that its entire development was controlled by individuals beholden to the state.[63] Birch further refuses to engage with the constitution of the Australian state beyond the narrow and violent structure he is willing to recognize, which would have eradicated all Indigenous peoples already, if taken to its logical conclusion. Furthermore, the criticism that the Uluru Statement from the Heart is symbolic is misplaced. The Uluru Statement from the Heart *is* symbolic, but it is more than that. It is an invitation to the Australian people to address the constitution of 'Australia', its symbolic and cultural existence, the power and effect of its institutions, and the structures of power and decision-making that make it what it is beyond the limited and unsatisfactory offerings provided by justice as equality. Unlike 'Recognise', the Uluru Statement from the Heart is both a refusal and an invitation; it addresses the symbolic and practical needs of reform by providing the respect and recognition that should be afforded to Indigenous peoples, that is, recognition rather than occlusion of inequality and difference, coupled with the required structural changes to ensure substantive reforms are achieved.[64]

Indigenous people should be building their resurgences and refusing to be recognized in limited ways. This includes refusing to accept justice as equality or idealized fairness and the limited, individual examples of success that are achieved as a result. Yet without addressing the relationship with non-Indigenous Australia, Indigenous people are unable to achieve the 'fresh and meaningful approaches to Indigenous/non-Indigenous relationships' that Birch supports.[65] My reflection is not meant to excuse continued oppressive practices nor advocate blind engagement with the Australian state. However, it does mean Indigenous people must take up the responsibility to engage with non-Indigenous people and institutions and clearly understand the demands of that task. This means emphasizing important Australian differences that too many adaptions of the North American experience, as represented by the likes of Coulthard and Simpson, fail to appreciate. We have not had the same history and experience of recognition (such as treaties that grant or recognize rights, now embedded constitutional institutions) that Indigenous people in North America have. These provide, even when understood in their limited and negative capacities, spaces for dialogue within the democratic institutions of those nations for Indigenous people and their claims to impact the power and the decision-making that takes place, including limited self-government. That does not mean that Indigenous people should not deploy refusal, but it does mean that there exist important institutional differences in Australia

63 Birch, 'On What Terms Can We Speak?' (n 53) 5.
64 See Davis and Williams (n 61).
65 Davis and Williams (n 61) 9.

with which Indigenous people must contend in forging new relationships with non-Indigenous Australia. We need to be able to develop institutional mechanisms, however limited they have been elsewhere, that enable Indigenous people in Australia to be recognized and respected, as well as providing the foundation upon which to negotiate our future relationship, beyond the limited offerings of justice as equality or idealized fairness.

My concern is that *absolute refusals* are incapable of engaging with the entanglements, no matter how unfair, of the relationship between Indigenous and non-Indigenous Australians. They leave Indigenous people as confined as the politics of recognition does. Both Coulthard and Simpson address this concern, accepting the continued need to engage the settler-state.[66] However, many Australian practices of refusal, such as Birch's, are more absolute and tend to mirror the violence of the settler state's own pretensions of sovereignty and right, those same absolute and universal demands that occlude from judgment and assessment the real aspects of our existence. By focusing too much on who is ideally recognized or limiting access to justice to those exclusionary ideals of justice as equality or fairness, the representational politics, structural forces, and material circumstances that produce the issues animating Indigenous demands remain occluded. Practices of refusal that refuse outright the other in our shared space are refusals of unfulfilled transformative potential.

4. Answering justice

What might a solution to Indigenous demands for justice look like? It should be clear that both outright refusal and ideal approaches focused on justice as equality or idealized fairness provide little hope for change in the here and now. Hope and the belief that our existence can and should be better matter. Of course, blind faith is something else, and abstract justice combined with glib restatements of principle and opportunity matter little when you suffer the injustice of extreme poverty and inequality and the refusal of your existence. I stress this point in the context of a popular nihilism that has taken hold in many decolonial spaces, especially Australia.[67] Nihilism, along with turning inward to the strength and support of one's own community and shared experience of being, is powerful, especially in the face of continued oppression and denial. But it can only ever be a temporary, transitionary state, which may be cyclical in that we revisit it again, towards a change in our relationship and attitude towards others, including the oppressed. Too much of the anger and rage involved in thumbing our noses at hope reaffirms and mirrors the injustices already faced and acts to further occlude the structures of power and decision-making that underlie and inform our relationships with others,

66 Coulthard (n 47) 179; Simpson (n 52) 177–94.
67 See, eg, Chelsea Watego, *Another Day in the Colony* (University of Queensland Press 2021).

leaving us focussed on battles that are incapable of achieving the change needed. It brings us closer to more rage and disagreement, rather than away from it, while also widening the gulf between Indigenous and non-Indigenous people. I agree with Shklar that 'nothing is more painful or soul-destroying than rage'—rage is not the ground upon which we can proceed justly.[68]

Proceeding differently is key. It means going beyond what accommodation and refusal offer. It also means embracing more seriously an obligation and responsibility that can and should be embedded in our democratic institutions and not just left to abstract statements of right or ideal measures and calculations of hypothetically free and equal citizens. This means starting from where we already are, not simply from a dominant standpoint or where we would be ideally. For Indigenous claims, this means not asking whether liberal states can accommodate Indigenous peoples and then proceeding with an abstract assessment of that accommodation. It means engaging with the ways this accommodation is already a reality and then proceeding to assess, judge, and implement, through a much more active culture of critique and change, how we can better improve the institutions of our democratic society by doing justice to the particular demands of inequality and difference that do exist.[69] The opposite of doing so is from behind a veil of ignorance. If those institutions are only ever judged in their formal capacity to deliver justice as equality and by their celebration of individual achievement and success, while ignoring inequality and difference, we simply 'confuse a common [and forced] culture with a harmony of political interests' that 'amounts to little but a sleight of hand'.[70] For Shklar, 'these intimations of shared meaning, as divined by prophetic or traditionalist avatars of the spirit of the people, are never checked against actual opinions, least of all those of the most disadvantaged and frightened people'.[71] These kinds of prophetic statements are all too familiar in response to the demands of Indigenous peoples in Australia.

The commitment to justice I have in mind entails embracing a universal orientation towards justice, a commitment to practice, which should be embedded in our democratic institutions. This may involve the implementation of rights and legal instruments to protect, enforce, negotiate, or otherwise recognize inequality and difference or specific cultural claims. But these are only the abstract vehicles we use to give expression to our existence other than by managing our relationships with one another and the claims to justice that we make from them. These abstractions cannot be allowed to rule or deny our existence. This means a commitment to an invigorated politics that refuses to accept or settle on justice as formal equality or idealized fairness in their most minimalist senses or an overarching and transcendental

68 Shklar (n 20) 49.
69 Again, creating the conditions for this is something else entirely.
70 Shklar (n 20) 115.
71 Shklar (n 20).

concept of justice that proceeds from ideal standards and makes no room for the reality of Indigenous justice claims. It involves a commitment to resolving existing and ongoing tensions through the building of required institutional relationships, keeping the structures of power and decision-making within clear view, and making credible adjustments to those institutions in the name of justice. This means a commitment to the transformative potential of political institutions to provide for what Tamara Jugov and Lea Ypi describe as an 'understand[ing] that empowerment means not to play by the rules (even when one individually benefits) but to be an equal contributor to their making'.[72]

Although, for Shklar, 'it would be childish . . . to imagine that democratic attitudes and institutions constitute an adequate response to the sense of injustice', they do provide us with the best means available of addressing it together.[73] As Shklar notes, the 'procedures of consent may be the best we can do, but they do not conquer the dominion of injustice'.[74] The point is that we may never eliminate disagreement, inequality and injustice, nor should we ever want to eliminate difference, yet we must have a way of being able to engage, while giving due respect to different justice claims. I am further guided by Jacques Derrida's words at the end of *The Politics of Friendship* on the achievement of this kind of justice and the attitudes and institutions required to realize it.[75] Derrida asks:

> is it possible to think and to implement democracy, that which would keep the old name 'democracy', while uprooting from it all these figures of friendship (philosophical and religious) which prescribe fraternity. . . . Is it possible, in assuming a certain faithful memory of democratic reason . . . not to found, where it is no longer a matter of founding, but to open out to the future, or rather, to the 'come', of a certain democracy?[76]

I think so. I think it is possible for the democracy that is 'Australia', rather than being irredeemably colonial and incapable of change, to look now to a democracy to come.

There exists within this politics a responsibility on the part of both Indigenous and non-Indigenous people that should not be denied. From within our own understandings and experience, responsibility exists not as a pure gift of justice but is thrust upon us imperfectly and unexpectedly by the fact of our existence together with others and our claims against one another.

72 Tamara Jugov and Lea Ypi, 'Structural Injustice, Epistemic Opacity, and the Responsibilities of the Oppressed' (2019) 50 J Soc Philos 7, 21.

73 Shklar (n 20) 91.

74 Shklar (n 20) 91.

75 Jacques Derrida, *The Politics of Friendship* (George Collins tr, Verso 2005).

76 Jacques Derrida, *The Politics of Friendship* (George Collins tr, Verso 2005) 306.

It is that forceful, imperfect, and unexpected demand of responsibility that makes it that much more important and impossible to deny and that makes the ongoing denial of inequality and difference in the face of an assertive justice as equality or idealized fairness so palpable. That responsibility requires us to engage across our differences and the tensions of our relations and to commit to institutions capable of facilitating meaningful dialogue. Our greatest responsibility, then, is attending to the difficulty of accompanying one another, of having to engage and acknowledge someone, not simply and violently by our own terms of reference, but via genuine engagements that respect one another and commit to a process of mutual engagement and transformation. That must be the universal standard of justice that governs our behaviour and inhabits our democratic institutions, rather than positing ideal principles that serve to benefit current and dominant practices and people at the expense of others.

Chapter 5

States of injustice and statuses of legality

Nicole Roughan[1]

1. Introduction

In *The Faces of Injustice*, Judith Shklar argued that 'the real realm of injustice is not in an amoral and prelegal state of nature.... It does not stand outside the gate of even the best of known states'.[2] While Shklar defended the principle of legality—law's constraints upon power—she argued that practices of injustice inhere in the law. Shklar argued that law's injustices are rooted in its abstraction, which leaves law inattentive to the sense of injustice felt by those persons to whom it is applied. The 'normal model of law' supports both 'passive' injustice—failures to act in the face of injustice—as well as the acute injustice of indifference to injustice itself.[3]

What Shklar sees as the normality of law's injustice is hardly news to those who recognize the Indigenous legalities that have been displaced and dominated by colonial impositions of settler legal orders. On its face, Shklar's critique of the faceless and abstracting institutions of law resonates with arguments that the model of law imposed (and perpetuated) by a colonial state not only fails to see and hear Indigenous faces and voices but cannot see and hear them in their own register.[4] The claim to procedural justice that is carried

1 I am grateful for the support of a Rutherford Discovery Fellowship from the Royal Society Te Apārangi, for research assistance from Kiraan Chetty; for detailed comments from Joshua Getzler, Coel Kirkby, and Arie Rosen; and the input of audiences at the Julius Stone Institute's workshop, *Responding to Injustice*, the University of Toronto, the University of Auckland Philosophy Department Seminar, and the Auckland Law Faculty Workshop. All errors are my own.
2 Judith N Shklar, *The Faces of Injustice* (Yale University Press 1990) 19.
3 Judith N Shklar, *The Faces of Injustice* (Yale University Press 1990) 3.
4 Influential and substantial critiques of the impact (upon Indigenous legalities) of the juridical forms favoured by the normal model of law include Ani Mikaere, *Colonising Myths—Māori Realities: He Rukuruku Whakaaro* (Huia Publishers 2011); Glen Coulthard, *Red Skin, White Masks: Rejecting the Colonial Politics of Recognition* (University of Minnesota Press 2014); Audra Simpson, *Mohawk Interruptus: Political Life across the Borders of Settler States* (Duke University Press 2014). These are representative examples of a much larger and linguistically/

DOI: 10.4324/9781032676159-6

within the normal model of imposed law also rings hollow, in light of both the imposition itself and state law's continuing inability—due to its claimed supremacy and its modes of abstraction—to attend to Indigenous claims to justice. Colonization (as a continuing phenomenon) may thus provide one of the clearest contexts in which law's agents are (just as Shklar suggested) agents of injustice. Those agents both operate the forms of injustice and display indifference in its face.[5]

The Faces of Injustice itself attended only barely and generically to the injustices faced by Indigenous peoples and the sense of injustice resulting from their forceful inclusion in settler states. It overlooked not only a specific concern for Indigenous faces and voices of injustice but also Indigenous forms and claims of justice. Shklar's broader work did not attend to Indigenous claims to the status of legality operating either independently or in interaction with the dominant (state) legal order. Indeed, for Shklar, the inclusive character of the liberal legal order is supposed to operate by diversifying and neutralizing—rather than intensifying and empowering—any affiliative preferences that treat persons as insiders or outsiders of particular groups.[6] Amidst Shklar's many insights as a critic of exclusion, her work may be criticized for its over-inclusion of persons within a state legal order. This is a familiar critique, but it resonates most strongly against Shklar's account in light of her own concern for the concrete experiences of victims of injustice. There is a core tension in posing a demand that responses to injustice see and hear persons in their concrete circumstances, without also seeing and hearing the independent and interacting claims to Indigenous legalities that are generated by concrete contexts of continuing colonization.

A rich vein of work responds to that tension, both (1) challenging liberal political theory to address Indigenous claims for self-determination and to redress the injustices of colonization; and (2) highlighting the particular injustice carried by the imposition and perpetuation of the normal model of law in the face of

geographically diverse field of literature, spanning beyond the mostly Canadian and New Zealand works cited here. The global field also uses different terminologies to capture the concept of indigeneity. Here I use the term 'Indigenous' except where citing other scholars, when their original terminology is retained.

5 Examined in concrete terms (and contemporaneous with Shklar's own work) in Moana Jackson, *Māori and the Criminal Justice System: A New Perspective He Whaipaanga Hou* (Policy and Research Division, Department of Justice 1987).

6 In Shklar's liberalism, 'the basic units of political life are not discursive and reflecting persons, nor friends and enemies, nor patriotic soldier-citizens, nor energetic litigants, but the weak and the powerful': Judith N Shklar, 'The Liberalism of Fear' in Nancy L Rosenblum (ed), *Liberalism and the Moral Life* (Harvard University Press 1989) 27. Shklar's aversion to nationalism in all its forms is summarized in Stanley Hoffmann, 'Judith Shklar as Political Thinker' (1992) 21 PT 172. On Shklar's distrust of democracy's tendency towards nationalist particularism, see Shefali Misra, 'Ugly Attachments: Judith Shklar and the Unattractive Face of Solidarity' (2022) 7 Glob Intellect Hist 685.

pre-existing and continuing models of Indigenous legality.[7] The present chapter does not aim to reiterate that work. Instead, its direct focus responds to Shklar's critique of the abstraction of the normal model of law (and its role in theories of justice), and her demand to provide for the faces and voices of concrete persons. I argue that, in the tension between abstraction and concretization, legality's tendency to abstraction offers more complex potential than Shklar's critique in *The Faces of Injustice* suggests. We can intervene more with the idea of legality (and offer more juridical responses to injustice) than Shklar allowed.

The chapter's primary claim is that abstracting the status of legality—away from concrete state law—allows us to see and hear interactive or overlapping claims to legality contesting the same mode of normative ordering. Such overlaps and interactions interrupt the recognition between officials and subjects of law that I argue is required for legality. The interaction of claims to legality generates either a matter of justice between competing claims or a matter of sheer force, in which one order dominates another. The latter outcome undermines law's claim to be a normative rather than merely powerful social institution. In the context of interacting state and Indigenous legalities, if law is to be something other than force, then the status of legality must be among the objects of justice—open to correction and redistribution in ways that recognize Indigenous legalities and respond to the injustice of their prior exclusion.

The chapter's second claim is that law's abstraction can suggest forms of 'interlegality'[8] that offer tools for addressing the interaction and intersection

7 Indigenous claims to self-determination became a central feature of debates over multicultural forms of liberalism (and their limits) following the influential collection of essays in Duncan Ivison, Paul Patton, and Will Sanders (eds), *Political Theory and the Rights of Indigenous Peoples* (CUP 2000). Influential early monographs include Will Kymlicka, *Liberalism, Community, and Culture* (OUP 1989); Andrew Sharp, *Justice and the Māori* (OUP 1990); James Tully, *Strange Multiplicity: Constitutionalism in an Age of Diversity* (CUP 1995). A shift from claims to political rights to claims to Indigenous legalities and forms of interaction with state legalities is marked across canonical contributions in different jurisdictions. In addition to the works cited in n 3 above, see, eg, John Borrows, *Canada's Indigenous Constitution* (University of Toronto Press 2010).

8 The term is often used without embracing the full critical ontology within which Boaventura de Sousa Santos presented it in Boaventura de Santos, 'Law: A Map of Misreading. Toward a Postmodern Conception of Law' (1987) J L Soc 279, 288. Klabbers and Palombella have elaborated a distinctive account of 'inter-legality' that addresses overlapping legal ordering by adopting the 'perspective of the case' rather than that of a single legal order: Jan Klabbers and Gianluigi Palombella, 'Introduction: Situating Inter-Legality' in Jan Klabbers and Gianluigi Palombella (eds), *The Challenge of Inter-Legality* (CUP 2019). For analysis, see Neil Walker, 'Legalising Inter-Legality' (2022) 1 Eur L Open 216. Klabbers and Palombella present inter-legality as a contender (alongside monism and dualism) for understanding relations between state and international (or other supra-state) legal orders. Essays in their collection, attuned to transnational and international instances of interlegality, do not examine state-Indigenous interlegality contexts, save for a brief mention by Besson of 'infranational' jurisdictional overlaps. Ralf Michaels has suggested that the vagueness of interlegality means it obscures more than it explains: Ralf Michaels, 'Tertiary Rules' in Nico Krisch (ed), *Entangled Legalities Beyond the State* (CUP 2021).

of legal orders and operating just institutions of justice (rather than mere force) in contexts of state–Indigenous interactions. While my full account of interlegality is defended elsewhere,[9] the present claim is that legality's forms of abstraction (the very forms Shklar criticized) can be used to imagine forms for just contestation, correction, recognition, and distribution of the status(es) of legality. If legality offers forms through which persons can see and speak to each other, forms for doing (and being recognized as doing) justice, then its counterpart interlegality offers such forms for relations between those who recognize different (state and Indigenous) legal orders. Interlegality's response to injustice does not turn away from abstraction, nor away from legal theory into political theory, rather looks further into theories of legality and the imaginative potential of law's forms of abstraction.[10]

These claims are defended in the next four sections. Section two argues that Shklar's call to address the faces and voices of injustice as personal encounters moves too quickly past forms and claims made against the state, as well as the status of legality that it assumes (and at times guards) for itself. Section three asks what it would take for those claims (and not simply voices) of injustice to be heard; for those forms (and not simply faces) of injustice to be seen. I suggest that legality itself can provide a particular mode for addressing the interaction of abstract and concrete claims of injustice, as well as the tension between abstract and concrete forms of recognition across interacting legal orders. These two concerns align in section four's account of the prospect of developing forms for contesting, correcting, recognizing, and distributing the status of legality between state and Indigenous legal orders, to correct the normal model of law by institutionalizing the humility that is required for legality to thrive in contexts of overlapping claims. Section five sets out a brief account of interlegality and the ways in which its abstraction can respond to a series of prominent objections about the recognition of Indigenous legality, including concerns about identity politics and 'ethno-nationalism' and the claim that historical injustices, while profound, have been superseded.

9 Nicole Roughan, 'From Interacting Legalities to Interlegality' in *Legalities* (unpublished manuscript).

10 On law's imaginative potential, see Maksymilian Del Mar, *Artefacts of Legal Inquiry: The Value of Imagination in Adjudication* (Hart Publishing 2020) and, in an interlegal setting, see the relational imagination of Horatia Muir Watt, 'Conflicts of Laws Unbounded: The Case for a Legal-Pluralist Revival' in Paul Schiff Berman (ed), *The Oxford Handbook of Global Legal Pluralism* (OUP 2020).

2. Revisiting *The Faces of Injustice*

The present work borrows both the tensions and insights of *The Faces of Injustice* and turns them upon the context of interaction of state and Indigenous legalities. This was not Shklar's own focus, so it is important to explain how that setting relates to Shklar's broader work.[11]

a. Shklar on personal and political injustice

Shklar argued that injustice is no mere precursor to justice, but a 'personal and political experience' that is 'a part of all societies known to history'.[12] According to Shklar, the peremptory treatments of injustice in both legal and political theories of justice serve to obscure the faces and voices of victims of injustice. Shklar argued that the faces of injustice can be given more attention in political theory, which can treat justice and injustice not only as juridical phenomena but also as personal and political experiences. In opposition to Shklar, the claim here is that turning too quickly away from theories of law lets branches of legal theory and legality itself off the hook. It also overlooks the potential of both legal theory and legal practice to respond to the injustices that surround the contestation and distribution of statuses of legality.

In Shklar's view, the normal model of law presents a particularly formal version of a principle of legality, in which the experiences of the concrete persons engaged in doing (and receiving) justice are not supposed to matter. Shklar thought that they do matter or, at least, that the personal and

11 Shklar scholars emphasize that her work is linked by her efforts to show that the liberal legal order is a precarious, imperfect, yet important tool to protect persons against cruelty; by her psychologically rich interests and approaches; and by her attention to history and its lessons: see, eg, Hoffmann (n 6) 172. The secondary literature has not focused upon state–Indigenous contexts for thinking about Shklar's work on injustice, but some proximate concerns examine the implications of Shklar's 'liberalism of fear' for thinking about postcolonial, multicultural, and cosmopolitan theories of democracy—see, eg, Jacob T Levy, *Multiculturalism of Fear* (OUP 2000)—and the implications of Shklar's thinking for international political theory—see, eg, Christof Royer, 'Introduction: Shklar's (Underappreciated) International Thought' (2022) 7 Glob Intellect Hist 639.

12 Shklar, *The Faces of Injustice* (n 2) 19. Shklar expressly sought to treat together the personal and political experiences of justice and injustice, following the lesson she took from Rousseau that 'overcoming the discrepancies between personal and public justice remains an essential aspect of any democratic ideal' (122). A political theorist of law, such as Shklar, cannot have as much distinctive faith in legality itself. On Shklar's political theory of law, see Samuel Moyn, 'Shklar Versus the International Criminal Court' (2013) 4 Humanity 473. See Shklar's original critique of the limits of an ideology that treats law as institutionally set apart, as having fora for contests that are not themselves open to contest, and ordered through juridical rationalities that are precisely not political: Judith N Shklar, *Legalism* (Harvard University Press 1964).

interpersonal experience of injustice (and not merely the abstract public personae of officials and subjects) are among the proper concerns for a theory of justice. Her account thus objected to theorists of justice who blindly accept the normal model of law, which engages both agents and victims of injustice as abstract legal persons—faceless amidst institutions that are celebrated as sites of 'juridical rationality, impersonality, fairness, and impartiality'.[13]

Shklar's attention to the persons who are the victims and agents of injustice carries forward her broader work's reasons to be sceptical about the more idealistic claims of liberalism, which are captured in her influential account of a 'liberalism of fear'.[14] Shklar sought to preserve what is valuable about liberal legality in the context of an inclusive democratic system, putting faith not in juridical but in democratic political institutions. The key task of the liberal state, for Shklar, is not to empower persons but to protect them from both public and private acts of cruelty.[15] Shklar showed, however, that the political order and its normal model of law are often cruel in themselves. This was evidenced, most profoundly, in Shklar's account of the stain on democracy in America left by both the era of slavery and failures to redress its wrongs.[16]

To supplement the normal model (or perhaps to supplant it), Shklar argued for attention to the concrete persons on whom injustice is wrought, and those who (actively or passively) administer injustice. The victims of injustice are neither served nor sated by the procedures designed to determine just outcomes according to the normal model of law. Instead, victims' senses of injustice should be given a 'privileged voice' in hearing their claims.[17] For all her concerns about the limitations of formal rituals of justice, Shklar

13 Shklar (n 2) 18 posits that this model is 'accepted by Aristotelians and Hobbesians, Kantians and utilitarians, liberals and conservatives, and most theologians as well'.

14 Shklar's term 'liberalism of fear' appeared first in Judith N Shklar, *Ordinary Vices* (Harvard University Press 1984) 1–6 and is fully elaborated in Judith N Shklar, 'The Liberalism of Fear' in *Political Thought and Political Thinkers* (Stanley Hoffmann ed, University of Chicago Press 1998). See also Moyn, 'Shklar versus the International Criminal Court' (n 12); Samuel Moyn, 'The Carlyle Lectures 2022—The Cold War and the Canon of Liberalism: Against the Enlightenment (Judith Shklar)' (University of Oxford, 25 January 2022) <www.history.ox.ac.uk/event/the-carlyle-lectures-2022-the-cold-war-and-the-canon-of-liberalism> accessed 19 June 2024; Samuel Moyn, 'Against the Enlightenment: Judith Shklar' in *Liberalism Against Itself: Cold War Intellectuals and the Making of Our Times* (Yale University Press 2023). There is a new wave of literature on the relation of Shklar's scepticism about value to a commitment to forms of egalitarian principles: see, eg, Bernard Yack, 'Political Liberalism: Political, Not Philosophical' (2017) 15 Perspectives on Politics 116.

15 The connection to Hobbes is explored by Elisabeth Anker, who criticizes Shklar's ousting of Hobbes from the tradition of liberal legality against which she presented her own account of the liberalism of fear. Elisabeth Anker, 'The Liberalism of Horror' (2014) 81 Soc Res 795.

16 Judith N Shklar, *American Citizenship: The Quest for Inclusion* (Harvard University Press 1991).

17 Shklar, *The Faces of Injustice* (n 2) 90. See also 109–10: the injuries we experience are specific and concrete, whereas courts as agents of the law must remain general and abstract.

acknowledged the value of procedural justice, provided it gives priority to the voices of victims. Accessible procedures can serve persons' psychological need for vindication, as well as building and inculcating a sense of justice.[18]

b. *Indigenous faces of injustice?*

Despite Shklar's interests in persons and their experiences of injustice, *The Faces of Injustice* touched only briefly upon the victims of colonization. Shklar offered a short critique of the fatalistic, racist, and inhuman recourse to beliefs in the 'biological and geographical necessity that doomed the Native American population to "removal"'.[19] This reference was presented alongside her critique of the belief in manifest destiny that propelled the American reach into Mexico, Cuba, and the Philippines, as 'well-known samples of political necessity'.[20] The faces of Indigenous victims of injustice are thus represented in the book as seen through the lens of the colonist's gleaming eye, which is moved both by greed and a belief in a cultural and political superiority that should be dispersed as widely as possible. Seeing the experience of Native nations in this way, through the colonist's actions, Shklar here made the same error that she pinned on theorists of justice, in which the acts of the unjust are given more attention than those of their victims.[21]

Looking beyond *The Faces of Injustice*, it is also striking that *American Citizenship*, Shklar's extended engagement with the historical and contextual circumstances of slavery,[22] did not grapple with the imposition of citizenship, its associated displacement of persons, and the exclusion or at least interference with Indigenous forms of citizenship. As far as I am aware, Shklar's only direct treatment of this topic appears within her posthumously published essay, 'The Boundaries of Democracy'.[23] There, Shklar described Jefferson's exclusion of Native Americans from his democratizing project. According to Shklar, Jefferson's view was that Native Americans:

> were to become good and obedient children, but quite obviously not citizens. The cultural boundaries of democracy were evidently as rigid as the geographic ones. The geographic expansion of democracy met a

18 Shklar, *The Faces of Injustice* (n 2) 178. Shklar reiterated that such procedures, however, are no 'cure for a sense of injustice'. Moreover, expressing the victim's sense of injustice does not mean that sense will be vindicated or will prevail.
19 Shklar, *The Faces of Injustice* (n 2) 74.
20 Shklar, *The Faces of Injustice* (n 2).
21 Shklar, *The Faces of Injustice* (n 2) 31–46.
22 Shklar, *American Citizenship* (n 16). The account did not engage with the enslavement of Native Americans.
23 Judith N Shklar, 'The Boundaries of Democracy' in *Redeeming American Political Thought* (Stanley Hoffmann and Dennis F Thompson eds, University of Chicago Press 1998).

> temporary obstacle in the Catholic Spaniards, but an absolute one in the Indian. He could never be remade into a New World citizen. I do not mention slavery, because it cannot be made into any vision of democracy at all, and Jefferson knew that perfectly well. He simply refused to think about it, and when that was not possible, did so with a mixture of fear, shame, and racism. The Indian could not yet be so readily ignored. He had to be considered, and so he was, in a way that had nothing to do with consent. He was left to his historic fate of dependence, which meant, in effect, removal and destruction.[24]

Shklar's examination of the polity-building project of early independent America painted it as an exemplar of the cruelty and violence that Shklar consistently associated with the excesses of idealized liberalism and its tendency to provoke exclusion.[25] Yet 'The Boundaries of Democracy' also offers a hint of a different concern for the distinctive Indigenous experience of injustice, which is the injustice of inclusion rather than exclusion. Immediately preceding the text quoted above, Shklar wrote:

> There was of course one large group of Americans who had no reason to look forward to Jefferson's programme with anything but terror. Indians were not ready to forget their ancestors, did not think of themselves as unattached individuals, and showed no disposition to be virtuous citizens of the United States. They were, nevertheless, incontestably a part of America.[26]

The passage presents Shklar's clearest acknowledgment of the experience of Indigenous rejection of the incoming order and its violent imposition. However, it also affirms Indigenous inclusion in the face of that rejection, and (most problematically) treats inclusion as being incontestable or inevitable. Perhaps Shklar meant that inclusion became practically incontestable, owing to the operation of force and the same belief in the perceived 'necessity' that she had deplored in *The Faces of Injustice*. Perhaps Shklar simply hadn't paid attention to the forms through which contestation could and did occur.[27] In either case, the passage touches the framing concern of the present paper: that a focus upon faces and voices of injustice does not fully capture

24 Judith N Shklar, 'The Boundaries of Democracy' in *Redeeming American Political Thought* (Stanley Hoffmann and Dennis F Thompson eds, University of Chicago Press 1998) 143. See also text at 95, discussing Jefferson's boast that he could bribe the Indians into submission.

25 See further Misra (n 6) 7.

26 Shklar, 'The Boundaries of Democracy' (n 23) 143.

27 Extensive recent literatures examine forms of contestation in different nations, both historically and in their continuing development. See, eg, the recent contribution from Justin B Richland, *Cooperation without Submission* (University of Chicago Press 2021). On the

the plural forms and claims to legality—and claims to do justice through law—that are central to responding to injustice in settler colonies. Contrary to Shklar's description, Indigenous responses to injustice include (and included) not simply personal unwillingness to 'forget ancestors' or embrace atomized individualism, but the rejection of claims to legal and political forms imposed upon their own. The boundaries of inclusion that result from such imposition, moreover, have been and remain deeply contested through both legal and political forms.

Beyond these brief references to the violence, racism, and cruelty used to impose settler legal ordering on Indigenous peoples, Shklar's work did not project forwards the histories of colonial or state-building encounters into her work on contemporary injustice.[28] More broadly, Shklar did not examine continuing contexts in which the very institutions of legality are challenged (over their claims to supremacy and/or exclusivity) in relation to other legal orders. Even in Shklar's response to the normal model of law, the institutions of legality may be criticized, but they go unrivalled—legality runs solo. While Shklar criticized the liberal state for the model of impersonal rationality through which it addresses victims of the injustices created by the very institutions designed to administer justice through law, it is not challenged for its claims to supremacy and the authority to do so.

The victims of injustice, meanwhile, are not treated as having organized or collective agency, nor as operating legal forms to rival the state legal order or make claims directly against it. They are regarded as whole and concrete persons (rather than the partial and abstract 'legal persons' of the normal model Shklar criticizes), but they are, in a sense, only persons, who can (in principle) be given an equal hearing in the juridical institutions of the (state's) law. The whole person to be seen and heard in *The Faces of Injustice* is detached from political claims either to affiliate with or to rival the state.

Shklar's work is, in this sense, a powerful representation of the liberal egalitarian commitments that reject divisions grounded upon ethnic or cultural lines, guarding against both extreme and more quotidian forms of nationalism. Her defence of liberalism (with all its flaws) and legality (with all its limitations) is mounted against the evils of both nationalism and totalitarianism,

rejection of citizenship forms, see Robert Williams Jr, *Savage Anxieties: The Invention of Western Civilization* (Palgrave Macmillan 2012).

28 The issue of Indigenous exclusion from the boundaries of democracy might have been explored in the fuller work on exile that Shklar was pursuing at the time of her death, though it does not arise among the kinds of 'internal' exile she examined in Judith N Shklar, 'Obligation, Loyalty, Exclusion' in *Political Thought and Political Thinkers* (Stanley Hoffmann ed, University of Chicago Press 1998). Skinner treats that paper as a sketch of the larger project: see Quentin Skinner, 'The Last Academic Project' in Samantha Ashenden and Andreas Hess (eds), *Between Utopia and Realism: The Political Thought of Judith N Shklar* (University of Pennsylvania Press 2019) 253.

as well as the violence of exclusion to which even more mild forms of communitarianism can lead.[29] As Misra characterizes Shklar's position,

> the state—the liberal state of her imagination—is meant precisely to be the big tent that serves as a sanctuary from the parochial tyrannies of other, smaller forms of community within the state, ranging from family and village to church and school.[30]

Shklar's rejection of parochial tyrannies included a critique of efforts to treat a state's democratic processes as either ends in themselves or as means for inculcating state-level nationalistic claims.[31] For all that Shklar cautioned about the limits of liberalism, finding its value in the avoidance of cruelty rather than more optimistic ideals, her emphasis on inclusion (and the cruelty of exclusion) embraced one sense of the normal model's (and liberalism's) preference for abstraction of the person. She celebrates an abstraction away from any hint of nationalism or tribalism.

Shklar did not, however, abstract away from history, which was crucial to her illustration of the ways in which liberalism can fail, as well as the need to prioritize resistance to both cruelty and nationalistic forms of exclusion and oppression. That commitment means that Shklar's near-silence on the topic of state–Indigenous interactions, with their associated forms and claims of Indigenous legalities, is indicative of more than the disciplinary blinkers that distanced much of the liberal canon of political theory (in Shklar's era) from supposedly more specialist scholarship on Indigenous rights, claims, and recognition.[32]

Could that omission be explained as a recognition of plural models of Indigenous legal ordering, treating the legal orders of Indigenous nations as being effectively beyond, despite being territorially within, the state (and thus outside of the normal model of state law against which her critique is

29 See, eg, her critique of Walzer's faith in community in Judith N Shklar, 'The Work of Michael Walzer' in *Political Thought and Political Thinkers* (Stanley Hoffmann ed, University of Chicago Press 1998). For commentary, see Hoffmann (n 6); Bernard Yack, *Nationalism and the Moral Psychology of Community* (University of Chicago Press 2016); Sanford Levinson, 'Is Liberal Nationalism an Oxymoron? An Essay for Judith Shklar' (1995) 105 Ethics 626.

30 Misra (n 6).

31 Misra (n 6).

32 Those blinkers were already shifting towards the end of Shklar's life. Contemporaneous with Shklar, see Iris Marion Young's representation of the differentiated legalities of American Indians in *Justice and the Politics of Difference* (Princeton University Press 1990) 181–4 (albeit arguing that fully fledged differentiation would require federal law to give up its ability to remove that differentiation). See also the emergence in generalist legal scholarship of attention to state-federal-tribal relations: eg, Judith Resnik, 'Dependent Sovereigns: Indian Tribes, States, and the Federal Courts' (1989) 56 U Chi L Rev 671.

directed)?[33] Even if such a pluralist reading of Shklar is plausible (which is doubtful, in light of Shklar's endorsement of liberal-state legality's comprehensively inclusive democratic procedures), it is not my aim here to examine or defend it. The point instead is to show how the injustice of the displacement of Indigenous legalities—borne directly and unequally by Indigenous peoples—highlights (in opposition to Shklar) both (1) the limits of a 'faces and voices' model of legality and injustice, and (2) the value of what I will call a 'forms and claims' model, with its prospect of abstracting legality away from state law.

3. Concrete faces or abstract forms of injustice?

Shklar's call for more attention to concrete persons foreshadows a central criticism of liberal political theory: the risk that liberal universalism abstracts away the very concrete circumstances of injustice itself.[34] However, it also sits in tension with liberal forms of abstraction; the demand to see and hear the individual's sense of injustice confounds a liberal desire for the public sphere to be shorn of both personal identities and identity politics.[35]

Setting aside (for now) those broader concerns in political theory, there is also a particular tension within liberal legal theory between the forms that abstract away from concrete persons in pursuit of egalitarian and inclusive institutions, and the forms that enable concrete persons to both participate in and to recognize the institutions of law and justice. To what extent can a demand to give priority to the faces (and voices) of injustice be pursued, without losing what is central and/or valuable to liberal legality itself? Addressing that tension means asking how (and how much of) the person, whose powers of recognition are tied up with the operations of legality and justice, can be recognized by the institutions that administer legality? How far can/should law recognize the faces and hear the voices of concrete persons?

Shklar implicitly embedded persons in their concrete circumstances to the extent these contour aspects of an individual's sense of injustice—her individual concern to be heard and seen. The concrete subject for Shklar thus appears as the traditional liberal subject: the individual, who is distanced

33 Shklar noted, after all, that 'in a pluralistic society, with many shifting rules and orders in conflict, it is not possible to formalize them all': *The Faces of Injustice* (n 2) 37.

34 Influential critiques of liberal theory's abstraction away from the circumstances of injustice include Susan Moller Okin, *Justice, Gender and the Family* (Basic Books 1989); Charles W Mills, '"Ideal Theory" as Ideology' (2005) 20 Hypatia 165; Charles W Mills, *The Racial Contract* (Cornell University Press 1997). For an account of the tensions surrounding abstraction and concretization in liberalism's reckonings with multiculturalism, see Jacob T Levy, 'Contextualism, Constitutionalism, and Modus Vivendi Approaches' in Anthony Laden and David Owen (eds), *Multiculturalism and Political Theory* (CUP 2007).

35 Both points are central to the defence of interlegality presented in section five.

from ethnic, cultural (let alone Indigenous) claims for self-determination, just as she is distanced from nationalist affiliations with the state.[36] This version of liberalism sees the faces and raises the voices of the victims of colonization, but not the prospect of their own political and legal orders. It does not provide for the claims that agents of Indigenous legalities make against settler state legal orders that have been imposed upon them.

A focus on persons' faces and voices demotes or even denies a particular kind of concrete attention to historicized as well as contemporary circumstances, which would reveal the distinctive forms and claims of Indigenous experiences of injustice. Shklar's own interest in the institution of slavery (and its continuing injustices), as well as her work on exile, demonstrated her concern for the impact (and not just the lessons) of history. Attending with the same care to the whole historicized context of colonialization means attending to overlapping state–Indigenous claims to legality; seeing and hearing persons' recognitions of Indigenous forms and claims of legality, as well as legal claims and forms rejecting state legalities. The concrete persons on whom settler colonial institutions have been (and are) imposed are not just individual members of groups displaced and dominated, but persons whose recognition of political and social institutions has been disrupted, their attendant statuses of legality denied and/or forcefully excluded by their forceful inclusion in the institutions of the state and its legal forms.

As the late Moana Jackson put it, writing of Aotearoa New Zealand but with resonance for other Indigenous and settler/colonial interactions:

> The colonisers' need to impose their laws and institutions on people who already had their own allowed no room for an honourable relationship. . . . Instead colonisation fomented injustice: a systemic privileging of the Crown and a relationship in which it assumed it would be the sole and supreme authority.[37]

Such historicized circumstances cannot be abstracted away because of their continuing impact upon persons and the way they recognize (and are recognized by) political and legal institutions. Attending only to the concrete faces of victims of injustice risks a failure to see those institutionalized forms and hear those claims of legality that cannot be recognized in the institutions of the colonizer. When legality is criticized but the status of legality is uncontested,

36 More expressly, Shklar's limited tolerance for membership and practices of groups is dependent upon their having clear and continuous exit options: Shklar, 'The Liberalism of Fear' (n 6) 115. For an argument that Shklar treats 'community as the main source of injustice', see Misra (n 6).

37 Moana Jackson, 'Where to Next? Decolonisation and the Stories in the Land' in Bianca Elkington, Moana Jackson, Rebecca Kiddle, Ocean Ripeka Mercier, Mike Ross, Jennie Smeaton, and Amanda Thomas (eds), *Imagining Decolonisation* (Bridget Williams Books 2020).

the voice of the subject-victim can be heard as such in the law's own institutions, but the voice that claims a distinctive legality in a community cannot be heard unless the claim to legality itself can be heard and contested.

The defects of independent statist legalities in this context are twofold. First, state juridical institutions cannot hear Indigenous claims because they are not contesting the content of the law imposed, nor the terms of its imposition upon their own concrete case, but making claims to independent practices of legality, authority, and subjecthood. These are not supplications, asking for a justification from the state for the law and conditions of justice it seeks to impose, but demands that the state not impose in this way—monistically—at all. Those claims cannot be heard and addressed within institutions that were consciously imposed to deny them, and which have continuously defended their own exclusivity or supremacy.[38]

Second, Indigenous claims and forms cannot simply be understood as voices or faces of *victims*. The complex discourse of victimhood amidst the variety of different Indigenous experiences of (and responses to) injustice requires far more care than the passing attention offered here.[39] However (and setting aside the question of whether a particular person or particular group represents themselves as a victim of colonization), there are distinctive claims to be made against the settler state that do not rest on victimhood. These include not only the claims to self-determination familiar from political theory (and to an extent from international law) but also claims to statuses of legality. Rather than resting upon victimhood, the claim is to compete, co-exist, and/or to coordinate with the state in the same project of ordering communities through legality, both empowering and protecting persons through law. Such claims bear not only the individual and collective voices but also the institutions and forms that organize and institutionalize authority and justice.[40] They present contrasting models of legality and contending claims to the status of legality.

The argument is not only that state institutions cannot *justly* hear such claims because natural justice requires that any direct contest between state and Indigenous legalities should not set up the state to be judge in its own

38 Annette Sykes, *The Myth of Tikanga in the Pākehā Law* (Nin Thomas Memorial Lecture 2020). See also Mikaere (n 4).

39 Shklar also noted that many persons will not see themselves as victims, nor represent themselves that way. The complex phenomenology of victimhood, self-recognition, and self-representation presents an important further avenue for addressing Shklar's theme of relating personal and political experiences of injustice.

40 See, eg, accounts from Val Napoleon, 'Thinking About Indigenous Legal Orders' in René Provost and Colleen Sheppard (eds), *Dialogues about Human Rights and Legal Pluralism* (Springer 2013); Jacinta Ruru, 'First Laws: Tikanga Maori in/and the Law' (2018) 49 VUWLR 279; Robert Joseph, 'Re-creating Legal Space for the First Law of Aotearoa New Zealand' (2009) 17 Wai L Rev 74, 85; Māmari Stephens, 'Kei a Koe, Chair!—The Norms of Tikanga and the Role of Hui as a Māori Constitutional Tradition' (2022) 53 VUWLR 463.

cause. Nor is it a version of the argument that even well-intentioned efforts to provide for the recognition of Indigenous legalities within state institutions risk causing still more injustice (for example, because of a lack of expertise or inapt procedures for applying Indigenous law). It is not a critique of efforts made to recognize Indigenous legality claims through settler legal doctrine, whether sourced in common law, custom, or statute. Those are all important (and in some sense complementary) concerns to be addressed together in a full substantive response to Indigenous claims of injustice.

The narrower (yet arguably stronger) version of the argument, for the present purpose, turns upon what it means to claim and to recognize legality in contrast to mere force.[41] The larger project from which this work draws[42] defends the claim that the recognition of legality needs to operate on both sides of legality relations—between agents and subjects of law—and on both sides of 'interlegality' relations—between state and Indigenous legal orders. That demand is not satisfied by the provision for tribunals, truth and reconciliation commissions, or other efforts to meaningfully provide for Indigenous faces and voices of injustice to be heard. While it remains crucial to find and develop such institutional forms, as well as to address the objections about natural justice, epistemic and procedural limitations, and doctrinal inadequacies in settler law, the injustice of the exclusion of Indigenous legalities also requires institutions for redressing, contesting, and redistributing the status of legality itself.

4. Statuses of legality

The broader project also attends with more care to the relationship between the question 'what is law' and what I have termed here the 'status of legality' as a variant of the orthodox jurisprudential debate over whether the concept of law necessarily entails the rule of law.[43] For the present work, it is enough that both the more austere notion of law and the richer accounts of the rule of law share the view that law/legality is something other than a gunman's

41 I argue elsewhere that statuses of legality are not reducible to whatever is conventionally operating as law. There are normative constraints upon what counts as legality, which turn not (as critics suggest) upon any universalizing tendencies of general jurisprudents' theories, but upon the normativity that is carried by recognition itself. These arguments are elaborated in a forthcoming project on *Legalities,* but also parallel the structural role of recognition defended in Nicole Roughan, 'The Recognition in Authority: Roles, Relations, and Reasons' (2023) 14 Jurisprud 171.

42 Nicole Roughan, *Legalities* (unpublished manuscript).

43 Whether understood as part of a general concept of law or as an ideal, legality is typically characterized by more or less similar lists of requirements. On the prevalence and limitations of list-based approaches, see Martin Krygier, 'Legal Pluralism and the Value of the Rule of Law' in Nicole Roughan and Andrew Halpin (eds), *In Pursuit of Pluralist Jurisprudence* (CUP 2017).

threat to his victim.[44] The impact of overlapping statuses of legality and the recognition challenges they raise does not turn on whether the rule of law is part of the concept of law.

That work on legality and law's normativity argues that a robust moral relation of legality is effected within normative practices of recognition between officials and subjects of law.[45] The full account of recognition between law's officials and subjects, and its centrality to legality, has key implications for the recognition of legalities when a legal order is faced with claims to the status of legality made by some other legal order.[46] When there are overlapping claims to the status(es) of legality, a response to injustice needs to provide for the possibility of contest, correction, and distribution of those statuses.

a. Recognition of legalities

Contests over the status of legality grapple not only with the impact of interaction of different and diverse legalities, but also with the implications of either withholding or recognizing the status of legality itself. Such contests alter what it takes for officials to claim legality (in recognition of subjects) and what it takes for subjects to recognize legality (in response to such claims). In both directions, the operation of alternative and competing forms of Indigenous legalities stand in the way of the recognition of (and by) state legal ordering.

44 Eg, HLA Hart, *The Concept of Law* (OUP 1961). More value-laden accounts offer different formulations of what the rule of law does to power. See Krygier's account of 'tempering power', elaborated in Martin Krygier, 'Tempering Power' in Maurice Adams, Anne Meuwese, and Ernst Hirsch Ballin (eds), *Constitutionalism and the Rule of Law: Bridging Idealism and Realism* (CUP 2017); and Martin Krygier, 'Why the Rule of Law Matters' (2018) 9 Jurisprud 146.

45 My recognition model is developed in full in a draft manuscript, *Officials*. See also Nicole Roughan, 'The Official Point of View and the Official Claim to Authority' (2018) 38 OJLS 191; Nicole Roughan, 'From Office-Holding to Officiality' (2020) 70 UTLJ 231. The account owes much to Gardner's work on the notion of the official of law (see, eg, John Gardner, 'How Law Claims, What Law Claims' in Matthias Klatt (ed), *Institutionalized Reason: The Jurisprudence of Robert Alexy* (OUP 2012); to Postema's work on the relations between officials and subjects, eg, Gerald Postema, 'Law's Ethos: Reflections on a Public Practice of Illegality' (2010) 90 BU L Rev 1847; and to Rundle's interpretations of Fuller's work on reciprocity in Kristen Rundle, *Forms Liberate: Reclaiming the Jurisprudence of Lon L Fuller* (Hart Publishing 2012). However, my work on recognition between officials and subjects departs from Postema's, Rundle's, and Fuller's reciprocity accounts, in part, by requiring less of the subject in that relation and (arguably) more of the official.

46 Recent case law in Aotearoa NZ includes Supreme Court judgments in *Trans-Tasman Resources Limited v The Taranaki-Whanganui Conservation Board* [2021] NZSC 127 (confirming the status of tikanga as 'other applicable law' under the Exclusive Economic Zone Act); *Peter Hugh McGregor Ellis v The King* [2022] NZSC 115 (the relevance of tikanga to a decision about continuance of a criminal appeal after the death of the appellant).

The core argument is that the imposition of one legal order in the face of another legal order's overlapping claims to the status of legality amounts to an exercise of force that disrupts the prospect of legality itself.[47] Such force is felt directly and indirectly by the persons who recognize the legal order that is being excluded or overpowered. In the state–Indigenous context, the point is not only that any individual person's recognitions of state claims to legality may be disrupted by their experiences or knowledge of the force perpetuated against Indigenous law by state law (though that is often and understandably the case).[48] The point is structural: the forms of legality present in Indigenous orders, operating independently as well as publicly interacting with the state legal order, interrupt the recognition of state law's legality. The claims and operation of the Indigenous order, replete with its distinctive forms and processes as well as its own practices of recognition of persons and statuses of legality, disrupts collective recognition of 'one law for all'. Instead, there are two legal orders, and the question (to which I return later) is whether there are/should be two laws for all, one law for some and one for others; or law for some and mere force for others.

The imposition of state legal ordering upon Indigenous legal ordering (in ways that perpetuate force rather than legality) not only upsets legality's recognition by subjects but also undermines the recognition that is required of those agents who manifest state claims to legality. The second implication of the recognition account (for contexts of overlapping legalities) is that persons in communities with legal orders that contest legality with the state cannot be recognized as subjects of independent state claims to authority, coercion, and justice in the same way as persons who do not recognize rival legal forms. In state–Indigenous contexts, a dominant state legal order's claim to independent legality (which simply treats Indigenous persons as subjects) is also a claim to supremacy over any legal ordering that those persons recognize. Furthermore, it asks persons to overlook the Indigenous legal order's forceful exclusion by the very state legal order that claims to be something other than force. Leaving open, for now, the question of whether a state's additional supremacy claim might be justified as a form of coercion rather than authority or legality,

47 As Mark Walters writes of the Canadian contexts, '[i]t would have been *absurd* and *tyrannical* to impose a new law upon a people with an established law. It would, in other words, introduce a degree of irrationality and arbitrariness inconsistent with the basic demands of normative order that we now associate with the rule of law.' Mark D Walters, 'The Judicial Recognition of Indigenous Legal Traditions: *Connolly v Woolrich* at 150' (2017) 22 Review of Constitutional Studies 347. I am grateful to David Dyzenhaus for drawing this piece to my attention. The point here is put in stronger terms, as the disruption of the recognition of legality (on both sides) affects not only a failure of the rule of law but also the more austere concept of law.

48 As occurs when persons brought before state criminal institutions argue that those institutions have no jurisdiction, no authority, or no legitimacy. See Jackson, *Māori and the Criminal Justice System* (n 5).

a state's claim to administer legality over Indigenous communities, *thereby overpowering Indigenous legalities*, is distinct from its claim to administer legality for all individuals within its jurisdiction. State law's recognition of Indigenous persons will be defective if those persons are simply treated as subjects of law without the recognition of the overlapping Indigenous legalities.

This structural feature not only alters what it takes for the state to recognize Indigenous persons as subjects of law rather than objects of force, but also casts doubt upon the extent to which the state's independent legality claims are made in good faith. The strongest version of this concern characterizes the state's claims to legality as being made despite agents knowing of (or being wilfully blind to) their defects, and thus in bad faith. Attention to the recognition engaged in statuses of legality, amidst overlapping claims to that status, reveals the importance of both law's claims and their reception, as well as the relation between claiming and receiving. For all the insight and the practical imperative of asking whether law has (and does not merely claim) authority, or whether an order achieves (and not merely claims) a status of legality, we should not overlook attention to the claims and their reception among law's persons.

This point responds, not merely in passing (and not only because of his involvement in the present collection), to the work David Dyzenhaus has done to draw a long 'arc' across the idea of legality.[49] Among that work's important insights, one is an insistence that an interest in the authority law *has* should trump the interest in the authority law *claims*. It is undoubtedly important to ask and to have tools for answering 'does law have authority?' However, claiming authority is no mere precursor to having authority. An official claim to authority both addresses (and intervenes upon) the subject and provokes her response. The claim and response manifest forms of recognition on both sides of law's differentiated official–subject relations. Examining law's claim to authority prompts us to ask: what must law be like in order to make this claim (Raz's question); but also, must the claim be made in good faith; and what would it take for the claims to be recognizable as claims to authority and not the mere wielding of force?

Examining the claim also re-shapes how we are to understand what Dyzenhaus presents as the subject's question: 'But, how can that be law for me?'[50]

49 David Dyzenhaus, *The Long Arc of Legality: Hobbes, Kelsen, Hart* (CUP 2022), argues for the priority of Hart's question over Raz's. Note that a key impact of Raz's very stringent authority theses is that law often has very limited legitimate authority and legality does not rescue it. This leaves open whether law might nevertheless be justifiably enforced.

50 David Dyzenhaus, *The Long Arc of Legality: Hobbes, Kelsen, Hart* (CUP 2022) 2. For other versions of the subject's question, see Hans Lindahl, 'Conflict of Laws: Asymmetrical Recognition of the Stranger (in Ourselves)' in Michael S Green, Ralf Michaels, and Roxana Banu (eds), *Philosophical Foundations of Private International Law* (OUP 2024) and my 'Plurality of Laws and Conflict of Laws: Reconciling through Recognition?' in the same volume.

The subject's question is asked in response to the purported authority's claim to intervene upon her, and so the claim itself bears direct examination, even in an account that starts with attention to the subject. The recognition of subjection that is carried by the claim to authority may itself be assertive or restrained, prompting different responses from the subject.[51] A restrained claim (for example, one that claims only relative authority or seeks to present an interdependent legality claim that recognizes a relation with Indigenous legalities) can be received (and thus recognized) differently from a claim to a legal order's exclusive authority. In context, the 'but' at the start of Dyzenhaus's version of the subject's question may be even more important than the 'for me' at its end. In contexts of overlapping claims to legality, the 'but' may be a rejection and an expression of non-recognition. One response to law's claim to authority is: '*no, because* how could *that* be law for me, *when I've got this other law*?' Or perhaps more strongly, as the present work suggests, the response is a robust rejection: 'but how can *that* be law *at all*?' In the context of state–Indigenous overlapping claims to legality, the purported subject of state legality is not asking for a justification, rather she is rejecting the state's claim to legality owing to its forceful displacement of the other claim that she recognizes.

b. Contest, correction, and distribution of legalities

If such overlapping claims to legality are not to be simply resolved through the imposition of force, then overlapping claims to legality (and the recognition they entail) invoke questions of justice with both distributive and corrective elements. Like the distribution of economic and social resources, and like the distribution of opportunities for public participation in governance and (thus) self-determination, the distribution of a status of legality calls for justification. In turn, histories of distortions or denials of claims to legality—most prominent in the exclusion of Indigenous legalities in common law settler states—also generate demands for corrective justice between those affected by such exclusionary interactions.

However, attention to the role of recognition here also affirms that there is an important constraint, perhaps a barrier, to treating either the status of law or legality as something that is 'distributed' at all. For a start, law itself is not an object or resource—it is a normative social practice, featuring institutions that depend for their effectiveness (and for an aspect of their legitimacy) on

51 On restrained self-assertion, see Hans Lindahl, *Authority and the Globalisation of Inclusion and Exclusion* (CUP 2018). cf Nicole Roughan, 'Meet Me in the Middle' (2019) 29 Duke J Comp & Int'l L 423 (on assertive self-restraint). For Lindahl's response, see Hans Lindahl, 'Authority and the Globalisation of Inclusion and Exclusion: Conceptual and Normative Considerations' (2019) 29 Duke J Comp & Int'l L 437.

their being recognized within communities by those who are subject to them. Legality is a matter of recognition, not distribution. However, legal institutions (and their agents) do claim to make authoritative determinations of what counts as law, and to back these up with coercive force. For instance, when courts pronounce on the law (especially in common law systems where a practice of precedent elevates their contributions, as officials, to determining sources of law and their evolution), they are positioned to determine that *this, not that*, counts as law. When direct claims to Indigenous legalities are brought before the courts, there are opportunities for the courts to claim authoritative distributions or corrections of statuses of legality. To the extent these influence wider recognitive practices, such institutions act as purported distributors as well as institutions for correction of mistakes or injustices generated over past denials of the statuses of legality.

Courts are but one type of institution engaged in the contestation, correction, and distribution of statuses of legality, operating alongside other state legal institutions as well as Indigenous legal institutions. The authority to recognize legality may itself be understood to be widely distributed (in the sense of being dispersed) among social institutions and among subjects of law—perhaps so widely that there's no real authority to recognize at all, just practices of recognition. However, even without distributors (and avoiding the terminology of distributive justice), the status of legality is positioned neither as a tool nor a structure through which justice is operated, but as a mode of power to be claimed, contested, and corrected. Seeing legality as among the objects of justice, in all its forms, captures the deliberateness of the recognitions and denials that colonial systems have variously deployed over Indigenous ones, as well as the deliberateness of efforts to do things differently.

The final point to be emphasized for present purposes is that the persons engaged in all of this recognition are, in some sense, abstractions. Although concrete persons occupy the roles of law's officials and subjects, in each legal order,[52] the roles themselves are abstract institutions, normatively constituted, burdened, and empowered. However, concrete persons do not disappear from the account. Concrete persons' individual practices of recognition feed into the forms of collective recognition of the roles of officials and subjects. Concrete persons' practices of recognition thus shape the content of the abstract roles within which collective recognition operates.

There is a further crucial sense in which the significance of recognition, contestation, distribution, and correction of statuses of legality requires a

52 The term 'official' is used to capture the role of law's institutional agents. The idea of 'officials of law' should not be narrowly construed as officials of state law, nor as having all the typical characteristics of officials in state legal orders. See Roger Cotterrell, *Law, Culture, and Society: Legal Ideas in the Mirror of Social Theory* (Taylor and Francis 2017) 37.

concrete focus. The significance of the gap between what is claimed and received likely depends upon context.[53] The challenge is to ask whether, in context, there is a way to rescue legality, removing the gap between what is claimed and received, that can preserve legality without the resort to force.

5. Interlegality: more abstraction, not less

How can and how should law respond to injustices in contexts of contested and overlapping statuses of legality? It may be helpful here to return to this chapter's engagement with Shklar, asking what is missed by attending to faces and voices of concrete persons, and what values abstraction still holds for responding to injustice.

As suggested earlier, if the challenge were only to find forms for hearing and responding to Indigenous faces of injustice, then a response might include setting up tribunals or other institutional forms that are designed to find ways of hearing claims against (and about) the injustices carried out by the state, which might be sufficiently independent from state legality. Designers of these institutions may seek to ensure that the institution's procedures, personnel, physical presence, and principles work to demote those of state law. Such efforts aim to redress the imbalance of power that state law projects and to provide for faces and voices of Indigenous persons to be heard. They may also be designed to bring together expertise not only in plural legal orders but also in history and other academic and practical fields outside of law, which are thought necessary to break the state lawyers' stranglehold on juridical efforts at justice.[54]

However, unlike providing visibility and voice for the faces of injustices that have already occurred, responding to the forms and claims of Indigenous legalities requires forward projection: ways of providing for the contestation, distribution, and correction of the recognition of statuses of legality. Responding to injustice requires more, not less, abstraction and more, not less, legality. More specifically, it involves abstracting both law and legality away from the concrete forms and claims of state law.

53 In Aotearoa New Zealand, where there are continuing contests over statuses of legality and ongoing questions of how to respond to injustice in light of those contests, the gap matters a great deal. It is examined in Nicole Roughan, 'Appendix 3: Interlegality, Interdependence and Independence: Framing Relations of Tikanga and State Law in Aotearoa New Zealand' in Te Aka Matua o te Ture | New Zealand Law Commission, *He Poutama* (NZLC Study Paper 24, 2023) <www.lawcom.govt.nz/assets/Publications/StudyPapers/NZLC-SP24-Appendix-3.pdf> accessed 20 June 2024.

54 Examples include the Waitangi Tribunal in New Zealand and truth and reconciliation commissions in Canada, South Africa, Argentina, Guatemala, and Chile. Note also the calls in Australia for a Makarrata Commission within the Uluru Statement from the Heart and, in Victoria, the Yoorrook Justice Commission.

In the context of overlapping claims to legality, the abstraction of the status of legality (away from the concrete manifestation of law in the dominant state legal order) provides space for practices of interlegality in which statuses of legality are open to contest, correction, and a kind of distribution. This makes the space of interaction itself a space for legality, rather than force or politics. Interlegality seeks forms through which legal orders can relate to one another not through force, nor through politics, nor through submitting to a superior third legal order, but through a form of legality that abstracts away from either legal order in order to govern their interactions and intersections.[55] Unlike legal forms that allow one order to unilaterally determine its relationship with the other (in the manner of conflict of laws), or legal forms that subject both legal orders separately to a higher legal order (in the manner of public international law), interlegality requires that the interaction and overlap between two (or more) legal orders is governed by rules of engagement and constraint that are determined and operated within both legal orders. Interlegality provides for interdependent legalities.

If interlegality's rules, principles, and institutions are to engage interacting legal orders, they need forms through which each order can recognize their relation. In simplified form, interlegality requires genuinely common law and genuinely shared law-making institutions. That conception allows that interlegality can operate to combine legalities from both orders and/or can operate legal forms for managing the relationship itself, such as jointly determining arrangements for either separating or sharing jurisdictions—special institutions for hearing disputes engaging both legal orders or for making rules to be applied in common across both orders. The particular mechanisms of interlegality will depend on context, with their design and processes likely to be controversial, but in its ideal form, interlegality would provide for statuses of legality to be both contested and administered by persons and institutions from both interacting orders.

However, while the concrete forms of interlegality will vary according to context, interlegality forms will in general need to be attuned to any existing imbalances between legal orders that threaten to revert to relations of power and politics. Responding to injustice through interlegality between state and Indigenous orders likely requires limiting the state's own claims to legality and institutionalizing humility in those claims. Political or even constitutional limits upon wielders of state power may not provide the necessary forms to prevent state legal orders from forcefully intervening upon Indigenous ones, or for remedying the power imbalance that typically renders Indigenous legalities vulnerable to

55 Echoing Klabbers and Palombella (n 8) 2, who argue that 'inter-legality' is a distinctively legal rather than political response: 'Inter-legality stays firmly within the law, within legal thinking, within legal practice.'

state legalities.[56] To rescue legality itself from a state's claims to independent or supreme legality, there needs to be some constraints upon state law's reach into Indigenous legalities. Concrete Indigenous legal orders in place—even when these are still being rebuilt, relearned, and revitalized by agents and subjects of those legal orders—will then require institutional forms (and perhaps new institutional forms) through which to relate to state legal forms.

I have not addressed here the normative question of whether such interlegality is the best response to the interactions of Indigenous and state legalities. Even if interlegality serves to rescue legality, it may not do enough to respond to injustice, and it would need to be evaluated and likely operated alongside other ways of doing so. I do not engage that full justificatory debate here, as my aim has been to represent (rather than to fully defend) an additional layer of abstraction beyond legality itself. However, within the present project's scope of testing the limits of concretization and the values of abstraction, an interlegality model can use its abstraction to respond to several prominent objections against the operation of Indigenous legalities in relations with the law of contemporary liberal states.

Responding to objections

Interlegality provides for responses to serious objections to the recognition and operation of Indigenous legalities. Two key objections present the view that the liberal democratic state is tasked with doing justice for all in the present by abstracting away from persons' particular identities as well as historical contexts. The first objects to any identity-based, ethnicity-based, or race-based forms of distinctions between persons and their entitlements in communities. The second argues that while historic injustices were inflicted upon Indigenous persons, they can be (and may have been) superseded by changes in circumstances. A third objection, which often appears alongside the first two, is a worry about the rule of law—that interlegality bears too much uncertainty or inconsistency to bear the name of legality at all and/or that it offends against a formal equality principle of one law for all. The fourth argument is a pluralist objection, namely that an Indigenous legal order does not seek or want forms of interaction with state law, and that plurality of laws (rather than interlegality) would better recognize the status of Indigenous legalities.

56 The potential for constitutional pluralism—constitutionality operating in both state and Indigenous traditions—means that the challenge of interlegality may not be straightforwardly addressed by constitutional mechanisms. Such mechanisms may need their own tools for relating to other constitutional orders. On the multiple constitutional traditions in Aotearoa New Zealand, see Andrew Sharp, 'This Is My Body: Constitutional Traditions in New Zealand' (2014) 12 NZJPIL 41; Carwyn Jones, 'A Māori Constitutional Tradition' (2014) 12 NZJPIL 187; David V Williams, 'Constitutional Traditions in Maori Interactions with the Crown' (2014) 12 NZJPIL 231.

An interlegality frame offers two complementary responses. The first response offers up the abstraction of legality (and interlegality) to address the first two objections, while the second response shifts the focus away from the recognition and legality of independent legal orders on to the recognition and legality of their relation, addressing objections three and four.

Space precludes engaging each of these in full. Instead, to complete the response to Shklar's own concerns, this final section focuses upon the first two objections, which both defend the view that, for all the injustice wrought upon Indigenous persons, the role of the contemporary state is to provide justice among those who are present (and perhaps those to come), whatever their provenance, identities, ethnicities, cultures, or beliefs. Both objections reject the position defended above, in which justice's attention to the whole person includes setting that person in historicized contexts instead of taking their formal membership of a liberal state community at face value. They also object (directly or indirectly) to claims to the operation of Indigenous legalities.

i. *Identity politics and ethno-nationalism*

Worries about identity politics and ethno-nationalism have long appeared at the heart of debates over liberal political theory's responses to claims to Indigenous rights and self-determination.[57] Their persistent concerns dispute whether political claims of Indigenous peoples clash with ideals and practices of multicultural liberal democracy.[58] Some responses elaborate the role of law in contested and overlapping plural communities,[59] or examine the range of prospects found in familiar statist legal forms—including forms of incorporation, delegation, or recognition—for giving effect to (or denying) Indigenous claims.[60] A recent and growing body of scholarship explores the

57 See, eg, the essays in Ivison, Patton, and Sanders (n 7) and the sketch of concerns presented in Will Kymlicka, 'Theorizing Indigenous Rights' in *Politics in the Vernacular: Nationalism, Multiculturalism, and Citizenship* (OUP 2001).

58 Prominent Indigenist responses regard the internal debates over whether liberal political theory can accommodate Indigenous claims as being marginal to the justification of the claims themselves. See, eg, Gordon Christie, 'The Supersession of Indigenous Understandings of Justice and Morals' (2022) 25 Crit Rev Int Soc Pol 427. See also Coulthard (n 4).

59 Jeremy Webber, 'Pluralism and Human Agency' (2006) 44 Osgoode Hall L J 167; Jeremy Webber, 'The Grammar of Customary Law' (2009) 54 McGill L J 579; Kirsten Anker, 'From Making Space to Being in Place' in Nicole Roughan and Andrew Halpin (eds), *In Pursuit of Pluralist Jurisprudence* (CUP 2017); Val Napoleon, 'Legal Pluralism and Reconciliation' (2019) Maori LR 1.

60 Eg, Jacob T Levy, 'Three Models of Incorporating Indigenous Law' in Will Kymlicka (ed), *Citizenship in Diverse Societies* (OUP 2000) and Jacob T Levy, *Rationalism, Pluralism, and Freedom* (OUP 2014). For a fresh review of delegation and recognition models in Canada, see the extra-judicial work from Sébastien Grammond, 'Recognizing Indigenous Law: A Conceptual Framework' (2022) 100 Can Bar Rev 1.

ways in which Indigenous legal forms themselves offer prospects for reimagining (and in some cases rescuing) democratic and constitutionalist ideals that have been hijacked and thus foreclosed by state domination of Indigenous legal and political orders.[61]

A full engagement with the rich potential in the new philosophies of interlegality cannot be offered here. The narrower claim is that the tools of interlegality (drawn out of legality's own efforts to abstract away from concrete identities) can recognize the forms and institutions of Indigenous legalities rather than the identities of persons or race-based categorizations of persons. Legality's abstraction houses its capacity to address the claims that are made from competing legalities. The restraint required by interlegality also echoes liberal legality's own effort to avoid encroaching too far into the personal activities or preferences of persons under law. Legality's conception of abstraction as neutrality may yet serve interlegality's abstract neutrality between legal orders.[62]

Interlegality presents an alternative to both nationalist demands and to denials of difference. It envisages institutions for recognizing statuses of legality rather than identities of persons. Importantly, interlegality avoids essentializing or over-determining the complex choices, preferences, and indeed preferred and practiced identities of persons who may (but need not) recognize Indigenous laws and reject state legality (or vice versa). It also avoids over-determining the significance of identity itself, or membership of a single rather than multiple overlapping communities. For instance, it would not recognize an Indigenous individual as having some special characteristics, entitlements, or indeed identity, vis-à-vis other persons in the community. It recognizes instead the distinctive as well as the interactive forms of Indigenous legal ordering and their implications for those persons who recognize and are recognized within that order. The abstraction of interlegality helps (just as the abstraction of legality serves) to abstract away from race/ethnicity/identity-based claims. It may thus ward off insidious forms of ethno-nationalism better than defective liberal claims to legality.

ii. Superseding historic injustice

The second objection rests on the 'supersession thesis', which has been advanced powerfully and consistently by Jeremy Waldron. Waldron argues that injustices wrought upon Indigenous persons, including forceful and

61 John Borrows, *Freedom and Indigenous Constitutionalism* (University of Toronto Press 2016); John Borrows, *Canada's Indigenous Constitution* (University of Toronto Press 2010); James Tully, *Public Philosophy in a New Key* (CUP 2008); Aaron Mills, 'The Lifeworlds of Law: On Revitalizing Indigenous Legal Orders Today' (2016) 61 McGill L J 847.

62 Here it is important that the claim is not that all legal orders are equally valuable or equally serve those who recognize them. As Webber, 'Pluralism and Human Agency' (n 58) explains, law's plurality calls out for (rather than avoids) the need for an evaluation of legal ordering.

deceitful appropriations of property,[63] sovereignty, and political authority,[64] as well as breaches of treaty-based rights and obligations,[65] can be superseded by changes in circumstances. This position accepts that injustices occurred historically (and that these may trigger entitlements to compensation) but rejects any reversion or restoration of Indigenous property, sovereignty, and authority when circumstances have changed in material and morally relevant ways.[66]

A number of responses to Waldron have challenged the supersession thesis.[67] The present work's focus upon the importance of forms and claims of legality gives rise to a distinctive response, which highlights the prospect of interlegality found in the form of state–Indigenous treaties. In 2006, Mark Bennett and I challenged Waldron's argument about the supersession of treaties, and specifically the Treaty of Waitangi, by arguing that circumstances arising from the forceful impact of colonization did not support the supersession of treaty obligations.[68] A treaty is supposed to establish or at least contour the content of the rules designed to protect and enable persons (and legal orders) to co-exist amidst the very challenges and changes arising from interaction.[69] Our earlier argument also raised a more foundational suggestion

63 As Waldron explains his supersession thesis: 'certain things that were unjust when they occurred may be overtaken by events in a way that means their injustice has been superseded', Jeremy Waldron, 'Settlement, Return and the Supersession Thesis' (2004) 5 Theoretical Inquiries in Law, 237, 240. A recent symposium revisited Waldron's account. See Lukas H Meyer and Timothy Waligore, 'Superseding Historical Injustice? New Critical Assessments' (2022) 25 Crit Rev Int Soc Political Philos 319. For Waldron's most recent account, see Jeremy Waldron, 'Supersession: A Reply' (2022) 25 Crit Rev Int Soc Political Philos 443, including a helpful explanation of the development of the thesis since its earliest iteration in Jeremy Waldron, 'Historic Injustice: Its Remembrance and Supersession' in Graham Oddie and Roy Perrett (eds), *Justice, Ethics and New Zealand Society* (Massey University Press 1990).

64 On sovereignty, see Waldron, 'Supersession' (n 63) and Jeremy Waldron, 'Supersession and Sovereignty' (Julius Stone Address, 3 August 2006, NYU School of Law, Public Law Research Paper No 13–33) <https://ssrn.com/abstract=2205708> accessed 20 June 2024.

65 On treaties, see Jeremy Waldron, 'The Half-Life of Treaties: Waitangi, *Rebus Sic Stantibus*' (2006) 11 Otago LR 161.

66 Waldron, 'Supersession' (n 63). Waldron's most recent account reaffirms, however, that an argument against restoration or reversion of Indigenous property is not also an argument against compensation or other forms of response to injustice, nor is it (by itself) an argument against Indigenous self-determination.

67 See Christie (n 58); Paul Patton, 'Historic Injustice and the Possibility of Supersession' (2005) 26 J Intercult Stud 255; Jimmy Casas Klausen, 'Jeremy Waldron's Partial Kant: Indigenous Proximity, Colonial Injustice, Cultural Particularism' (2014) 46 Polity 31; Julio Montero 'Colonialism and Rights Supersession: A Kant-Inspired Perspective' (2022) 25 CRISPP 331.

68 Mark Bennett and Nicole Roughan, '*Rebus Sic Stantibus* and the Treaty of Waitangi?' (2006) 37 VUWLR 505.

69 Mark Bennett and Nicole Roughan, '*Rebus Sic Stantibus* and the Treaty of Waitangi?' (2006) 37 VUWLR 505. See also Michael Coyle, 'As Long as the Sun Shines' in John Borrows and Michael Coyle (eds), *The Right Relationship: Reimagining the Implementation of Historical Treaties* (University of Toronto Press 2017).

that the context surrounding treaty obligations (and their contemporary outworking) involves a complex interplay of international law, constitutional law, and Indigenous law—an argument that might be redescribed as an argument invoking interlegality.[70]

By abstracting from a singular legal order (whether the international legal order governing treaties, the constitutional legal order of the contemporary state, or an Indigenous legal order), an interlegality frame enables us to ask which combinations of legal materials, and which combinations of legal orders, can justly be applied to an interaction of legalities. It enables us to ask: what would be just institutions of justice fit to respond to injustices arising from the overruling and domination of one legal order by another? A treaty between legalities then appears among the candidate forms of interlegality—relating legal orders to one another—rather than subjecting both to the operation of constitutional or international law that one party either unilaterally determines, or is powerful enough to ignore.

An interlegality model can concede the argument that interacting peoples cannot and should not be segregated, but insist that the abstract forms of legal ordering can still be rearranged—and abstract statuses of legality recognized, attributed, and distributed—in ways that people and places cannot. The generations of persons who have arrived since settlement cannot justifiably be removed without further cause, but exclusionary or supremacist legal forms can be removed and Indigenous legal forms can be renewed.[71] Interlegality then requires forms for their interactions and intersections. A treaty is just one form for such a practice of interlegality, and my claim is not that it is necessary or sufficient to support interlegality's responses to injustice.[72] The forms for constructing and realizing interlegality will be deeply contextual and will have their own inter-relationships—for example, treaty forms interacting with Indigenous forms, as well as with the particular legal rules, principles, and institutions drawn from each of the interrelating orders. Despite this diversity, interlegality offers a distinctive response to the supersession thesis, showing that the concrete interaction of persons and the entanglements of their activities and entitlements do not set the limits of the abstract responses that legality (and its derivative interlegality) makes possible.

70 We described these as 'signposts'. Bennett and Roughan (n 68) 506.

71 The renewal might itself be operated as a form of correction for the injustice of exclusion. Space has precluded the full elaboration of this aspect of the account.

72 Other legal forms, including forms from tikanga Māori as well as common law and legislation, also offer direction and content for law's constraints on political relationships. As is well-documented, treaty forms lend themselves to a range of readings and approaches, let alone implementations, which are then defended either as an aspect of that form or on other grounds. For analysis of some of these issues, see the essays in John Borrows and Michael Coyle (eds), *The Right Relationship: Reimagining the Implementation of Historical Treaties* (University of Toronto Press 2017).

6. Conclusion

Acknowledging the limits of an abstract account of interlegality prompts a conclusory return, somewhat apologetically, to Shklar. Shklar's scepticism about the normal model of law, her limited yet principled faith in legality itself, and her discomfort with ethnic and other affiliative forms of nationalism, have all been somewhat unfairly instrumentalized here in the course of getting from the faces of injustice to the forms of interlegality. Shklar's work has been taken to provoke attention to the forms and claims of Indigenous legalities, by representing concerns that I take to be central to the strongest claims made against their recognition.

The more direct engagement with Shklar offered here has responded to her criticism of the abstraction of legality with a sketch of the possibilities such abstraction offers for responding to the injustices that continue to pervade the interactions of state and Indigenous legal orders. Abstraction harbours the potential to abstract faces and voices into forms and claims, and to abstract away from a singular legality into the domain of interlegality. Interlegality adopts the potential of abstraction to respond to injustices by enabling contenders for legalities to relate without domination, as well as to avoid essentializing persons' identities, celebrating forms of nationalism, or separating people into insiders and outsiders. Interlegality may in this way serve the goals that Shklar herself demanded of a theory of injustice.

Chapter 6

Bringing heaven down to earth

Rights and inclusion in Rawlsian public reason

Patrick Emerton and Jayani Nadarajalingam[1]

This chapter provides a theoretical account of the capacity of liberalism to respond to claims to *inclusion* as a component of justice. Bringing together Karl Marx's famous essay 'On the Jewish Question'[2] and John Rawls's account of public reason, rights, toleration, and the social bases of self-respect, we argue that the demands that these liberal commitments impose are best understood as manifestations of an ongoing historical process. This process, one that accepts contingency and is driven by political action, is the working out of liberal commitments, including an ongoing working out of the boundary between (1) what is public and hence subject to the demands of public reason, and (2) what is private and hence outside such scope. If the actors that make up the liberal state participate in the process in a principled manner, the process drives the liberal state in the direction of ever-greater recognition and inclusion of diverse identities. In Rawlsian terms, this is a mechanism of procedural justice.

As is well-known, Marx adopts a historicized account of political relationships and political possibility. However, in 'On the Jewish Question', he argues that the liberal state has gone as far as a distinctively *political* arrangement can go in universalizing human power and freedom—ensuring that all citizens enjoy the same abstract rights in the 'heavenly' political sphere—and that it has done so by alienating those things from the actual, 'earthly' site

1 We thank participants at the Julius Stone Institute conference 'Responding to Injustice' (8 December 2022), IVR Bucharest (7 July 2022), the Deakin Law School Legal Theory work shop (6 May 2022), the Alfred Deakin Institute workshop 'Constitutionalism and Civil Religion' (9 December 2021) and the Deakin Law School conference 'The Future of Freedom of Speech and Religion after Israel Folau' (7 December 2019) for their comments on earlier versions of this chapter, particularly Guy Baldwin, David Dyzenhaus, Matt Lister, Ben Golder, Triantafyllos Gkouvas, John Morss, Colleen Murphy, Henry Richardson, Manuel Rodeiro, Wojciech Sadurski, Ashwini Vasanthakumar, Miguel Vatter, Kevin Walton, David Winterton and Duncan Wallace. We also thank Julian Sempill, John Sebastian, and an anonymous reviewer for their comments, and Kirsty Wilson and Jack Fagan from the Melbourne Law School Academic Research Service for their assistance.

2 Karl Marx, 'On the Jewish Question' in *Writings of the Young Marx on Philosophy and Society* (Loyd De Easton and Kurt H Guddat eds and trs, Anchor Books 1967).

DOI: 10.4324/9781032676159-7

of human life—'civil society'—which is characterized by what he describes as the 'unbridled' pursuit of particular concerns, producing not only possible but actual conflict and division. Marx therefore concludes that human emancipation is *impossible* while such a state of affairs endures.[3] Marx's conclusion is powerful and, to our knowledge, remains neglected in the literature on political liberalism. This chapter thus puts forward two claims that take Marx's conclusion as a starting point.

First, and contrary to Marx's conclusion, the liberal state is able to 'bring heaven down to earth'—at least some of heaven—by imposing requirements of universality upon the everyday world of civil society. These requirements are imposed in response to demands of reciprocity that make themselves felt through the actions of those whose identity has led to them being denied full participation in some or other aspect of civil society; their continued prosecution of these claims results in their subsequent recognition within public reason. Certain, typically early, stages in this process reveal a tension in liberal commitments to the toleration and inclusion within a common citizenry of diverse forms of life and the values and commitments associated with them; Marx takes this tension to be a *paradox* (or *contradiction*) that cannot be resolved within the confines of the liberal state. We argue that these tensions are the manifestations of the ongoing *process* just described, and we show how Rawls's framework can be developed to incorporate and explain this process.

One important aspect of the process that we describe is that the recognition within public reason of new claims to inclusion is frequently accompanied by necessary developments in some of the comprehensive doctrines that participate in the overlapping consensus that underlies public reason. This is because, as long as the separation between the 'heavenly' realm of universal citizenship and the 'earthly' realm of civil society endures, someone somewhere will be suffering unhappy experiences or consequences of particularity. As we just observed, this will lead them to make claims of justice upon the political sphere, and while not all of these claims will be immediately successful, liberalism has no principled basis for denying them. They therefore generate a continual pressure to revise the content of public reason, and thus the parameters of the overlapping consensus of reasonable comprehensive doctrines. This leads to our second claim: a correct understanding of how liberalism accommodates claims to inclusion requires abandoning Rawls's suggestion that the content of rights is identified simply by reference to existing liberal-democratic practice. Rather than a priori reflection, the persuasive political action of those making such claims establishes what their participation requires, including by way of the content of rights that ensure just

3 See also Wendy Brown's discussion, influenced by 'On the Jewish Question', of the limits of emancipation within the confines of the liberal state in Wendy Brown, *Regulating Aversion: Tolerance in the Age of Identity and Empire* (Princeton University Press 2008) ch 3.

inclusion. Indeed, the existence of this process shows that it would be quite *complacent* to think that the project of constitutionalism, or human rights, can *ever* be completed. This second claim is the more important of the two. To the extent that the process of bringing heaven down to earth is unable to be completed, Marx's concern about the incompleteness of human emancipation retains force, whereas our conclusion about the proper Rawlsian conception of the relationship between political action and the content of public reason is of immediate and unavoidable significance to Rawlsian political philosophy.[4]

Our development of Rawls's framework in this fashion responds to 'agonistic' criticisms of political liberalism.[5] Like 'agonistic' approaches to politics, our approach foregrounds an ongoing working out—in the real world and by real political actors—of the public/private distinction. Whilst 'agonistic' approaches, particularly those that are deeply pluralist, are typically sceptical of consensus approaches to politics, our approach reconciles pluralism and consensus in a way that does not entail the disappearance or even sidelining of political action. Further, whilst our account is proceduralist, we adopt an *expansive* understanding of procedure—one that incorporates political activities and processes that 'agonistic' approaches typically *contrast* with procedure (narrowly understood to only refer to procedures that are established and controlled by the state).

Section one consists of an outline of the Rawlsian framework that we draw on. Section two sets out the relevant ideas from Marx and presents an argument as to what they tell us about the way liberalism addresses claims to injustice arising out of the relationship between universality and particularity. Section three, after showing why Marx's argument is wrong, argues that the content of public reason and of rights in Rawlsian liberalism must be understood as a matter of procedural justice. While our argument operates at a reasonably abstract level, several real-world examples in this section, including the change in the application of the Fourteenth Amendment of the United States Constitution from *Plessy v Ferguson*[6] to *Brown v Board of Education*,[7] illustrate our key claims.

4 Chad Flanders is one of the few philosophers we are aware of who has seriously grappled with how the content of public reason comes about and, importantly, how it changes: see Chad Flanders, 'The Mutability of Public Reason' (2012) 25 Ratio Juris 180. Like us, he emphasizes a 'bottom-up' mechanism of change that is driven by political action.

5 For well-known 'agonistic' approaches to politics, see William Connolly, *The Ethos of Pluralization* (University of Minnesota Press 1995); James Tully, *Strange Multiplicity: Constitutionalism in an Age of Diversity* (CUP 1995); Chantal Mouffe, 'Deliberative Democracy or Agonistic Pluralism?' (1999) 66 Soc Res 745; James Tully, *Public Philosophy in a New Key, Volume I: Democracy and Civic Freedom* (CUP 2008); James Tully, *Public Philosophy in a New Key, Volume II: Imperialism and Civic Freedom* (CUP 2008); Bonnie Honig, *Political Theory and the Displacement of Politics* (30th anniversary edn, Cornell University Press 2023).

6 *163 US 537 (1896).*

7 347 US 483 (1954).

1. The relevant Rawlsian framework

Rawls argues that, in a liberal society, *the right is prior to the good*: members must understand and accept that they may have to subordinate certain aspects of their own conception of what is good or bad as part of the process of fully and equally accommodating others who have their own, possibly different, conceptions.[8] That subordination manifests itself in *the priority of the reasonable over the rational.*[9] People are reasonable in one important respect:

> when, among equals . . . they are ready to propose principles and standards as fair terms of cooperation and to abide by them willingly, given the assurance that others will likewise do so. . . . The reasonable is an element of the idea of society as a system of fair cooperation and that its fair terms be reasonable for all to accept is part of its idea of reciprocity. . . .
>
> Reasonable persons . . . desire for its own sake a social world in which they, as free and equal, can cooperate with others on terms all can accept. They insist that reciprocity should hold within that world so that each benefits along with others.[10]

Reciprocity is thus central to Rawls's conception of a liberal society; it imposes limits on the pursuit of people's own 'private' ends, that is, *the rational.*[11] The reasonable and the rational do not operate in different spheres; rather, they intersect in the one *social world.* Although there is a normative dimension to Rawls's account of the *reasonable* and its priority, it is also a claim about social feasibility: a society in which the rational is *not* subordinated to the reasonable is not one that is able to be stable for the right reasons and thus able to ensure widespread support for its own institutions.[12]

Rawlsian liberalism does not demand that individuals set aside their differences or that they avoid all conflicts of ends: accommodating others does not mean that there will not be (for instance) planning disputes around where churches are to be built or the possibility of rules that regulate when they may ring their bells.[13] But it does require 'mutual respect' and accommodation

8 John Rawls, *Political Liberalism* (rev edn, Columbia University Press 1996) 176 n 2. See also John Rawls, *Justice as Fairness: A Restatement* (Erin Kelly ed, Harvard University Press 2001) 141 and John Rawls, *A Theory of Justice* (Harvard University Press 1971) 449, 563–64.

9 Rawls, *Justice as Fairness* (n 8) 82.

10 Rawls, *Political Liberalism* (n 8) 49–50.

11 Rawls, *Political Liberalism* (n 8) 54, 60–61, 156–57. The priority of the right over the good and the subordination of the rational to the reasonable are thus closely connected to Rawls's notion of social unity: see Rawls, *Political Liberalism* (n 8) 134.

12 Rawls, *Political Liberalism* (n 8) 134, 390–92; Rawls, *Justice as Fairness* (n 8) 180–202.

13 The boundary between legitimate disputes of the sort described in the main text and active repression of religious practices is not always clear-cut. Rehan Abeyratne discusses a Sri Lankan case where nuisance (noise pollution) is seemingly used to repress an Islamic house

and identifies the capacity 'to meet others halfway' as a preeminent social virtue.[14] A family of reasonable *political conceptions of justice* makes this possible and provides the content of public reason.[15] These conceptions have three main features:

> First, a list of certain basic rights, liberties and opportunities . . .;
> Second, an assignment of special priority to those rights, liberties, and opportunities, especially with regard to the claims of the general good and perfectionist values;
> Third, measures ensuring for all citizens adequate all-purpose means to make effective use of their freedoms. . . .
> Each of these liberalisms endorses the underlying ideas of citizens as free and equal persons and of society as a fair system of cooperation over time. . . . They are required to specify . . . substantive ideas of fairness involving fair opportunity and ensuring adequate all-purpose means. . . .[16]

In addition, 'the criterion of reciprocity' acts as a 'limiting feature'.[17] Rawls characterizes a putatively liberal conception that does not have the third feature as one in which the basic liberties 'are properly criticized as purely formal' and as consequently 'lack[ing] the criterion of reciprocity and allow[ing] excessive social and economic inequalities as judged by that criterion'.[18] Rawls identifies the following list of all-purpose means:

a. basic rights and liberties;
b. freedom of movement and free choice of occupation against a background of diverse opportunities;

---

of worship: Rehan Abeyratne, 'Rethinking Judicial Independence in India and Sri Lanka' (2015) 10 Asian J Comp L 99, 125–26.

14 Rawls, *Political Liberalism* (n 8) 156–57.

15 Rawls suggests that, at least for many liberal views, the scope and application of public reason have the same basis as its content: Rawls, *Political Liberalism* (n 8) 225–26. See also John Rawls, *The Law of Peoples; with 'The Idea of Public Reason Revisited'* (Harvard University Press 1999) 143–44.

16 Rawls, *The Law of Peoples* (n 15) 140–41. Much the same formulation is found in Rawls, *Political Liberalism* (n 8) 6 and Rawls, *The Law of Peoples* (n 15) 14, 49, although only the latter expressly stresses the importance of reciprocity: see below, text to n 18. Rawls suggests that his own particular form of liberalism, *justice as fairness*, has a particular salience in the family of liberal conceptions identified in the quoted passages, as distinctively egalitarian and hence distinctive in its capacity to reconcile potentially opposed social and economic interests: Rawls, *The Law of Peoples* (n 15) 14 n 5, 142 n 27; Rawls, *Political Liberalism* (n 8) 6, 167–68. In the context of this chapter, as we go on to show, a focus on *the social bases of self-respect*—which is implicit in any conception of justice conforming to the requirements of reasonableness as articulated by Rawls—is sufficient to make out our argument.

17 Rawls, *The Law of Peoples* (n 15) 140–41.

18 Rawls, *The Law of Peoples* (n 15) 49. See also Rawls, *Political Liberalism* (n 8) lecture viii.

c. powers and prerogatives of offices and positions of responsibility in the political and economic institutions of the basic structure;
d. income and wealth; and
e. the social bases of self-respect.[19]

The lattermost are further characterized as 'those aspects of basic institutions normally essential if citizens are to have a lively sense of their worth as persons and to be able to advance their ends with self-confidence'.[20] Humans are social beings whose sense of their own worth and identity, and whose wants and aspirations are significantly shaped by the social structures to which they are subject. Thus, for many people at least, part of having a sense of living a good life comes from having that affirmed by others.[21]

There is some duplication—for instance, basic rights and liberties are mentioned in the first feature but also occur as components of the third—but this is not a problem for understanding the content of public reason.[22] In later works, Rawls states that '[t]he criterion of reciprocity is normally violated whenever basic liberties are denied'[23] and that the social bases of self-respect include 'the public recognition of that fact [that citizens have equal basic rights] and that everyone endorses the difference principle, itself a form of reciprocity'.[24] In this chapter, we do not consider the difference principle in its specific detail, but we note that *public recognition and honouring* of equal basic rights and of reciprocity, whatever particular additional institutional form the latter might take, are themselves manifestations of public reason. So there is a circularity—not vicious but one of mutual reinforcement—between the content of public reason and its actual role in public discourse. This takes us to the *scope* of public reason.

In his later work, Rawls is ambiguous as to the extent to which reasoning by state officials and voting decisions by citizens ought to be responsive to public reason. He tends to discuss the practical working of the basic rights and liberties through the lens of constitutional guarantees, judicially

19 Rawls, *Political Liberalism* (n 8) 181. See also 76, where offices are not mentioned but fair equality of opportunity is, and 308–09; Rawls, *Justice as Fairness* (n 8) 58–59; Rawls, *A Theory of Justice* (n 8) 62, 92.

20 Rawls, *Justice as Fairness* (n 8) 59.

21 Rawls, *A Theory of Justice* (n 8) 440–42; Rawls, *Political Liberalism* (n 8) 269, 318–19.

22 In *A Theory of Justice*, Rawls identifies some complexities around the inclusion of the social bases of self-respect in the list of all-purpose means, arising from the possibility of envy resulting from differences of income and wealth: Rawls, *A Theory of Justice* (n 8) 545–46. See also 178–79, which suggests a more expansive understanding of the social bases of self-respect.

23 Rawls, *The Law of Peoples* (n 15) 138.

24 Rawls, *Justice as Fairness* (n 8) 60. The same point is made in Rawls, *Political Liberalism* (n 8) 319–20.

enforced,[25] and thus neglects their role in public reason more generally. He says that the ideal of public reason:

> is realized . . . whenever . . . government officials, as well as candidates for public office, act from and follow the idea of public reason and explain to other citizens their reasons for supporting fundamental political positions in terms of the political conception of justice they regard as most reasonable.[26]

This suggests that the demands of public reason apply only in respect of 'fundamental political questions'.[27] However, in *A Theory of Justice*, Rawls states that a law, if it is to be binding simply in virtue of its enactment, must be

> so far as one can ascertain, within the range of those that could reasonably be favored by rational legislators conscientiously trying to follow the principles of justice . . . [because] those who disagree with the decision made cannot convincingly establish their point within the framework of the public conception of justice.[28]

The reason for the negative framing is that legislation 'frequently depends upon speculative political and economic doctrines and upon social theory generally', meaning that '[o]ften the best that we can say of a law or policy is that it is at least not clearly unjust'.[29] Thus, while public reason does not, in itself, settle all political questions, it establishes clear limits on the scope of political discourse. Some discourse and some legislative proposals may fall outside the 'allowed bounds' and hence be demonstrably unjust within the parameters of public reason.[30] The legitimacy of legislation, then, is a matter of quasi-pure procedural justice,[31] that is, the fact of its enactment by a constitutionally conforming legislature acting within the allowed bounds is sufficient to make legislation binding.[32] This is not a question of constitutional permissibility in a formal legal sense but whether legislators, who

25 See, eg, Rawls, *Political Liberalism* (n 8) 232, 338, although cf the disclaimer at 234–35.

26 Rawls, *The Law of Peoples* (n 15) 135. See also Rawls, *Political Liberalism* (n 8) l–li, 217–18.

27 Rawls, *Political Liberalism* (n 8) 137, 217, 219–20, 247; cf Rawls, *The Law of Peoples* (n 15) 135.

28 Rawls, *A Theory of Justice* (n 8) 362.

29 Rawls, *A Theory of Justice* (n 8) 199. See also 201. It may be that Rawls intends his remarks about the relationship of public reason to fundamental questions to mean that those questions do not require any appeal to 'speculative' doctrines and hence can be affirmatively and not merely negatively settled entirely within public reason; this seems to be what Rawls means when he characterizes public reason as 'complete': Rawls, *Political Liberalism* (n 8) 225, 241, 244; Rawls, *The Law of Peoples* (n 15) 144–45.

30 The phrase 'allowed bounds' occurs in *A Theory of Justice*, where Rawls says that legislators must 'select a policy within the allowed bounds': Rawls, *A Theory of Justice* (n 8) 362.

31 Rawls uses this phrase without defining it: Rawls, *A Theory of Justice* (n 8) 201, 362.

32 cf Samuel Freeman, 'Democracy, Religion & Public Reason' (2020) 149 Daedalus 37, 45–46.

have a political duty to justify their support of legislation within the 'allowed bounds', are able to justify their legislative decision-making in such cases. Further, what counts as a fundamental political question itself requires articulation in terms of public reason; we return to this point later.

Samuel Freeman discusses relatively banal cases of legislation enacted in apparent pursuit of perfectionist values, such as various sorts of education (for example, scientific knowledge and aesthetic appreciation), public facilities (for example, museums and sports grounds), and subsidized events (for example, the performing arts and athletics events), and says that these may be justified within public reason because of their contribution to the capacity of citizens (1) to formulate and pursue their own conceptions of the good, and (2) to do so within a framework of commitment to the priority of the right over the good.[33] Even in such cases, we may ask whether (for instance) promoting and celebrating the athleticism and sporting achievement of some sends an implicit signal to others who live less physical lives that their lives are not as good? Does conferring recognition and status on those who succeed at formal education send an implicit signal that a less-educated life is a less-worthwhile one? Some of these questions are answered by the reality of the contexts in which we live. For instance, given the realities of the contemporary Australian economy, some minimum degree of education is probably necessary for any sort of flourishing life. This makes education and concomitant socialization into the ways of urban and bureaucratic life *all-purpose means* on a par with the other primary goods.[34] But tensions may still arise. One person's education and socialization may lead them to affirm a conception of the good that excludes exactly the life that some other person has found, through their experience of those same social processes, to be the good for them. In these circumstances, what sort of forbearance is owed by who to whom?

Rawls states that the ideal of public reason does not apply in the 'background culture' or 'the culture of civil society',[35] that is, in political discussion that takes place in non-public forums.[36] However, he also notes that the political principles of justice impose essential constraints on the family and non-public associations to ensure that they do not impermissibly burden the basic rights and liberties and the freedoms and opportunities of their members.[37] This reiterates the contrast between the reasonable and the rational in

33 Samuel Freeman, 'Democracy, Religion & Public Reason' (2020) 149 Daedalus 44, 46, 48. The 'moral powers' to which Freeman refers are the capacities mentioned in the text: see Rawls, *Political Liberalism* (n 8) 19.

34 For Rawls's discussion of education as a primary good, see Rawls, *Political Liberalism* (n 8) 184.

35 Rawls, *The Law of Peoples* (n 15) 166.

36 Rawls, *The Law of Peoples* (n 15) 166. See also Rawls, *Political Liberalism* (n 8) l, 14, 220–21. Lawrence Solum agrees and argues further that the ideal should not extend to 'public discussion of moral and cultural matters': Lawrence Solum, 'Constructing an Ideal of Public Reason' (1993) 30 SDLR 729, 752.

37 Rawls, *The Law of Peoples* (n 15) 158–60.

social terms, as the boundary between the public (and political) and the background culture; but until the demands of reciprocity have been worked out, the scope of reasonableness and its demands remain unclear, as does the boundary between what counts as 'public' and what counts as 'background culture'.

We finish this section with an important point regarding basic rights and liberties. Rawls states that the basic rights and liberties can be given by a list, based on those 'normally protected' in the constitutions of democratic states, paying particular attention to 'those constitutions which have worked well'.[38] The rights and liberties, he says, 'are characterized in more or less the same manner in all free regimes'[39] and, when compared to principles that govern social and economic inequalities, '[i]t is far easier to tell whether these essentials are realized' and '[i]t [is] much easier to gain agreement about what the basic rights and liberties should be, not in every detail of course, but about the main outlines'.[40] We disagree.

Basic rights and liberties and their affirmation in public reason serve two functions: they create a space of liberty in which individuals are permitted to pursue their private aims, affirming their own conceptions of the good;[41] but, as we have seen, they also provide the basis of self-respect, by allowing individuals not only to pursue their own aims but to have the worth of their choice and pursuit of aims affirmed.[42] Thus, there is an evident possibility of both a *theoretical* and a *practical* tension: in a pluralist society, it may be hard to have one mode of life affirmed as *good* without, perhaps implicitly, suggesting that other ways of living are *not* so good. Tensions of this sort continually emerge and they cannot be resolved simply by looking to past lists.

This takes us to Marx.

2. Marx's criticism of the liberal state

This section sets out Marx's analysis of the way that liberalism grapples with the relationship between particularity and universality and presents an argument as to what this tells us about the way that liberalism addresses claims to injustice arising out of that relationship.

Framed as a reply to Bruno Bauer's writing on the same topic, the starting point of 'On the Jewish Question' is the debate over the emancipation of the Jewish minority.[43] Although there is a sense in which 'the Jewish question' is

38 Rawls, *Political Liberalism* (n 8) 292–93.
39 Rawls, *Political Liberalism* (n 8) 228.
40 Rawls, *Political Liberalism* (n 8) 230.
41 See, eg, Rawls, *Political Liberalism* (n 8) 308; Rawls, *A Theory of Justice* (n 8) 542–43; Rawls, *Justice as Fairness* (n 8) 105, 112–13.
42 Rawls, *A Theory of Justice* (n 8) 440–41; Rawls, *Political Liberalism* (n 8) 318–19. Marx does not address this function of civil rights.
43 Marx, 'On the Jewish Question' (n 2).

not Marx's central concern, the concerns that underlie that 'question'—matters of identity, particularity, belonging, citizenship, and the like—*are* central to his argument. One important issue, brought out in the first half of 'On the Jewish Question', is that of the *reciprocal* dimension of emancipation: is the call by a religious minority for inclusion a request for special privileges?[44] (Some critics of multiculturalism seem to think so.[45]) Is addressing such a call via non-radical politics—for example, by engaging *with the state*—an endorsement of the political status quo?[46] Perhaps most generally, is there a paradox in seeking recognition and acceptance of *difference* within the *universal* framework of civic inclusion via citizenship?[47] Marx answers 'Yes' to this last question. His reasoning rests primarily on an account of the social and psychological processes that underlie human particularity.

Although pluralism and identity extend well beyond the domain of religion, Marx sees religion and politics as closely related. He sees their social and psychological structures and processes as similar, even to a significant extent identical: both are expressions of *alienation*.[48] Thus, the critique of religion leads to the critique of politics.[49]

Marx is influenced by the Feurbachian and, ultimately, Hegelian analysis of religious belief as a type of alienated human self-understanding,[50] but he is also cognizant of the widely recognized social changes that constitute modernity: the end of uniformity of religious conviction and cultural practices more generally as a source of social integration; and the search for new, more self-conscious forms of establishing and governing human communities. Marx's analysis of religion as a social and psychological phenomenon leads him to an early account of the communist ideal: humanity self-consciously united in knowledge, power, and benevolence as the result

44 Marx, 'On the Jewish Question' (n 2) 216–20.

45 See, eg, John Gray, *Enlightenment's Wake* (Routledge 1995) 35–38; Brian Barry, *Culture and Equality: An Egalitarian Critique of Multiculturalism* (Harvard University Press 2001).

46 Marx, 'On the Jewish Question' (n 2) 217. See Bauer's criticism of Jewish calls for emancipation, as paraphrased by Marx: John Gray, *Enlightenment's Wake* (Routledge 1995) 35–38; Brian Barry, *Culture and Equality: An Egalitarian Critique of Multiculturalism* (Harvard University Press 2001).

47 This question is suggested, for instance, in John Gray, *Enlightenment's Wake* (Routledge 1995) 35–38; Brian Barry, *Culture and Equality: An Egalitarian Critique of Multiculturalism* (Harvard University Press 2001) 222–26.

48 John Gray, *Enlightenment's Wake* (Routledge 1995) 35–38; Brian Barry, *Culture and Equality: An Egalitarian Critique of Multiculturalism* (Harvard University Press 2001).

49 Marx, 'Toward the Critique of Hegel's Philosophy of Law: Introduction' in *Writings of the Young Marx on Philosophy and Society* (Loyd De Easton and Kurt H Guddat eds and trs, Anchor Books 1967) 249–51.

50 See the discussions in Shlomo Avineri, *The Social and Political Thought of Karl Marx* (CUP 1968) 11–2; David MacGregor, *The Communist Ideal in Hegel and Marx* (University of Toronto Press 1984) 57–60.

of an (inevitably revolutionary) 'un-inverting' of the everyday world.[51] The central premises in Marx's argument are *neither* normative *nor* conceptual: (1) that religious feeling and longing are genuine, but (2) are misdirected, because of the alienation of human beings from one another and hence from their collective capacity in the real world. The un-inversion of the world via communism will enable these sentiments to be realized free of alienation. Importantly for our purposes, Marx's argument retains much of its force even if one does not accept one or both of premises (1) and (2). As we show in the next sub-section, Marx's account of the failure of reciprocity in the liberal state as arising from a type of alienation of people from their own social circumstances and collective capacity can be advanced without relying on any parallel account of religious feeling and belief.

a. The critique of the liberal state and its universal citizenship

Marx diagnoses a paradox in *political emancipation*, that is, in the inclusion of difference within a liberal framework of universal citizenship. The diagnosis is expressed as a criticism of both the *particularity* that political emancipation permits and of the *demands of universality* that it imposes.[52] In making this diagnosis, Marx follows Bauer in recognizing that liberal citizenship demands some sort of relinquishing of claims grounded in particularity—just as does Rawlsian *public reason*. But he differs from Bauer in focusing on whether political (in contrast to human) emancipation offers a viable alternative in exchange. Marx makes it clear that he is less concerned with normativity and more with feasibility: the liberal state, no matter how inclusive, cannot eliminate particularity.

Religion remains a concern for Marx in this respect, and he argues that 'the existence of religion implies a *defect*'.[53] The starting point for understanding why is as follows: due to the liberal state 'relegat[ing] religion to . . . civil society', religion is (or becomes) a manifestation of particularity.[54] And,

51 For discussion of this early account of the communist ideal, see Avineri (n 50) 31–38.

52 Marx, 'On the Jewish Question' (n 2) 220–21.

53 Avineri (n 50).

54 Avineri (n 50) 228. This is of course not a *general* claim: some societies are characterized by a very high degree of, even near-total, religious homogeneity. But in such societies religion will not have been relegated to civil society and, conversely, such homogeneity cannot obtain in a society in the circumstances of liberal modernity, in which the question of the emancipation of members of minority religions has become a serious topic of political debate. In the case that Marx is familiar with—that is, the emergence of the liberal state concurrently with the working out of the Reformation—more intricate questions of cause and effect do not arise, but in cases where the state emerges (or is imposed) via a different pathway, the question of causal priority takes on greater significance. We suggest, in light of what Marx argues (and as we have explained in the text) that the fundamental characteristic of liberal modernity in this instance is the relegation of religion to civil society. It is this rendering of religion into a matter of private choice that opens the door to pluralism and hence the breakdown of near-total

according to Marx, the fact that particularity endures even in a fully inclusive, fully liberal state shows us the true direction of causation.[55] The liberal state *presupposes* difference and particularity among its members because the equal citizenship that it universally confers is a status distinct from the everyday life of the individual. The liberal state presupposes that a citizen is not *only* a citizen but is also an individual with private interests, pursuits, convictions, and so on. These differences, which include the continued existence of religion and hence of religious difference not only separate people from one another but (potentially and in actuality) give rise to conflict, both with other citizens in their private capacities and with the individual's relationship to the political community as a whole.[56]

There are many ways in which such conflicts might manifest. The notional concern of Marx's essay is minority religious status, but we could equally point to people who squat in abandoned buildings in breach of their legal obligations to their fellow citizens because they have nowhere else to live; to people who would have to give up an hour of work to go and vote and thus either fail to fully participate in collective, political life because of their need to earn a wage or else compromise their role in the complex system of production and distribution in order to perform their duties as citizens; or to people who vote for a government that will reduce the regulation of their business activities, thus allowing an increase in profitability, even though they can recognize that this will increase the burden of externalities generated by those activities.

Marx regards this endurance of *particularity* as a defect because he regards it as incompatible with genuine human emancipation. He has a demanding conception of the latter. Marx expounds Bauer thus: 'How is an antagonism to be resolved? By making it impossible'.[57] Marx does not criticize Bauer on this point. Rather, Marx's threshold for successful political inclusion and universality is that *anything less should be impossible.* Rephrased in terms of reciprocity or social unity[58]—what Marx calls 'species-life'

homogeneity. Rawls's account of public reasons rests explicitly on the premise of pluralism: see, eg, Rawls, *Political Liberalism* (n 8) 36–37, 63.

55 Marx, 'On the Jewish Question' (n 2) 222–23, 226.

56 Marx, 'On the Jewish Question' (n 2) 225–27, 232, 241.

57 Marx, 'On the Jewish Question' (n 2) 218.

58 Rawls uses the phrase 'social unity' in the index to *Political Liberalism* to describe the goal of his political philosophy: *Rawls, Political Liberalism* (n 8) 460. That goal is to articulate an account 'of society as a fair system of social cooperation between free and equal persons viewed as fully cooperating members of society over a complete life' without 'the oppressive use of state power [being] necessary for political community', to ensure that '[a] society united . . . remain[s] so': Marx, 'On the Jewish Question' (n 2) 9, 37. In *A Theory of Justice*, Rawls articulates a similar idea using the phrase 'social union': Rawls, *A Theory of Justice* (n 8) 523–27. Rawls argues that this sort of social unity can be achieved while honouring 'the rights of man' and permitting private property (subject to Rawls's well-known 'difference principle' and a requirement of fair equality of opportunity) and thus that his political philosophy has an answer to Marx's objections: Rawls, *Justice as Fairness* (n 8) 176–78.

and 'species-being', the alternative to the sorts of conflict that particularity permits[59]—this demanding standard entails that anything less than *utter reciprocity resulting in the impossibility of conflict* is not reciprocity at all. Marx thus concludes 'On the Jewish Question' with a concomitantly radical call for genuine human emancipation.[60]

b. Civil rights, civil society, and the limits of the political

The following passage sets out the contrast between individual particularity and universal citizenship that obtains in the liberal state:

> The state abolishes distinctions of *birth*, *rank*, *education*, and *occupation* in its fashion when it declares them to be *non-political* distinctions, when it proclaims that every member of the community *equally* participates in popular sovereignty without regard to these distinctions, and when it deals with all elements of the actual life of the nation from the standpoint of the state. Nevertheless the state permits private property, education, and occupation to *act* and manifest their *particular* nature as private property, education, and occupation in their *own* ways.[61]

Marx then identifies the following problem:[62] one way that the liberal state expresses its presupposition of particular pursuits is through guarantees of 'natural rights' or 'the rights of man',[63] which include liberty, property, and 'the *right to be religious* according to one's liking and to practice a particular religion . . . [as] a *universal human right*'.[64] According to Marx, these civil rights are premised on the prospects of conflict, arising from what today we would describe as differences of *identity* but also differences in more banal features of social life, such as educational opportunity and attainment, occupation, and differences in the relationship to property, both in general and in particular instances.[65]

But Rawls does not squarely address Marx's argument that the liberal state is unable to resolve the conflicts that it permits and, indeed, is premised on, between universality and particularity.

59 Marx, 'On the Jewish Question' (n 2) 225–28, 231, 237.

60 Marx, 'On the Jewish Question' (n 2) 241.

61 Marx, 'On the Jewish Question' (n 2) 224–25, 237 (emphasis added). Rawls rejects such a picture as an adequate account of human sociability: Rawls, *A Theory of Justice* (n 8) 522–23.

62 Marx, 'On the Jewish Question' (n 2) 237.

63 Marx discusses these extensively in Marx, 'On the Jewish Question' (n 2) 233–37, 240.

64 Marx, 'On the Jewish Question' (n 2) 234 (emphasis added).

65 Marx, 'On the Jewish Question' (n 2) 224–28, 235–37, 239–40. For a thoroughgoing discussion and elaboration of this aspect of Marx's argument, see Christoph Menke, *Critique of Rights* (Polity Press 2020).

Having set out the problem, Marx states that it is 'easily settled'.[66] Marx's 'settling' of the problem begins with his version of the generally understood proposition that the liberal state and the modern industrial economy together dissolve (or sometimes brutally disintegrate) other forms of social organization and social intermediation. Marx observes that '[f]eudal society was dissolved into its foundation, into *man*. But into man as he actually was the foundation of that society, into *egoistical* man'.[67] 'Thus', says Marx, 'none of the so-called rights of men goes beyond the egoistic man, the man drawn into himself . . . and separated from the community'.[68] This then leads into an analysis of the relationship between the individual and the state:

> This man, the member of civil society, is now the basis and presupposition of the political state. He is recognized as such by the state in the rights of man.
>
> But the freedom of egoistic man and the recognition of this freedom is rather the recognition of the unbridled movement of the spiritual and material elements forming the contents of his life.
>
> Thus man was not freed from religion; he received religious freedom. He was not freed from property. He received freedom of property. He was not freed from the egoism of trade but received freedom to trade.
>
> Actual man is recognized only in the form of the egoistic individual, authentic man, only in the form of abstract citizen.[69]

Marx's analysis leads him to a definite conclusion: the liberal state has gone as far as a distinctively *political* arrangement can go in universalizing human power and freedom, and it has done so by alienating those things from the actual site of human life—'civil society' characterized by the 'unbridled' pursuit of particular concerns, producing conflict, and making emancipation impossible while this state of affairs endures.

It is important to note that the failure of human emancipation that Marx diagnoses, which results from the conflict described earlier, is universal. The 'winners' in social conflicts have also failed to achieve emancipation, because they are not reconciled to their own sociality: they know (or are in a position to know) that they are treating others without full regard to those others' equal membership of society.[70] The owner of the polluting business who votes

66 Marx, 'On the Jewish Question' (n 2) 238.
67 Marx, 'On the Jewish Question' (n 2) 238–40.
68 Marx, 'On the Jewish Question' (n 2) 236–37.
69 Marx, 'On the Jewish Question' (n 2) 240.
70 GA Cohen makes a similar point in his criticism of Rawls's accommodation of market incentive structures into his formulation of the difference principle: GA Cohen, *If You're an Egalitarian, How Come You're So Rich?* (Harvard University Press 2001) 126–27, 134–35, 207 n 31. Rawls repeatedly emphasizes that the difference principle is necessary to ensure that society can be understood by *all* its members as a system of fair cooperation—a social

for a lessening of regulation is failing to achieve genuine emancipation just as much as the worker who cannot afford to take time off in order to cast a vote.[71] And it is because exercising one's 'natural rights' is *nothing but* a mode of particularity rather than universality that Marx does not think that Jewish people must give up their identity in order to enjoy liberal citizenship. (This could be read as an embrace of multiculturalism, but in a decidedly lukewarm fashion!)

In the next section, we explain why we do not accept Marx's conclusion and why his argument nevertheless has important implications for Rawlsian liberalism.

3. How heaven is brought down to earth

We begin by explaining how we differ from Marx in our conception of history and processes. This difference, combined with actual developments in liberal states, leads to our rejection of Marx's conclusion in 'On the Jewish Question'. But a consideration of those actual developments and the manner in which they show Marx to have been wrong also shows why the content of public reason and of rights, in Rawlsian liberalism, must be understood as a matter of quasi-pure procedural justice.

a. *History and processes*

When Marx discusses the *trajectory* or *tendency* of a political idea or situation, he is making an assertion about both the *logic* or *interrelationships and connections* of concepts and also *the development of human society and self-consciousness*. This Hegelian understanding of the way in which 'spirit' manifests through the historical doings of particular individuals and collectives permits Marx to treat particular statements and theorizations of political problems as having a truth—even if it is a distorted or occluded truth—that is grounded not in *their accuracy as reports of particular states of affairs* but rather *their emergence from particular states of affairs*. A similar Hegelian understanding leads Marx to assert that '[t]he [proper] formulation

---

union—characterized by fraternity and reciprocity: Rawls, *A Theory of Justice* (n 8) 101–03, 105–06, 178–79, 315, 498–502, 527–29, 535–57, 544–46; Rawls, *Political Liberalism* (n 8) 318, 320–26; Rawls, *Justice as Fairness* (n 8), 76–77, 125–26, 139. This is what generates the force of Cohen's critique and, contrary to Cohen's own interpretation (at *If You're an Egalitarian, How Come You're So Rich?* 136 and 209 n 7), does so even within the scope of political liberalism.

71 Marx reinforces this point, in the context of relations of production, in Karl Marx, 'Economic and Philosophic Manuscripts (1844)' in *Writings of the Young Marx on Philosophy and Society* (Loyd De Easton and Kurt H Guddat eds and trs, Anchor Books 1967) 295–97.

of a question is its solution'.[72] In Rawls's terminology, then, Marx regards history as (ultimately) a process of perfect procedural justice.[73]

Rawls does not take the same view of history. Some critics of Rawls argue that his account of political ideals is overly (even completely) divorced from social and historical reality.[74] We reject such criticism. Rawls's later work[75] is grounded in certain particular historical circumstances: that some but not all societies are those in which the fact of reasonable pluralism obtains.[76] Rawls emphasizes the origins of liberalism in early modern Europe, where, following the Reformation and the Wars of Religion, religious pluralism became an ineliminable fact of life. The endurance of religious difference, in spite of attempts to impose uniformity by a combination of war and law, led to a new form of social life being invented. That new form of social life separated concepts like *good citizen* and *law-abiding person* from particular religious ideals. Over time—Catholic emancipation came to Britain in the early nineteenth century, while as Marx's essay shows, Jewish emancipation was still a topic of debate in the mid-nineteenth century—it made these transformed concepts a real part of social life: people could vote, stand for office, study at educational institutions, and take up jobs, regardless of their religious beliefs or lack thereof.[77] *A Theory of Justice* also rests on certain historical and social premises: that society has a basic structure with the capacity to establish and maintain background justice[78] and that this structure is to be achieved in part by the distribution of certain all-purpose means, including the social bases of self-respect.[79] Taken

72 Marx, 'On the Jewish Question' (n 2) 216–20. For a critical discussion of this aspect of Marx's thought, including in the context of his later development of dialectical materialism, see Cohen (n 70).

73 Rawls, *A Theory of Justice* (n 8) 85. Rawls describes perfect procedural justice as resulting from a procedure that has been 'devised': Marx, 'On the Jewish Question' (n 2) 216–20. History, in Marx's conception of it, has not been devised but does have an internal logic *as if it were* a device.

74 See, eg, Michael Sandel, *Liberalism and the Limits of Justice* (2nd edn, CUP 1998); Raymond Geuss, *Outside Ethics* (Princeton University Press 2005) chs 1, 2.

75 Beginning with John Rawls, 'Justice as Fairness: Political Not Metaphysical' (1985) 14 Philos Public Aff 223.

76 For a discussion of this feature of Rawls's later work, see David A Reidy, 'Rawls on International Justice: A Defense' (2004) 32 PT 291.

77 Rawls, *Political Liberalism* (n 8) xviii–xix, xxiv–xxviii, xxxix–xli, 154, 303–04; Rawls, *The Law of Peoples* (n 15) 11–12, 16, 124–25. It was only in the 1960s that Yale University ended its restriction of Jewish enrolment. See Dirk Johnson, 'Yale's Limit on Jewish Enrollment Lasted Until Early 1960's, Book Says' *New York Times* (New York, 4 March 1986) Section B 1 <www.nytimes.com/1986/03/04/nyregion/yale-s-limit-on-jewish-enrollment-lasted-until-early-1960-s-book-says.html> accessed 21 June 2024.

78 Rawls, *A Theory of Justice* (n 8) 84–88, 274–80.

79 See above, text to n 19.

together, and perhaps unsurprisingly given Rawls's concerns as a philosopher, these underpinnings of Rawls's political philosophy correspond to the conditions of liberal modernity.

Thus, Rawls's philosophy not only has a particular audience (namely, those of us who live under those conditions)[80] but identifies demands of justice that arise under those conditions.[81] Rawls does not regard history as a process of perfect or even imperfect, procedural justice because he offers no account of what justice demands that is independent of the particular social developments that take place over time. Nor does he argue that there must be a particular historical trajectory in which ideas and social reality are unified.[82]

We accept a Rawlsian rather than a Marxist approach to historical processes.[83] But Marx does not give any reason, independent of his historicism, for thinking that the 'rights of man' must be fixed in their content and their capacity to thwart claims emerging from the political sphere and that 'none of the so-called rights of men goes beyond the egoistic man, the man drawn into himself . . . and separated from the community'.[84] Likewise, he has no independent argument that the liberal state *must* 'permit[] private property, education, and occupation to *act* and manifest their *particular* nature as private property, education, and occupation in their *own* ways'[85] or that political emancipation *must* be 'the emancipation of civil society from politics, from the *appearance* of a general content'.[86] These conclusions about the limits of the liberal state depend upon his conception of the dialectic.

As the next sub-section argues, the actual development of liberal conceptions of citizenship and belonging suggests that neither claim is true.

80 For Rawls's discussion of the way in which political philosophy always addresses a particular audience, see John Rawls, *Lectures on the History of Political Philosophy* (Samuel Freeman ed, Harvard University Press 2007) 1, 103.

81 The idea that particular social and historical circumstances might generate distinctive and important normative demands, the satisfaction of which is not *inevitable*, but which is possible given the circumstances that give rise to them, is a familiar one in social theory: see, eg, Emile Durkheim's discussion of the anomic and forced divisions of labour in Emile Durkheim, *The Division of Labor in Society* (Steven Lukes ed and WD Halls tr, Palgrave Macmillan 2014) and Philip Selznick and Philippe Nonet's discussion of the rule of law in Philip Selznick and Philippe Nonet, *Law and Society in Transition: Toward Responsive Law* (Routledge 2001).

82 This is made clear in Rawls, *The Law of Peoples* (n 15) 54–57, 59–62, 122–23.

83 In particular, we accept as sound Cohen's criticisms of Marx's method: see Cohen (n 70).

84 Marx, 'On the Jewish Question' (n 2) 236–37.

85 Marx, 'On the Jewish Question' (n 2) 225 (emphasis added).

86 Marx, 'On the Jewish Question' (n 2) 239 (emphasis added).

b. *Reciprocity and inclusion as an open-ended series of demands on the liberal state*

Many contemporary societies are characterized by pluralism of not only religion but also occupation, language, cultural outlook and aspiration, race, and sexuality, just to pick up on some of the more salient factors of our contemporary human identity. We use the word *identity* in a capacious fashion to capture these various manifestations of human difference and social pluralism. In respect of many of these identities, the political has extended itself, in various ways, into civil society: heaven has brought itself into communion with earth. A crisp illustration of this point, in relation to race, is the change in the application of the Fourteenth Amendment of the United States Constitution from *Plessy* to *Brown*.

Consider the following quote from *Plessy*:

> [The Fourteenth Amendment's] main purpose was to establish the citizenship of the negro, to give definitions of citizenship of the United States and of the States, and to protect from the hostile legislation of the States the privileges and immunities of citizens of the United States. . . .
>
> The object of the amendment was undoubtedly to enforce the absolute equality of the two races before the law, but, in the nature of things, it could not have been intended to abolish distinctions based upon color, or to enforce social, as distinguished from political, equality, or a commingling of the two races upon terms unsatisfactory to either. Laws permitting, and even requiring, their separation in places where they are liable to be brought into contact do not necessarily imply the inferiority of either race to the other. . . .
>
> The distinction between laws interfering with the political equality of the negro and those requiring the separation of the two races in schools, theatres and railway carriages has been frequently drawn by this court. . . .
>
> If the two races are to meet upon terms of social equality, it must be the result of natural affinities, a mutual appreciation of each other's merits, and a voluntary consent of individuals. . . .
>
> Legislation is powerless to eradicate racial instincts or to abolish distinctions based upon physical differences, and the attempt to do so can only result in accentuating the difficulties of the present situation. If the civil and political rights of both races be equal, one cannot be inferior to the other civilly or politically. If one race be inferior to the other socially, the Constitution of the United States cannot put them upon the same plane.[87]

87 *Plessy* (n 6) 543–45, 551–52.

This reasoning is consistent with Marx's account of the liberal state: equality and universality are principles that operate to ensure that all citizens enjoy the same abstract rights, but in the everyday world of travelling on trains, attending school, and otherwise interacting with one another, principles of universality have no work to do. Nor, say the judges, is there any prospect of politics intervening in civil society to transform it in a more universal direction. The law at issue in *Plessy* did not prohibit anyone from purchasing a ticket to travel by train; in this respect, it is different from the sorts of status-conferring laws that were common in 'pre-modernity' and exemplified its intermingling of political and civil life.[88] This is why the majority judges are able to present it not as going to citizenship but rather as merely giving effect to 'established usages, customs, and the traditions of the people' (analogously to a public decency law).[89]

Even at the time *Plessy* was decided, however, the reasoning just quoted was not all that could be entertained. In his dissent, Justice Harlan said the following:

> [W]e have before us a state enactment that compels, under penalties, the separation of the two races in railroad passenger coaches, and makes it a crime for a citizen of either race to enter a coach that has been assigned to citizens of the other race. . . .
>
> Everyone knows that the statute in question had its origin in the purpose not so much to exclude white persons from railroad cars occupied by blacks as to exclude colored people from coaches occupied by or assigned to white persons. . . . The fundamental objection, therefore, to the statute is that it interferes with the personal freedom of citizens. . . . If a white man and a black man choose to occupy the same public conveyance on a public highway, it is their right to do so, and no government, proceeding alone on grounds of race, can prevent it without infringing the personal liberty of each. . . .
>
> In respect of civil rights, all citizens are equal before the law. . . . The law regards man as man, and takes no account of his surroundings or of his color when his civil rights as guaranteed by the supreme law of the land are involved. . . .
>
> The arbitrary separation of citizens on the basis of race while they are on a public highway is a badge of servitude wholly inconsistent with the civil freedom and the equality before the law established by the Constitution. It cannot be justified upon any legal grounds.[90]

88 Marx, 'On the Jewish Question' (n 2) 239.

89 *Plessy* (n 6) 550.

90 *Plessy* (n 6) 553, 557, 559, 562. The reasoning we have quoted does not depend upon an assertion that the Constitution, or public reason more generally, must be colour-blind, as

Justice Harlan bases his conclusion on 'civil rights', which he takes to extend to an entitlement to choose to travel, in public, as part of a mixed-race group. *Travelling in public* is not, in general, a manifestation of individuals' 'heavenly' life (an exception might be travelling so as to cast one's vote). It is conduct undertaken in civil society. Thus, the implication of Justice Harlan's argument is that civil society may not organize itself in such a way as to systematically deny participation on the grounds of race.

The Court in *Brown* accepted that participation in civil society includes not just public transportation but also public education, and it more overtly identified the social bases of self-respect as a key basis on which to determine the content of the relevant civil rights:

> To separate [children] from others of similar age and qualifications solely because of their race generates a feeling of inferiority as to their status in the community that may affect their hearts and minds in a way unlikely ever to be undone. . . .
>
> [I]n the field of public education, the doctrine of 'separate but equal' has no place. Separate educational facilities are inherently unequal.[91]

In the case of schooling, the content of civil rights reflects the role of education in ensuring that its recipients can participate in both civic and social life, thus enjoying crucial all-purpose means.[92]

Anti-discrimination law has extended the insistence on universality to other domains of civil society, such as the opportunity to be employed and the provision of goods and services in general.[93] In the United States, the extension of the principle stated by Justice Harlan and by the *Brown* Court to privately

Harlan J asserts: *Plessy* (n 6) 559. The commentary on the Justia website notes that 'Justice Harlan's dissent is the most notable element of *Plessy*, although its rhetoric is less progressive upon closer analysis than some suggest': 'Plessy v. Ferguson, 163 U.S. 537 (1896)' <https://supreme.justia.com/cases/federal/us/163/537/> accessed 21 June 2024.

91 *Brown* (n 7) 494–95.

92 In *Runyon v McCrary* (1976) 427 US 160, a majority of the Supreme Court found that a commercially operated private school's refusal to admit Black students was a breach of Title 42 USC. § 1981, which confers equal legal status, including to accept contracts offered to the general public, regardless of race.

93 Tarunabh Khaitan identifies bearers of non-discrimination duties as actors who have a 'sufficiently public character', with a weak interest in negative liberty and who are 'gate keepers of opportunities': Tarunabh Khaitan, *A Theory of Discrimination Law* (OUP 2015) 195–213. In Rawlsian terms, this might be seen as characterizing the basic structure, although Khaitan does not follow through with the full implications of that characterization. It is important to acknowledge that there are ways in which racism manifests that are not straightforwardly captured by anti-discrimination/inclusion norms, the most obvious of these being policing/criminal justice. Such cases can still be understood within our framework; policing is one way of distributing (or withholding) the social bases of self-respect. Tommie Shelby analyzes these matters using a broadly Rawlsian framework in Tommie Shelby, *Dark Ghettos:*

operated hotels, restaurants, and other entertainment venues, and to (some) employers, depended upon Congressional exercise of its power to legislate in respect of interstate commerce.[94] This legislation restricts the rights of some to deal with their property as they wish (for example, by not serving those towards whom they hold a racial animus) in order to ensure that others' participation in civil society is not burdened by their racial particularity.

The obvious argument, within public reason, for the conception of civil rights found in Justice Harlan's dissent, in *Brown*, and in anti-discrimination law, is that it enforces the subordination of the rational to the reasonable that is required by the priority of the right to the good. But this argument takes as a premise that the public conception of justice—in virtue of the basic rights and liberties it affirms and that underlie its commitment to the social bases of self-respect—requires racial equality of this sort. This is not a self-evident or self-actualizing proposition, as is shown by the majority decision in *Plessy*. Its subsequent recognition in *Brown* and the *Civil Rights Act 1964* was not the result of a priori reflection. It resulted from the political action that made clear *what* was necessary to satisfy the basic rights and liberties and to ensure the social bases of self-respect for Black citizens in America.[95] The trajectory that we see in these developments, therefore, is that the demands of reciprocity make themselves felt—through the actions of those whose identity has led to them being denied full participation in some or other aspect of civil society[96]—and while these demands are not able to be satisfied to the extent of making conflict *impossible*, more and more requirements of universality are placed upon the everyday world of civil society. Thus, what Marx takes to be a paradox (or contradiction) that cannot be resolved within the confines of the liberal state actually manifests as an ongoing tension that drives the liberal state in the direction of greater inclusivity of diverse identities. Opponents of such political intervention may sometimes characterize it as indulgently or even impermissibly perfectionist: pursuing one particular conception of the good at the expense

Injustice, Dissent, and Reform (Harvard University Press 2016) 201–51. We leave full consideration of these important matters to a subsequent occasion.

94 *Civil Rights Act 1964*, Titles II, VII; *Heart of Atlanta Motel, Inc v United States* (1964) 379 US 241. On the technical issue of state action in the context of the Fourteenth Amendment, see Jud Mathews, *Extending Rights Reach: Constitutions, Private Law, and Judicial Power* (OUP 2018), especially ch 5.

95 This argument is, at least in part, a development of Patricia Williams's characterization of the role played by Black political action in giving life to rights: see Patricia Williams, *The Alchemy of Race and Rights* (Harvard University Press 1991). Somewhat similarly, Steve Biko argues for the priority of Black action and decision-making in ensuring the social bases of self-respect for Black people in apartheid South Africa: Steve Biko, *I Write What I Like* (40th Anniversary Edition, Picador Africa 2017), especially ch 14.

96 *Plessy* (n 6) itself was a test case instigated by a committee of concerned citizens wanting to overturn the Louisianan law.

of other, plural conceptions.[97] Establishing that such intervention is, in fact, a matter of justice—to use Rawls's terminology—or is a bringing of heaven down to earth—to use Marx's metaphor—is itself a matter of political action. That is not to say that it is arbitrary—arguments for liberal inclusion orient themselves in relation to liberalism's history and trajectory—but it is not self-revealing and self-realizing.

Recognizing the existence of this tension and the political trajectory that it generates is important even for those who are more sympathetic than Marx is towards constitutionalist and human rights ideals.

c. *The content of public reason and of rights: a matter of quasi-pure procedural justice*

Rawls observes that:

> Justice as fairness, by contrast [with Marx's idea of a full communist society], assumes that given the general facts of the political sociology of democratic regimes (such as the fact of reasonable pluralism), the principles and political virtues falling under justice will always play a role in public political life. The evanescence of justice . . . is not possible.[98]

We argue that *the role played by principles and political virtues falling under justice*, which, according to Rawls, will not fade from the public political life of a liberal society,[99] must be understood as incorporating the trajectory described earlier: as long as the separation between the 'heavenly' realm of universal citizenship and the 'earthly' realm of civil society endures, someone somewhere will be suffering unhappy experiences of or consequences of particularity, leading them to make claims upon the state to intervene in pursuit of universality, genuine reciprocity among citizens, and thus non-discriminatory inclusion in respect of some or other element of social life. Within the Rawlsian framework, these are claims to the enjoyment of adequate all-purpose means and, in particular, to the social bases of their self-respect. Contrary to Marx's conception of the relationship between the state and civil society, a central role of the former is to generate principles that constrain conduct in the latter, beyond simply

97 See, eg, John Gray, 'The Problem of Hyper-Liberalism' *The Times Literary Supplement* (30 March 2018) <www.the-tls.co.uk/articles/problem-hyper-liberalism-essay-john-gray/> accessed 21 June 2024.

98 Rawls, *Justice as Fairness* (n 8) 177.

99 Rawls uses 'constitutional democratic society' and 'liberal society' interchangeably: Rawls, *The Law of Peoples* (n 15) 12. In the quoted passage, 'democratic regime' likewise has the same meaning.

protecting property and security;[100] the state must ensure that these claims are satisfied.

It follows from this that the demands that the reasonable places on the rational are not given once and for all and not by a priori reflection. Rather, the 'rights of man' have their content settled by the political process we have described. As new claims to reciprocity are made, the persuasive political action of those making those claims will establish what reciprocity requires.[101] Not all such claims will be immediately successful (as *Plessy* illustrates), but liberalism has no principled basis for denying them. Only in this way is Rawls's philosophy able to account for the accommodation of new forms of pluralism within liberal society, just as, historically, it accommodated religious pluralism.

This takes us, also, to the question of the scope and application of public reason. What public reason precludes is likewise continually up for grabs. The liberal demands of toleration thus also must be understood as the product of an open-ended process. Just as was the case in achieving the accommodation of religious pluralism, and just as Justice Harlan in *Plessy* would have had it and as the Court in *Brown* did have it, recognizing and giving effect to claims to reciprocity may not leave every element of civil society unchanged. As heaven is brought more and more down to earth, the boundary between what is 'public' and what is 'background culture' will continue to move and the demands of reciprocity as a response to experienced injustice will place new constraints on action undertaken within civil society.

We do not suggest that it is historically *necessary* that any particular trajectory should play out and justice in some abstract sense actually be realized. The debates that take place within liberal political discourse and the ways that these are resolved are not historical inevitabilities. Rather, this process should be understood as an example of quasi-pure procedural justice, somewhat comparably to Rawls's account of legitimate legislation. The *process* is that of political action undertaken with the aim of appealing to the sense of justice of those who have the power to effect political change. We draw here on Rawls's distinction of civil disobedience from resistance[102] but with the following important qualification: whereas Rawls envisages civil disobedience as a response to *injustice* and hence as something to be addressed as part of

100 Which is Marx's characterization of the 'rights of man': Marx, 'On the Jewish Question' (n 2) 235–37. See also above, text to n 69.

101 For a powerful social-existentialist account of political action, see Lewis R Gordon, *Fear of Black Consciousness* (Penguin 2022), particularly ch 12.

102 Rawls, *A Theory of Justice* (n 8) 363–68, 372–73. It is important to note that, within the Rawlsian framework, it is possible to express the demands of the reasonable using the vocabulary of particular comprehensive doctrines *without* violating public reason. This is because what underlies public reason is an overlapping consensus of reasonable comprehensive doctrines. It is thus not an objection to our view that a lot of civil disobedience actors use language drawn from their own, or that are at home in a, comprehensive doctrine. See Rawls, *The Law of Peoples* (n 15) 143–44.

non-ideal theory,[103] our theorizing is located within *ideal* theory. The process we describe is analogous to pure procedural justice because there is no prior conception of what a just satisfaction of political claims to inclusion would consist in. But it is only *quasi*-pure because, just as legislators must aim at justice within the allowed bounds, so the political actors who are seeking inclusion must be aiming to achieve justice through ensuring their enjoyment of adequate all-purpose means, particularly the social bases of their self-respect.[104]

Once we understand the content of rights and of public reason in this fashion, we can see how *complacent* it would be to think that the project of constitutionalism or human rights can *ever* be completed. We can nevertheless make some general remarks about certain consequences or implications of this process.

First, as Rawls emphasizes, the development of toleration did not take place *independently of* religion: for this new form of social life to work, toleration and reciprocity must be firmly grounded and stable,[105] and this meant that religion itself had to change, recognizing pluralism as permissible or even desirable, rather than simply putting up with it as a regrettable but unavoidable failure of the aspiration to impose uniformity.[106] The ongoing movement of claims of particularity into the 'background culture' is a further sign of change in existing comprehensive doctrines: it involves both a change in their content (an 'internal' change) such that they no longer burden universality and a change in their location in relation to the 'fundamental political questions governed' by public reason (an 'external' change). We suggest that this is a more thoroughgoing form of 'privatization' of claims of particularity within the liberal state than even Marx anticipated.

Second, cultural leaders who refuse to engage meaningfully with the (ever-emerging) demands of pluralism, while appealing to existing freedoms as if they were some self-standing principles of human affairs, are engaged in a particular form of hypocrisy, seeking to claim the benefits of the liberal trajectory as if it could be frozen at a particular point in time. That is a type of repudiation of the reasonable rather than a manifestation of it. Just as Marx regards even the 'winners' in civil society as suffering from a failure to be fully emancipated as humans, so this sort of hypocrisy precludes those who engage in it enjoying genuine social unity within a pluralist, liberal society. They are, in effect, affirming a reactionary conception of social unity that is not achievable, given the fact of reasonable pluralism that characterizes modernity.

103 Rawls, *A Theory of Justice* (n 8) 363, 382–83, 391.

104 Thus, political actors seeking inclusion (and legislators) are importantly different from card dealers at casinos. For Rawls's discussion of gambling as an instance of pure (not quasi-pure) procedural justice, see Rawls, *A Theory of Justice* (n 8) 86.

105 Rawls, *Political Liberalism* (n 8) 38–40, 65; Rawls, *The Law of Peoples* (n 15) 150; and see also above, text to n 12.

106 Rawls, *The Law of Peoples* (n 15) 21–22, including n 15, 126–27, 149–52, 154 n 52.

Chapter 7

Beginning from injustice

Ashwini Vasanthakumar

1. Introduction

Iris Marion Young, a prominent theorist of structural injustice, introduced readers to Sandy.[1] Sandy is a single mother with two children. She needs to find a place to live now that her current apartment has been bought by a developer and will be remodelled into condominiums. A sales clerk at a suburban mall, Sandy commutes for about three hours a day from her current apartment. Sandy wants to live closer to work in a neighbourhood that is safe for her children, but the only affordable options involve long bus commutes, so she decides to lease a car, even though monthly car payments will mean less money for rent. After a few months' searching, and with the assistance of an enthusiastic realtor, Sandy settles on an apartment—smaller than she wanted, no playground for her children—that she can afford. Because she used her savings on a down payment for a car, however, Sandy does not have the funds to pay the required deposit of three months' rent. With the end of her current tenancy looming, Sandy and her children face homelessness.

Sandy's predicament is not the result of malevolent individuals or a predatory state, nor is it simply a matter of bad luck; certainly, it has not arisen because of her feckless behaviour. Rather, Young urges us to see, it results from her position in a structure—of law and economic policy, the enduring legacy of historical practices and urban planning, and ongoing social norms—that means she is especially vulnerable to homelessness. For Sandy's predicament arises from the following features of contemporary life in liberal democracies: urban planning decisions that make commutes long, socio-cultural norms that mean women are paid less and tend to end up in poorly paid jobs, the financialization of housing that makes affordable housing scarce, the various ways that mothers are penalized in the workforce, and the absence of affordable childcare and healthcare. Young notes that Sandy has made decisions that contribute to this predicament—she did not attend

1 Iris Marion Young, *Responsibility for Justice* (OUP 2011) 43–45.

DOI: 10.4324/9781032676159-8

university, she left her husband[2]—but the fact that these decisions render her vulnerable to homelessness results from structural injustice.

Young's account widens the scope of injustice in several respects. Rather than interpersonal or interactional wrongs or discrete periods of political injustice, injustice is more amorphous: it might begin in a state's discriminatory legal system but persist long after legal reform, and its mechanisms are not limited to institutions and individuals, instead extending to cultural norms, prevailing stereotypes, and everyday interactions. Good intentions and earnest efforts cannot prevent one from being a victim, beneficiary, or contributor, which complicates individual agency and moral responsibility without doing away with either.

Among other things, this means that there are many more victims of injustice than standard accounts of justice contemplate. Philosophical discussions give us some indication of these victims. Sandy joins a pantheon of victims of oppression: *Deferential Wife*, *Uncle Tom*,[3] *Shreya*, and *Chloe*,[4] to name a few. *Deferential Wife* fails to form her own preferences and projects, instead fully taking on her husband's as her own; *Uncle Tom* is obsequious to White people, offering no complaint or seeing anything amiss when he is unfairly treated, saving his ire instead for other Black people; *Shreya* is a racialized female attorney who is given various 'housework' tasks in the firm and expected to provide emotional labour without recognition or recompense; *Chloe* acquiesces to sex with her husband even when she does not want to in order to avoid conflict.

These figures can be seen as a partial response to Judith Shklar's question, 'What of the victims of injustice?'[5] Shklar points to a tendency in political philosophy to focus on justice and to 'take it for granted that injustice is simply the absence of justice, and that once we know what is just, we will know all that we need to know';[6] where injustice is considered, it is only as a 'surprising abnormality'.[7] As a result, Shklar notes, there is little interest in victims: 'the unjust person has a character, the victim does not even have a role'.[8] Victims of injustice warrant greater interest, however. A better understanding of victims might be needed in order to construct a more fulsome

2 We don't know more, but these decisions may have been shaped by structural injustice. College is unaffordable without crushing student debt; there may not be sufficient opportunities for young mothers to attend college; enforcing childcare payments is costly and rarely effective, meaning that single mothers are the sole providers for their children.

3 See Thomas E Hill Jr, 'Servility and Self-respect' (1973) 57 Monist 87.

4 See Serene Khader, 'Self-Respect Under Conditions of Oppression' in Richard Dean and Oliver Sensen (eds), *Respect: Philosophical Essays* (OUP 2021).

5 From her 1988 Storr's Lectures at Yale University. See Judith N Shklar, *The Faces of Injustice* (Yale University Press 1990).

6 Judith N Shklar, *The Faces of Injustice* (Yale University Press 1990) 15.

7 Judith N Shklar, *The Faces of Injustice* (Yale University Press 1990) 17.

8 Judith N Shklar, *The Faces of Injustice* (Yale University Press 1990) 35.

account of injustice.[9] As structural accounts of injustice suggest, injustice is the norm rather than a 'surprising abnormality'; focusing on victims thereby provides a more accurate account of the standard case or the average individual. Put another way, many more people—perhaps *most* people—are Sandys, Shreyas, Uncle Toms, and Chloes.

What would it mean to begin with injustice and its victims? What types of characters and roles do victims play? And should we explore these characters and roles with a view towards alleviating injustice? In this chapter, I explore these questions both substantively and methodologically. First, I begin with an account of victims' duties in the face of their oppression and the roles they are thereby required to play. Against a general tendency to focus on resistance, which aims at ending oppression, I explore duties of self-respect and assistance, and the roles and responses these duties call for. These duties undergird relations of mutual support and deliberation amongst victims of oppression that enable victims to navigate and even flourish in the midst of their oppression. Second, I consider key objections to these arguments and their methodological implications. I address the claim that accounts of victims' duties are in tension with anti-oppression theorizing because they are overly burdensome in theory and, by contributing to practices of victim-blaming, also in practice.

The chapter is structured as follows: section two defines key concepts I will draw on; section three illustrates what duties of self-respect and assistance require; and section four addresses with objections of over-demandingness and victim-blaming.

2. Definitions

Structural injustice refers to social processes that tend towards the disadvantaging and advantaging of particular groups. Here, I use the terms 'structural oppression' and 'structural injustice' interchangeably. Social processes include institutions, laws, norms, social conventions, and arise in the dynamic interactions among individuals and between individuals and processes. These processes often seem natural or given—indeed, they might be motivated by principles of equal dignity—but their operation nevertheless produces unjust outcomes. Structural injustice persists, therefore, even in liberal democracies where political and legal institutions are expressly committed to principles of equality and freedom and even when institutional offices are occupied by individuals who embrace those principles earnestly. Despite an official commitment to equality, ideologies persist that generate epistemic distortions about different social groups and that justify how the social and political

9 Judith N Shklar, *The Faces of Injustice* (Yale University Press 1990): 'Unless one takes a full account of [victims'] experience, the picture of injustice is incomplete.'

order is structured. If women are, by nature, ill-suited for public life, then it is untroubling that so few hold political office; if Black people are prone to violence and criminality, then their disproportionate presence in the criminal justice system is inevitable; and if the upper class is more virtuous, then it is only fitting that it dominates cultural, social, and political institutions. In the context of structural oppression, these ideologies circulate through unofficial 'master-narratives': 'stories found lying about in our culture that serve as summaries of shared social understanding . . . consisting of stock plots and readily recognizable character types, and we use them not only to make sense of our experience but also to justify what we do'.[10] How we interpret events and interactions, and the patterns of treatment to which we subject others and to which we are ourselves subject, are partly mediated through these 'master-narratives'.

There are various formulations and refinements of the idea of structural injustice,[11] but the following key features are common. First, unjust outcomes result from a complex interaction of institutions and practices, arising through the cumulative actions of individuals working within these processes. This makes structural injustice *epistemically indeterminate*: it is not clear whether a particular outcome is the result of structural injustice nor what actions will avoid or mitigate this outcome. Second, these unjust outcomes rarely are intended or even countenanced by individuals—indeed, individuals may not be able to avoid contributing to, benefiting from, or being a victim of structural injustice. Structural injustice lends itself to *moral indeterminacy*, in that the connection between individual agency and unjust outcomes is unclear, not only because social processes constrain individuals' options and their ability to pursue them, but also because these processes can damage individuals' rational capacities for agency. Finally, victimhood is *intersectional.* Victims of structural injustice often include those who are members of subordinated groups, such as racial minorities, women, gender and sexual minorities, and the poor and class-oppressed. This is not to say, however, that they cannot *also* be beneficiaries and contributors. Intersectional analyses of oppression often focus on the ways that victims of multiple forms of oppression face singular injustices that are not mere aggregates of these different forms nor are remedied by addressing each form alone. However, intersectionality also allows us to recognize that someone can be a victim of one form of oppression whilst simultaneously

10 Hilde Lindemann Nelson, *Damaged Identities, Narrative Repair* (Cornell University Press 2001) 6. See also James C Scott's discussion of public transcripts and hidden scripts—James C Scott, *Domination and the Arts of Resistance: Hidden Transcripts* (Yale University Press 1990)—and José Medina, *The Epistemology of Resistance: Gender and Racial Oppression, Epistemic Injustice, and Resistant Imaginaries* (OUP 2012).

11 See, eg, Anne E Cudd, *Analyzing Oppression* (OUP 2006); Robert E Goodin, *Perpetuating Advantage: Mechanisms of Structural Injustice* (OUP 2023).

being privileged by others in ways that inform without erasing their victimhood. If Sandy is a White woman, she will enjoy racial privilege; but, while this might mitigate her various vulnerabilities to structural injustice and oppression, it does not shield her from them or do away with them entirely. As an attorney, it might be safe to say that Shreya is not housing insecure even though her educational background and class position will not disqualify her from 'housework' tasks at the workplace or shield her from intimate partner violence at home. Individuals are privileged and disadvantaged along particular axes, which informs *how* they are privileged and disadvantaged along other axes but without altering the fact that they are. Victims' agency means they can be complicit in their own oppression as well as the oppression of others. Given that victims are so numerous, it follows that there will be great variety amongst them. The intersectionality of victims will not do away with their duties but will inform how they discharge these duties and, in particular, how they ought to relate to one another when they discharge these duties together.

3. Victims' duties

When philosophers attend to victims' duties, they usually understand these as duties to resist.[12] I want to examine other responses that victims make to their oppression and the moral duties that require these responses. I focus on victims' duties of self-respect and assistance, which I argue call for more localized responses to their oppression, and that undergird moral relations of reciprocity and solidarity amongst victims that can, but need not always, lay the ground for resistance. I do not provide an exhaustive discussion of each duty nor do I justify each duty from first principles; instead, my aim here is to illustrate some of victims' roles in the context of injustice and shed some light on victims' moral lives and relations to one another on the ground.

a. Duties of self-respect

As moral agents, victims are subject to duties of self-respect: the duty to treat themselves with appropriate respect. I define self-respect as a *robust appreciation of one's worth*. There are two distinct senses in which I can appreciate my worth: my intrinsic moral worth and equal standing with respect to others—call this *recognition self-respect*—and my worthiness in the sense of attaining

12 See, eg, Bernard R Boxill, 'The Responsibility of the Oppressed to Resist Their Own Oppression' (2010) 41 J Soc Philos 1; Carol Hay, *Kantianism, Liberalism, and Feminism: Resisting Oppression* (Palgrave Macmillan 2013); Daniel Silvermint, 'Resistance and Well-Being' (2013) JOPP 405; Ashwini Vasanthakumar, 'Recent Debates on Victims' Duties to Resist Their Oppression' (2020) 15 Philos Compass 1.

standards that I have come to endorse—call this *appraisal self-respect.*[13] I will restrict my discussion here to recognition self-respect. There are two aspects of recognition self-respect worth highlighting. First, appreciating one's worth is not a purely cognitive exercise; instead, it involves a richer affective dimension and is an orientation to the world. Self-respect is not simply something I believe but something I feel; it is a way of being in the world.[14] Second, this affective dimension means that self-respect is fostered with others: my appreciation of my self-worth is developed through interactions, experiences, and relationships, and while this appreciation can be changed, it is not straightforwardly subject to rational revision. In short, my belief that I am worthy of equal respect is not invulnerable to persistent mistreatment from others.

Oppression undermines victims' self-respect in several ways. Liberal democracies enact laws and policies predicated on liberal values of equality and autonomy as well as laws that prohibit discrimination; the equal moral worth of every individual is publicly asserted and different forms of oppression routinely are condemned. But these public affirmations are contradicted by 'master-narratives' that say otherwise and that shape victims' interactions with others—that shape their experience and social reality. Victims of structural oppression are told one thing but treated in a way that communicates something else—and because appreciating one's worth is not purely cognitive, these interactions, especially when they are persistent, will shape how victims see themselves. Under contexts of structural oppression, as Anita Superson puts it, victims have reason to be confused.[15] Their responses to this confusion—feeling shame for something even when they know they are not to blame, hesitating to speak up even when they are sure they know the right answer—can, as Dillon notes, generate second-order responses of shame and embarrassment, as they blame themselves for the misalignment between what they believe and how they feel and behave.[16] Structural oppression therefore has a tendency to *damage* victims' self-respect: victims' have some sense of their worth, but this sense is burdened or deformed.[17]

What does the duty of self-respect require of victims of structural oppression? One prominent view is that self-respect requires protest: an overt act that registers a public complaint about mistreatment.[18] Protest may be seen to be constitutive of self-respect, to be evidence of self-respect, including to

13 Stephen L Darwall, 'Two Kinds of Respect' (1977) 88 Ethics 36.
14 Robin S Dillon, 'Self-Respect: Moral, Emotional, Political' (1997) 107 Ethics 226.
15 Anita Superson, 'The Deferential Wife Revisited: Agency and Moral Responsibility' (2010) 25 Hypatia 253.
16 Dillon (n 14) 232–34.
17 This is a tendency of structural oppression, which does not preclude the possibility that there will be victims who have no self-respect whatsoever as well as those whose self-respect is not at all damaged.
18 Bernard R Boxill, 'Self-Respect and Protest' (1976) 6 Philos Public Aff 58.

oneself, and to be a means of undermining the oppressive norms and practices that undermine one's self-respect. With respect to victims' duties, protest may be over-determined. As others have pointed out, however, protest is not always possible—at least, not without sacrificing oneself—and in any case, it is not necessary to evidence one's self-respect.[19] Sandy might tolerate the dismissive treatment of her superiors at work because she cannot afford to jeopardize her job but joke about them with her friends afterwards.[20] James C. Scott has illustrated that behind the apparent complacency of the oppressed lies a rich world of mockery, anger, and subversion.[21] A second view contends that victims' self-respect requires resistance: actions that will contribute to the demise of oppressive institutions and practices. Carol Hay provides a Kantian account for why victims have duties of self-respect to resist their oppression.[22] She argues that victims' self-respect arises, ultimately, from their rational capacities and directs them to respect these capacities, which entails protecting them. Given the several ways that structural oppression undermines victims' rational capacities,[23] and given victims' duty to protect these rational capacities, victims have a duty to resist their oppression.[24]

Victims' rational capacities, however, may well already have been undermined; in this case, *repairing* these capacities will therefore be the first point of order. I argue that duties of self-respect call on victims to *repair* their self-respect.[25] I use the term repair broadly to refer to processes that enable something to perform its intended function, even when it does so in an idiosyncratic manner. A repaired item may therefore bear the scars of the damage it has sustained or may accommodate this damage through modification. To repair something is not to mimic a state of being pristine. Nor is this fact lamentable. A repaired item is not necessarily the inferior of its never-been-damaged counterpart, and in fact might be more resilient, acquire additional capabilities, and have special aesthetic value. When victims repair their self-respect, then, their aim is not to foster self-respect as though it never was damaged nor is it to mimic some ideal of the properly self-respecting person. Rather, repairing self-respect aims at approximating the features and securing the functions of self-respect in light of past and ongoing threats to victims' self-respect.

19 Tommie Shelby, 'Reflections on Boxill's *Blacks and Social Justice*' (2010) 41 J Soc Philos 343.
20 Khader (n 4).
21 Scott (n 10) 23–28.
22 I consider objections to Hay's account in greater detail in section 4.
23 Hay outlines several ways that oppression damages and restricts victims' rational capacities, for example, by encouraging self-deception, denying the material resources required for rational deliberation, and exacerbating tendencies of *akrasia*.
24 Hay (n 12) 122–26.
25 Ashwini Vasanthakumar, 'Victims' Reasons and Responses in the Face of Their Oppression' (2021) 28 Harv Rev Philos 143.

This functional approach to self-respect points to how victims might repair damaged self-respect. Where damage arises out of unsteady epistemic resources that can undergird victims' self-respect, repair calls for marshalling alternative epistemic resources. Recall that structural oppression is undergirded by 'master-narratives' that, among other things, normalize structural oppression. 'Master-narratives' can be undermined by 'counter-stories': 'purposive acts of moral definition developed on one's own behalf or on behalf of others'.[26] Counter-stories can be a tool of resistance: if there is sufficient uptake by non-victims, then the master-narrative is weakened, as are the oppressive norms and practices it underwrites. But master-narratives often have a grip on victims, and counter-stories can aid in victims coming to recognize their oppression as such and to reject the demeaning characterizations of themselves upon which their mistreatment is predicated. This recognition not only strengthens victims' beliefs *that* they are worthy; it also helps them to identify insulting interactions or unjust outcomes as an instantiation of structural oppression. Among other things, this helps to minimize the damage that arises from the dissonance between what victims believe and how they feel. It can also repair the damage wrought by this dissonance by prompting victims to challenge or alter demeaning interactions, asserting themselves in ways that change how they are in the world.[27]

b. *Duties of assistance*

As moral agents, victims are subject to duties of beneficence: when they can assist someone at relatively low cost to themselves, they have a *pro tanto* duty to do so. When there are several capable bystanders, there are different principles by which to allocate the duty, for example, on the basis of moral responsibility, capacity to assist, or a prior special relationship.[28] Which principle operates will be context-specific and can change over time: as David Miller notes, addressing urgent needs may be allocated in the first instance to the agents most capable of efficaciously providing assistance, with more sustained or long-term assistance falling to others. When allocated on the basis of capabilities alone, the duty to assist is exclusively forward-looking: it only considers who is presently capable of providing assistance without inquiring into who is morally culpable for the needy stranger's plight or how the capable bystander came to acquire their capabilities. The duty to assist falls to the person who is in the 'wrong place at the wrong time with the right resources'.[29]

26 Lindemann Nelson (n 10) xiii.
27 Ashwini Vasanthakumar, unpublished manuscript.
28 David Miller, 'Distributing Responsibilities' (2001) 9 JOPP 453.
29 Dale Jameison, 'Rights, Justice, and Duties to Provide Assistance: A Critique of Regan's Theory of Rights' (1990) 100 Ethics 349, 353.

Many of these principles will converge on perpetrators and bystanders, who may be morally responsible for victims' plight and who often will be in a better position to assist in terms of having greater resources and being less vulnerable to retaliation. For example, when Shreya is asked to buy the leaving gift for a colleague, it is easier for her senior male colleague to intervene than it is for her female colleagues or for Shreya herself. But perpetrators and bystanders may be unwilling to intervene or be unaware of the need to do so. In the context of structural oppression, injustice occurs in plain sight but often is not recognized as such. Her senior male colleagues may not notice that Shreya routinely is given 'housework' tasks; they may not recognize that these tasks reflect gendered and racialized norms of labour; or they may not appreciate that these norms of labour come with professional and personal costs. Indeed, they may think Shreya is a caring colleague who is enthusiastic about birthdays.[30]

Why might we expect her female or other racialized colleagues to notice that something is amiss? In virtue of their own experience of oppression, victims generally will have forms of epistemic privilege: in general, they are better aware that there are victims in need of assistance and better aware of how to assist. First, victims have information: they are aware that there are victims in need of assistance. The harms of structural oppression occur in plain sight but are rendered invisible, understood as 'harmless' fun or the ordinary operation of the law or the market. Second, victims have a better understanding of the harms that oppression causes. They appreciate the extent to which seemingly normalized practices are humiliating, dangerous, and inhibitive. They are aware of the cumulative effects of these harms, how they can grind victims down by diminishing their self-respect, and how they can get in the way of victims' pursuit of different life plans. And finally, victims have better insights into what assistance looks like.

What does assistance entail? Assistance is necessarily a limited response. The capable bystander is expected only to mitigate harm—not to address the root causes of the needy stranger's plight or to secure all her interests, which instead are addressed through the duty of justice. Instead, the duty to assist works in tandem with the duty of justice, providing for an *ad hoc* response to those contexts of need where institutional responses are inappropriate or unavailable. Thus, in the paradigmatic case of rescue, assistance only involves securing the needy stranger's basic interests; it does not extend to assisting them beyond this or to addressing the causes of their distress. In the case of Shreya, it would mean mitigating the burden on Shreya without necessarily

30 To be sure, these interpretations might be in bad faith or reflect their own gender norms, but the duty to assist is driven by the need for assistance and is therefore allocated in the first instance to the capable and conscientious agent; they, and the victim, may have a complaint later against those who did not notice and intervene and be entitled to redress from them, but this does not alleviate them of the initial duty. See Ashwini Vasanthakumar, 'Epistemic Privilege and Victims' Duties to Resist Their Oppression' (2018) 35 J Appl Philos 465.

addressing the unjust allocation of responsibilities, the possible retaliation that would follow from overtly rejecting these responsibilities, or the norms that undergird both. Thus, other victims might volunteer to do some of these tasks, they might suggest alternative methods of allocating these tasks, or they might suggest alternatives to gift-giving. What make these instances of assistance, rather than resistance, is that they mitigate the harmful impact of an oppressive practice without calling attention to that practice or targeting it.

A few caveats are in order. First, not all victims will be capable bystanders. Victims' epistemic privilege may be limited. For those victims who have internalized oppressive norms and think that these types of tasks simply are 'women's work', they will not notice that anything is amiss. Victims must recognize oppression—theirs and others—in order to be capable of providing assistance.[31] And victims will generally have fewer resources with which to assist and be particularly vulnerable to retaliation should it arise. The relative costs of providing assistance, therefore, generally will be higher for victims. Female and racialized colleagues may be hesitant to intervene lest they be dismissed as bossy or aggressive.

Second, there are limits on what the duty to assist can demand of capable bystanders. One limit arises from burdensomeness. Since the gendered and racialized division of labour is ongoing, so too is the need for mitigation. Mitigating the harm to Shreya thereby becomes an ongoing burden to other victims: even when they are not taking on some of the labour Shreya is expected to perform, they are still burdened with being vigilant, with assessing how they ought to respond, with actually responding, and then with contending with any of the fallout that follows. Shreya's burden becomes theirs. In addition, this burden is unfairly borne. Non-victims are clueless or apathetic or wilfully ignorant and are, as a result, further privileged. The distribution of the duty to mitigate helps one victim in the short-term but at the expense of perpetuating oppressive norms over time and thereby harming many other victims. Mitigation is, both morally and practically, a limited strategy. At some point, targeting the practice—resistance—will be necessary.[32]

c. *Compatibilities and conflicts*

There is much more to say about how victims ought to repair their self-respect and render assistance to one another. Is it permissible for victims to call out an insult to repair their self-respect, even if they do so in a way that is

31 A female colleague who volunteers to assist Shreya out of kindness would not be discharging a duty of assistance because she does not recognize that Shreya is being harmed.

32 This is not to deny that mitigation can sometimes have the effect of changing the practice. Without realizing it, the allocation of these responsibilities might change through persistent intervention, but that is serendipity rather than design.

disproportionate to the insult and express inappropriate reactive attitudes to the putative wrongdoer? May victims generate counter-stories that are morally objectionable or false, even if they are effective at repairing their self-respect? When providing assistance, should capable bystanders defer to the preferences of putative beneficiaries in how to provide assistance or should they do what they believe to be in the latter's best interests? How should victims take into account the ways that their assistance might expose putative beneficiaries to further risk or otherwise harm them? How can victims avoid acting as saviours for other victims? I consider these questions in greater detail elsewhere;[33] here, I want to mention two general features relevant to the question of how victims should discharge their duties: the ways that these duties can be compatible but can also conflict, and the interpersonal and collective dimensions of discharging these duties.

There are obvious compatibilities between victims' duties. Victims need to recognize their oppression as such in order to reject their oppression and repair their self-respect, but also to appreciate when another victim is in need of assistance. When victims protest their mistreatment, for example, they help other victims recognize these interactions as morally objectionable, model different ways of being in the world—of being self-respecting rather than servile—and contribute to the long-term change by challenging the norms and assumptions that underlie these interactions. If Shreya were to complain about the 'housekeeping' tasks she routinely is assigned, she demonstrates self-respect, she alerts others to the invisible labour that often is performed by women and racialized colleagues, and she challenges the norms that undergird these assignments. Repairing, mitigating, and resisting, however, can be in tension with one another. When Shreya calls out her supervisor for constantly giving her insignificant matters that will not advance her career, she may easily be labelled a 'troublemaker' or 'over-sensitive'. Even if Shreya decides that doing so is warranted for her self-respect, she might now be less able to assist others effectively—in fact, when she intervenes on behalf of another victim it is to that victim's detriment—or to help bring about long-term change because she has been discredited. As Khader describes her, Shreya is aware of these trade-offs and decides to accept disrespectful treatment in order to pursue her other aims, which could, moreover, enable her to bring about more lasting change within the workplace. While it might be *unfair* that victims must contend with these trade-offs, it does not diminish the fact that they must do so and must thereby deal with the moral residue of the duties they fail to discharge.

Questions about how victims should discharge these duties and navigate the conflicts between these duties point to the importance of deliberative communities *amongst* victims. Victims will often rely on alternative communities,

33 Vasanthakumar, unpublished manuscript.

which can be found or chosen.[34] Found communities are those into which individuals are born and raised, such as families, social groups, nations, and neighbourhoods, and chosen communities are those that individuals seek out or create, such as political and civil society groups, friendship groups, and families.[35] Alternative communities need not be stable or self-consciously created as such. An informal WhatsApp group of women at the workplace can constitute an alternative community. Alternative communities provide the resources to generate counter-stories that provide alternative interpretations of victims' circumstances, interactions, and relationships. They provide a social context in which victims can assert themselves, speaking and behaving in ways that might otherwise attract comment or criticism. And they provide a forum where victims can come to appreciate certain occurrences and features as instantiations of injustice and come to some mutual understanding of how best to mitigate harm. In short, alternative communities help victims discharge their duties to themselves and to other victims, to appreciate the ethical and practical constraints they should consider when they do so, and to be held accountable.

4. Victims' duties and anti-oppression theorizing

There are two objections to victims' duties I want to consider: that these duties are over-demanding and that they sustain practices of victim-blaming. The objection of over-demandingness is internal to arguments about victims' duties and questions whether it is *accurate* to attribute these duties to victims; the objection of victim-blaming focuses not on these arguments' internal consistency but instead on their political implications.

a. *Over-demandingness*

While morality may be demanding, it cannot be over-demanding—and burdening victims of oppression with duties to respond to their oppression will strike many as both unfair and unduly demanding. One response to this objection is to stipulate that victims' duties are limited. First, moral agents are not morally required to discharge a duty when they lack the resources to do so or when doing so would be excessively costly. Sandy may not have the capacity to attend a local organizing meeting, and she may not complain about insulting treatment at work because she cannot risk her job. To speak of victims' duties is not, therefore, to demand that victims engage in self-sacrifice. The burdensomeness of victims' duties is further mitigated by

34 Lindemann Nelson (n 10) 9.

35 The distinction between these is not hard, but instead reflects different degrees of choice that members have in creating and exiting these groups.

the discretion victims have over *how* to discharge their duties. Hay, for example, argues that victims' duties are imperfect duties: victims are duty-bound to adopt the end of resisting their oppression but have leeway in determining how and when to act. And indeed, the epistemic indeterminacy of structural oppression is such that there are many ways victims could discharge their responsibilities. In any given context, there is no single act that a victim's duty of self-respect requires of her; instead, there will be a range of actions that could discharge this duty. Victims' duties do not require self-sacrifice, then, and they can be discharged through a range of means.

Although this partly responds to the initial worry about over-demandingness, it does not mean that victims' duties are not demanding. First, the epistemic indeterminacy of oppression that grants victims' discretion in *how* to respond to their oppression also increases the burden of doing so—not because the response itself is costly, but because of the deliberation that is required before a response is decided on and made. Victims' duties require victims to be vigilant with respect to social interactions and with respect to themselves, interrogating themselves about how they responded to a particular comment, whether they are engaging in bad-faith rationalizations or otherwise succumbing to self-deception. The deliberation does not end here, for once a victim has determined that some set of circumstances is an instantiation of oppression, she then must determine how to respond, which calls for reflection on the efficacy of different actions and the likely costs she will face—determinations that are difficult to make given the epistemic indeterminacy of victims' oppression. In short, victims' duties can be exhausting.

This relates to a second worry: victims' duties can lead to 'second-order oppression'. Jean Harvey notes that, even if we were to eliminate concerns about resources and costs, victims' duties can lead to a 'saturation of focus'.[36] Harvey focuses especially on how non-victims' deference can generate second-order oppression: well-meaning non-victims routinely ask a victim for her views on oppressive circumstances or events, they consult her and put her forward for speaking engagements and committees, and they refer others to her. As Harvey notes, 'someone can gradually slide into devoting herself just about entirely to working against the kind of oppression experienced, not because of a fully aware, personal choice (which can happen), but in response to the persistent moral expectations of others'.[37] Even in the absence of deferential others asking victims to share their insights, victims' duties can generate this 'saturation of focus', and indeed might seem to require it. If oppression constrains victims' life-chances by hemming in their options and identities, and responding to their oppression requires vigilance and deliberation, then responding to their oppression can, perversely, further hem in their

36 Jean Harvey, 'Victims, Resistance, and Civilized Oppression' (2010) 41 J Soc Philos 13, 19.
37 Jean Harvey, 'Victims, Resistance, and Civilized Oppression' (2010) 41 J Soc Philos 19.

options and identities. Victims' oppression crowds out other aspects of their identities and life-plans—only now it is doing so through the mechanism of victims' duties to respond to their oppression.

These concerns qualify *how* victims' duties can be discharged and place moral constraints on others: moral deference can easily become a form of exploitation.[38] And the epistemic burden of victims' duties can be mitigated through alternative communities, which provide victims with shared epistemic resources. But victims' duties will be demanding, and this demandingness is an unavoidable aspect of being a moral agent. Being subject to duties simply is a feature of moral agency; insofar as victims remain moral agents, then they will be subject to moral duties. Non-victims will also be subject to these duties with the attendant requirements of vigilance, deliberation, and introspection; living in the midst of structural oppression places moral demands on all moral agents. Of course, some victims of oppressions may not be moral agents—the cumulative harms inflicted by structural oppression, or the traumatic violence to which victims are especially vulnerable, may render some incapable of moral agency or sufficient moral agency to ground responsibility. While this is an undeniable feature of structural oppression, we should be cautious about drawing this conclusion too broadly, since structural oppression often is predicated on the view that victims lack moral and rational capacities. Relieving victims of demanding duties comes at the expense of recognizing their moral agency.

b. Victim-blaming

Even with these caveats in place, and even if it is accurate to attribute duties to victims, a focus on victims' duties might be misplaced for other reasons. Serene Khader recently has argued that philosophical arguments about victims' duties to resist their oppression often are in tension with anti-oppression theorizing.[39] This line of criticism is concerned less with the niceties of logical consistency and more with the political implications of such arguments; as such, this criticism is especially salient to an attempt to pursue philosophical inquiry from the fact of injustice and the perspective of victims. Khader's critique focuses on Carol Hay's arguments, which I outlined briefly earlier. To recap, Hay argues that victims have a duty to respect their rational capacities, which entails a duty to protect these capacities when they are under threat. Oppression undermines victims' rational capacities in myriad ways, so victims have a duty to resist their oppression. Hay outlines what she means by resistance, which includes overt resistance, such as joining movements and opting out of oppressive norms and practices, and internal resistance, which

38 Nora Berenstain, 'Epistemic Exploitation' (2016) 3 Ergo 569.
39 Khader (n 4).

can be done by building up mental walls against oppression's encroachments, or simply recognizing that something is wrong with their situation.[40] Hay prefers overt acts of resistance but recognizes that, in some cases, merely recognizing one's plight might be all that a victim can do.

Khader argues that Hay's account and arguments about victims' duties more generally perpetuate oppressive practices. First, Khader argues, these accounts overstate the scope of individual responsibility for oppression and thereby contribute to victim-blaming: the practice of blaming victims for the circumstances they suffer rather than appreciating the social and political contexts that over-determine those circumstances. Take the argument that victims ought not to comply with oppressive norms because doing so ultimately harms them and sets back their interests and projects. Khader questions the underlying empirical assumption that victims generally can refuse to comply with oppressive norms. Instead, Khader argues, it is a feature of structural oppression that victims *routinely* are placed in double binds: choice situations where victims' self-respect comes at the expense of their well-being, which she understands as their ability to develop their talents and to pursue their goals.[41] As she notes, 'fighting small battles against everyday racism and sexism . . . can become a way of not investing in [victims'] own talents'.[42] When a victim decides to comply with oppressive norms in order to further her other ends, Khader adds, it can be done knowingly: it need not reflect adaptive preferences, the internalization of oppressive norms, or other forms of damaged rational capacities.[43] Oppression does not operate solely through bad beliefs about oneself, but instead through a 'set of pervasive material rewards and punishments that limit what oppressed agents can and cannot pursue';[44] by failing to appreciate this empirical reality, accounts of victims' duties exaggerate the degree of choice that victims have and mistakenly attribute victims' compliance with individual defects of reasoning. Furthermore, Khader notes, developing an account of victims' duties that is predicated on damaged rational capacities creates the impression that this is a widespread phenomenon: suggesting that victims need to do more to preserve their rational capacities implies that many victims' rationality is under threat. As a result, Khader argues, Hay's arguments support tendencies

40 Hay (n 12) 140–43.

41 I understand these double binds as compelling victims to compromise one form of self-respect for another, and identify this as one form of damaged self-respect, since victims might blame themselves for compromising their self-respect and not see themselves as properly self-respecting. For a systematic discussion of double binds, see Sukaina Hirji, 'Oppressive Double Binds' (2021) 131 Ethics 643. I understand double binds as partly arising from tensions between the two kinds of self-respect.

42 Khader (n 4) 235.

43 Khader (n 4) 236.

44 Khader (n 4) 242.

to blame victims and their defective moral and rational capacities for their oppression, rather than to focus on the structural obstacles they encounter.

Khader's second, related critique is that Hay prescribes a course of action—non-compliance—that undermines victims' well-being and their ability to resist their oppression. 'Standing up for oneself', she notes, can get in the way of victims pursuing their life plans, including by organizing to resist their oppression; it promotes episodic grandstanding over concerted collective action; and it prioritizes grandstanding that communicates to privileged groups over less overt acts—an eyeroll, a grimace—that appear compliant to privileged groups but communicate dissent to others. By calling for overt non-compliance, Khader warns, Hay prescribes self-sacrifice, which interferes with victims' capacity to engage in resistance and which is not asked of the privileged. 'Anti-oppression theorists', Khader concludes, 'have a right to consider the burdens a moral theory assigns to the oppressed as a strike in favour of or against that theory'.[45]

I do not endorse Khader's interpretation of Hay, whose arguments have the resources to respond to some of Khader's substantive concerns. Hay, moreover, considers the dangers of victim-blaming, suggesting that she is also attentive to the political consequences of her argument.[46] However, I take some of Khader's objections to be instructive for the project of exploring victims' duties more generally: in particular, Khader's denial that victims' apparent compliance should be taken to reveal defects in their rationality; her worry that paying philosophical attention to a problem, such as victims' damaged rational capacities, implies that it is widespread; and that, in assessing a normative theory, theorists committed to dismantling oppression are right to consider the consequences of these theories. I address these objections in turn.

First, it is not clear how standard Khader's Shreya is. As Khader presents her, Shreya is completely self-aware and has good reason to comply with oppressive norms in order to pursue her other ends, including her well-being. In fact, grandstanding over everyday sexism and racism might get in the way of her promotion within the workplace, a position from which presumably she could bring about more far-reaching institutional and structural change. Using Shreya, Khader demonstrates that apparent compliance can instead result from victims' clear-eyed view of their predicament and the choices they make, fully aware of the oppressive norms at play and rejecting them even as they comply. Indeed, Khader's Shreya is an exemplar of the oppressed individuals James C. Scott describes, who deploy the 'weapons of the weak' while remaining outwardly complacent.

Certainly, victims' compliance with oppressive norms need not mean they have internalized these norms or suffer from other rational deficits; this does

45 Khader (n 4) 245.
46 Hay (n 12) 130–31.

not mean, however, that it never does. After all, as anti-oppression theorists, including Khader, are quick to stress, structural oppression does not only constrict the options and resources available to victims, but also aims to 'psychically dominate' victims so that they 'internalise the gaze of the oppressor' and see themselves as inferior.[47] Indeed, Khader insists that merely recognizing one's oppression is a resistant act given the psychic domination to which victims are subject. It seems likely, then, that at least some of the time, if not often, victims' compliance reveals the internalization of oppressive norms or the battery of damaged rational capacities Hay outlines.

Consider these alternative Shreyas. Shreya might enthusiastically perform the 'housework' tasks she is assigned and enjoy the approbation she thereby receives for fulfilling feminine stereotypes. She enjoys being one of 'the good ones'. Or Shreya might believe, as some of her colleagues apparently do, that her most helpful contribution in meetings is to take notes as others speak and that she should buy the office presents and bring coffee for others because their time should be spent on more important tasks. Or Shreya might bristle at being assigned these tasks but be too afraid to reject them—not because she fears retaliation but because she does not want her male colleagues to think she is a 'nag' or 'unpleasant'. Or Shreya might comply for any number of reasons but convince herself that she is playing the long game, biding her time until she has attained a degree of power and control before instigating change—only, of course, for that time never to come. If anti-oppression theorists insist on the ubiquity and harm of structural oppression, then they must recognize that these alternative Shreyas, with their internalized oppression and bad-faith reasoning, are not uncommon.[48]

Recognizing that Khader's Shreya is not standard may go some way to addressing Khader's other methodological concern: that focusing on a phenomenon implies that it is widespread. If, as I and Khader argue, victims of oppression are subject to 'psychic domination', then many victims' rational capacities will in fact be undermined by oppression. The implication Khader criticizes might well be warranted. Furthermore, it is not the only implication that can be drawn. Philosophers direct their attention to phenomena for several reasons. A phenomenon might be under-theorized relative to its actual

47 Khader (n 4) 240.

48 Moreover, the 'psychic domination' of victims means that there is always the danger of damage to victims' rational capacities. Khader's depiction of Shreya relies on a distinction between belief and behaviour that may be difficult to sustain over time. Her Shreya is canny, wearing a mask of compliance whilst maintaining her self-respect internally, calculating how best to achieve her ends, and expressing this self-respect overtly through conversations with female colleagues. But while such masks can be an important tool of self-preservation and navigation, there is also the danger that the wearer's face comes to fit the mask. Shreya might become habituated to the compliance she once deployed as a tactic, unable to recognize or shed her habits of compliance.

incidence in the world, even when that incidence is not widespread. Here, philosophical attention corrects an oversight. Or philosophers may scrutinize unusual phenomena precisely because they are marginal and can therefore illuminate the more central cases, providing fresh insight. When philosophers scrutinize victims of oppression, then, it might be to correct the oversight that Shklar observed, to engage earnestly with the moral claims victims make, or to better refine conceptions of agency and self-respect in non-victims. Philosophical scrutiny does imply that the topic under study is worthy of scrutiny, but it can be worthy for many reasons.

Even if all of this is true, it might be beside the point. Khader urges us to look beyond the internal consistency and rationale of philosophical arguments to their *consequences*, both in terms of how they distribute burdens and whether they contribute to agents' ability to resist their oppression. Khader writes: 'If philosophical prescriptions about oppression are likely to get in the way of social change that would end oppression, we should take this as a strike against those prescriptions'.[49] And she argues that arguments about victims' duties do get in the way, first, by encouraging practices of victim-blaming that deflect attention from structural causes and, second, by prescribing courses of action that will undermine victims' well-being and their ability eventually to engage in anti-oppression activities. I take issue with the consequences Khader attributes to arguments about victims' duties, and I have reservations about the role she gives to these consequences in philosophical inquiry—including for anti-oppression theorists.

At most, Khader can demonstrate how these arguments *can* get in the way of social change—not that they necessarily or even often do so. A case could equally be made for why arguments about victims' duties contribute to social change. Attending to victims' duties is to take victims' moral and political agency seriously; failing to do so not only reiterates oppressive tropes about victims' lack of agency but also places them in the role of being moral patients. This role is morally and politically unattractive. It places victims in relations of dependency, passively awaiting assistance and rescue from others. And it is inaccurate, failing to capture the political reality of victims being the agents of change in actual contexts of oppression. Failing to recognize the agency of victims is an act of philosophical erasure that can have dangerous political consequences. In her work on poor-led anti-poverty social movements, Monique Deveaux illustrates the dangers of ignoring victims' moral and political agency.[50] Philosophers, focusing on the moral agency of the affluent and conceiving of poverty as resource deprivation, have argued for extensive duties of assistance to the poor, who typically are understood as passive beneficiaries—in the paradigmatic case, they are

49 Khader (n 4) 241.
50 Monique Deveaux, *Poverty, Solidarity, and Poor-Led Social Movements* (OUP 2021).

likened to toddlers drowning in a pond. This is in stark contrast to the poor's conception of poverty, Deveaux argues, which emphasizes poverty as a set of social and political relations of domination. On the latter's view, addressing poverty requires social transformation rather than top-down solutions of resource-transfer that leave intact unequal relations of domination.[51] One consequence of de-emphasizing victims' duties is that moral and political agency is associated with non-victims, often in ways that reiterate oppressive relations, that produce misdiagnoses of oppression, and that thereby prescribe solutions that will not go far enough or will be counter-productive.

Khader would likely agree that these outcomes are undesirable. My point only is that it is plausible that arguments about victims' duties help avoid such outcomes and that avoiding talk of victims' duties, while avoiding 'victim-blaming', might generate its own oppressive dynamics. Given the epistemic indeterminacy of structural oppression, and the multiple mechanisms and dynamics that reflect and engender oppressive relations, it would be difficult to determine whether a philosophical argument will 'likely get in the way' of social change. Appealing to the consequences of a philosophical argument, especially in the context of structural oppression, is not a helpful criterion of assessment, especially as philosophers might tend to overestimate the consequences, desirable or otherwise, of their arguments. Furthermore, it is unclear that philosophers *ought* to consider the desirability of an argument's consequences when formulating their argument. Doing so presupposes that philosophers know, *ex ante*, what the goals of social change ought to be and what methods will be most effective in achieving this change; philosophical inquiry merely supplies reasons for conclusions they already know to be correct. But philosophers, including those committed to dismantling oppression, are fallible. Citing Margaret Urban Walker's work on 'epistemic rigging', Khader notes that 'because moral philosophy is continuous with social practices of assigning responsibility, philosophers may, intentionally or unintentionally, contribute to social practices that keep oppressed people in their place'.[52] There is no reason to believe that anti-oppression theorists are immune from epistemic rigging, and philosophers committed to anti-oppression movements disagree amongst themselves. Trans-exclusionary and trans-inclusionary feminists, for example, ostensibly are committed to anti-oppression theorizing but disagree on what that looks like. The surprising or counterintuitive or politically unpalatable consequences of a philosophical argument demand that we revisit the argument, but this speaks in favour of philosophical rigor rather than philosophical rigging.

51 To be clear, Deveaux is reluctant to dwell on the poor's duties to engage in anti-poverty efforts, which I criticize. See Ashwini Vasanthakumar, 'On Why the Poor Have Duties, Too' (2023) 16 CRISPP 8.

52 Khader (n 4) 241.

5. Conclusion

In *Invisible Child: Poverty, Survival, and Hope in an American City*,[53] Andrea Elliott follows Dasani, a child who lives in a New York homeless shelter. Over the course of eight years, Elliott traces Dasani's challenges at school, her favourite teachers, some of whom will also experience homelessness, her changing bond with her siblings, the family's encounters with social services and the legal system, and Dasani's eventual enrolment in and expulsion from a boarding school that is meant to be her ticket out of poverty. Like Sandy, Dasani's circumstances illustrate vividly the dynamics of structural oppression and their interaction with historical injustices that endure into the present. But, because Dasani is not a hypothetical intended to illustrate the phenomenon of structural injustice, readers are invited into a much more intimate portrayal of life in poverty and the myriad vulnerabilities and uncertainties the poor must navigate.

Dasani and her family navigate these obstacles with a combination of ingenuity, defiance, and despair; they are fiercely loyal to one another, even as they let one another and themselves down. They take themselves to be moral agents, even when this agency sometimes is exercised in violent or self-destructive ways, and even when this agency is heavily constrained and burdened. And, as scholars of poverty have long argued, the poor *are* agents, whose agency, moreover, is central to combatting the relations of domination and exploitation that constitute poverty.

In this chapter, I have attempted to heed Judith Shklar's appeal to attend to victims, sketching what areas of inquiry might follow and reflecting on the methodological and political consequences of such an inquiry. Victims of oppression warrant greater attention for a few reasons. If injustice is more pervasive than standard accounts contemplate, including in well-ordered liberal democracies, then there are many more victims of injustice than might seem apparent. Victims are not special cases or exceptions—insofar as moral and political philosophy aims to illuminate political life and reflect on our relations with one another and with social and political institutions, then addressing victims is essential. Marginalized figures in politics and philosophy are not peripheral figures. Second, theorizing moral agency in the context of oppression and victimhood complicates standard conceptions of agency and autonomy and advances non-ideal theorizing not simply to examine what is required of individuals and institutions when there is imperfect compliance with the requirements of justice but to revisit more fundamentally these conceptions in the context of pervasive injustice.

53 Andrea Elliott, *Invisible Child: Poverty, Survival, and Hope in an American City* (Random House 2022).

Some scholars, such as Khader, powerfully illustrate the ethical and political stakes of pursuing this inquiry. Among other things, emphasizing the agency of victims might seem to diminish the badness of oppression—to celebrate the resilience of a child like Dasani is to distract from the fact that she should not need to be so resilient. And emphasizing the agency of victims opens the door to holding them responsible *for* their oppression: to blame the victim. By clarifying how victims can discharge their duties, I have sought to show how victims' agency and the resulting responsibilities and accountability that follow are distinct from holding victims blameworthy for their own oppression. And I have gestured to the dangers of ignoring or minimizing victims' agency, particularly as it relates to dismantling the social and political mechanisms of oppression. Moral agency and moral responsibility are demanding at the best of times, and they seem especially onerous for victims of oppression. But duties are not only burdens that get in the way of individuals' life-plans; they can be precursors to these life-plans that ground relations of solidarity and resistance.

Chapter 8

Injustice and the moral obligation to obey the law

Jonathan Crowe[1]

1. Introduction

It is commonly thought that injustice undermines the moral obligation to obey the law. This idea is captured, for example, in the classical natural law slogan that 'an unjust law is no law at all'.[2] However, as Judith Shklar has observed, injustice is ubiquitous in legal and social institutions; law, even at its best, merely 'puts injustice into temporary remission'.[3] This has the potential to fundamentally undermine the obligatory character of legal standards. If there is no moral obligation to obey unjust laws, then it may turn out that few if any laws impose moral obligations. Does the ubiquity of injustice therefore entail philosophical anarchism?

The present chapter responds to this problem by advancing a multilayered account of the moral obligation to obey the law, developing and extending my previous work in this area.[4] Legal obligation, on this view, is responsive to injustice but is not determined by it. There is therefore no simple answer to the question of whether citizens must obey an unjust law. Rather, the moral obligation to obey a law depends upon three primary factors: the law's salience as a mode of social coordination, its reasonableness, and its capacity to promote common goods. The injustice of a law is relevant to each of these criteria.

The ubiquity of injustice, on this view of legal obligation, does not entail philosophical anarchism. Some deeply unjust laws are incapable of imposing moral obligations because they fail on the three criteria just outlined.

1 This chapter has benefited greatly from the insightful suggestions offered by the participants at the Responding to Injustice Conference held at the Julius Stone Institute, University of Sydney on 8–9 December 2022.

2 The provenance of this claim is disputed, but a version can be found in Augustine, 'On the Free Choice of the Will' in *On the Free Choice of the Will, on Grace and Free Choice, and Other Writings* (Peter King ed and tr, CUP 2010) 1.5.11.33. See also Cicero, 'On the Laws' in *On the Commonwealth and On the Laws* (James EG Zetzel ed and tr, CUP 2017) 2.14.

3 Judith N Shklar, *The Faces of Injustice* (Yale University Press, 1990) 22.

4 Jonathan Crowe, *Natural Law and the Nature of Law* (CUP 2019) ch 10; Jonathan Crowe, 'Coercion and the Prima Facie Duty to Obey the Law' (2020) 81 Persona y Derecho 11.

DOI: 10.4324/9781032676159-9

However, other unjust laws may be salient and even reasonable modes of promoting common goods. This somewhat paradoxical conclusion—laws may be both unjust and morally obligatory—helps to shed light on an overlooked form of moral harm inflicted by governments on their subjects.

Governments can—and often do—employ coercive and manipulative measures to bootstrap unjust laws into moral obligations. They have extensive, although not unlimited powers to render their laws salient and reasonable, while crowding out rival common goods. These techniques are pervasive in liberal democracies as well as totalitarian regimes, encouraging the ubiquity of what Shklar calls 'passive injustice', that is, 'the refusal of both officials and . . . private citizens to prevent acts of wrongdoing when they could and should do so'.[5] This kind of moral manipulation constitutes a serious and understudied harm to both individuals and societies. To recognize and combat this harm, we must first understand how it occurs—and this requires grasping the complex relationship between unjust laws and moral obligations.

2. Common goods

The normative foundation for the view of legal obligation developed in this chapter is the notion of *common good duties*: each person has weighty pro tanto reason to follow salient social norms where these represent reasonable modes of pursuing common goods within their community. I will therefore begin by outlining the components of this idea before applying it to unjust laws. I will first explain the notion of common goods, then discuss how it generates reasons to comply with salient and reasonable social norms.

The notion of the common good plays a prominent role in natural law political theories.[6] The common good, as typically understood, is the situation where all members of a community can enjoy flourishing lives. This situation would be good for everyone; hence the name 'common good'. The common good is good for everyone because everyone has an interest in living a flourishing life; the situation where everyone can live a flourishing life is therefore beneficial for all. The legitimate interests of community members, on this analysis, are at least potentially coincident. The situation where they converge is the common good.

The term 'the common good' is normally used in the singular. I have used it this way myself in past work.[7] However, I have come to think it is more illuminating to speak of 'common goods' in the plural.[8] The common good,

5 Shklar (n 3) 5.
6 See generally Crowe, *Natural Law and the Nature of Law* (n 4) ch 4.
7 Crowe, *Natural Law and the Nature of Law* (n 4) ch 4.
8 I am grateful to David Dyzenhaus for pressing me on this issue.

in the singular, designates the abstract state where everyone in a community can enjoy a flourishing life. However, in practice, the common good takes different forms in diverse communities. Each society has its own way of realizing the common good for its members. There is, in this sense, no single or unified common good guiding all communities; there are, rather, manifold common goods.

Different communities, then, have various common goods. This pluralism is reinforced when one considers the nature of communities. We are accustomed to think about communities as coextensive with polities, such as nations, provinces, and so on. However, there is an important sense in which large communities, such as nations, contain many smaller overlapping communities. These local communities are not necessarily structured around formal institutions, but are better viewed as communities of practice.[9] They are, nonetheless, communities in the sense that they have their own common goods.

Many people (if not all) will be participants in multiple overlapping common goods. A particular person may be a member of a nation, a workplace, a religious community, and a cultural group. These groups will have their own distinctive, albeit intersecting, local common goods. They will each adopt norms and practices they regard as conducive to the flourishing of members of that community. The members of the group have reason to follow these practices as modes of promoting the flourishing of themselves and other members.

We can understand this notion of plural common goods by drawing an analogy with goods for persons. There are, plausibly, certain things that are good for all humans by virtue of their nature—health, pleasure, friendship, play, and so on.[10] However, there are also a range of things that are good for a specific person without necessarily being good for all. It is very good for me, for example, to have time and peace to write, because I like writing and do it for a living, but the same thing may not be good (or *as* good) for someone else.

Similarly, some elements are plausibly universal to all common goods, insofar as they aim at human flourishing, but other things are part of the common good for only some communities, due to their distinctive character. All genuinely common goods, for example, value and protect the health and safety of their members. However, the common good of my local football club may also promote optimal conditions for playing football. This is good for the members of the group and helps them thrive, but it is not necessarily good for people outside the club, who do not enjoy football so much or find satisfaction in it.

9 For discussion of this distinction in relation to small-scale communities, see Jonathan Crowe, 'Two Models of Mediation Ethics' (2017) 39 Syd LR 147.

10 Crowe, *Natural Law and the Nature of Law* (n 4) ch 2.

3. Common good duties

I have so far sketched a pluralistic conception of common goods and the communities that pursue them. Common goods are valuable since they advance the flourishing of community members. A potential challenge, however, arises from the fact that the flourishing of some people does not necessarily depend on the flourishing of all. Why should people prefer common goods—that is, the situation where everyone in a group can flourish—to the situation where only they can flourish? The latter situation might have other benefits for them personally; they might, for example, enjoy a higher standard of living by exploiting others.

Various responses have been offered. John Finnis, for example, argues that the common good (which he treats as singular) transcends the value each individual places on living a flourishing life. A and B might both have an interest in some goal X; this gives them reason to cooperate to achieve it.[11] A true community, however, does not arise from this kind of instrumental cooperation. A true community, rather, arises when both A and B act at least partly for the well-being of the other. A cooperates with B to achieve X not merely because this is good for A but also because it is good for B; and B likewise acts partly from concern for A. Their interests cease to be merely coincident; rather, they form a genuine community.[12]

Finnis's picture is attractive to those who share its basic assumptions. However, he offers very little substantive explanation of why we should care about common goods *for other people's sake* in the way he suggests. Rather, this is posited as a self-evident component of practical reasonableness.[13] It does indeed seem to be a central feature of our experience of practical choice that the moral status of our actions depends on how they affect not only our own interests but also those of other people. It is helpful, however, to offer an explanatory context for this idea, rather than relying on appeals to self-evidence.

I have argued in previous work that at least three possible stories supply an explanatory context for the claim that we have reason to pursue common goods for the sake of other people, as well as ourselves.[14] The first—and, to my mind, most fundamental—story connects these reasons with the fundamental value of openness to human flourishing.[15] I have reason to consider the interests of other people in pursuing basic human values, on this view, because cultivating an attitude of openness to human flourishing in all its forms is an integral component of a meaningful and fulfilling life.

11 John Finnis, *Natural Law and Natural Rights* (2nd edn, OUP 2011) 139–40.
12 John Finnis, *Natural Law and Natural Rights* (2nd edn, OUP 2011) 143–44.
13 John Finnis, *Natural Law and Natural Rights* (2nd edn, OUP 2011) 125. See also 106–09.
14 Crowe, *Natural Law and the Nature of Law* (n 4) 64–66.
15 Crowe, *Natural Law and the Nature of Law* (n 4) 39–41.

A second and related story focuses on the basic good of friendship. I have reason to consider the interests of other people, on this account, because it is good for me to engage in mutually supportive social relationships.[16] Social connectedness is a fundamental aspect of human flourishing that extends to both close relationships and wider social bonds. I frustrate this good if I fail to value other people's flourishing for its own sake.

The third possible story focuses not on the role that other people play in my own participation in intrinsic values (such as friendship), but rather on the values themselves. It is because goods like friendship and health are valuable for humans generally that I can recognize their value in my own life. My life plan would fail to be intelligible outside this wider context.[17] My realization that the goods are valuable therefore goes beyond recognizing that they are worth pursuing for me. It entails recognizing their value for other people.

Any combination of these stories can ground the idea that people have an obligation to promote common goods not merely for their own sake but for the sake of other people as well. The duty to promote common goods, on this view, is a weighty one, since it combines the reasons that people have to ensure flourishing lives for both themselves and others. Common goods, being states of affairs where everyone can flourish, aggregate the reasons each person possesses to promote both their own flourishing and that of each other member.

What precisely, then, does this duty require us to do? It obviously rules out certain types of behaviour. We should not do anything that directly frustrates somebody else's chances of living a flourishing life—such as murdering or enslaving them, for example. These negative duties, however, are only a small part of what common goods entail. We also have a positive obligation to create the conditions necessary for all members of our communities to flourish. Plausibly, this requires more than just leaving them to their own devices. Sometimes, they will need our assistance if their pursuit of a fulfilling life is not to be denied.

4. The role of social norms

The obligation to supply everyone with the conditions of a flourishing life belongs to all of us. It does not attach to any individual on their own. We therefore do not each have a duty to do everything necessary to constitute common goods by ourselves—which would, in any case, be impossible—but rather a duty to do our share alongside other members of the community.

16 Crowe, *Natural Law and the Nature of Law* (n 4) 45–48.

17 For discussion of the notion of intelligibility employed here, see Jonathan Crowe, 'Intelligibility, Practical Reason and the Common Good' in Jonathan Crowe and Constance Youngwon Lee (eds), *Research Handbook on Natural Law Theory* (Edward Elgar 2019) 298–300.

This represents another sense in which common goods are properly described as common. They are not only beneficial for everyone, but also serve as a source of genuinely communal obligations. We must work together to bring common goods about.

The next issue that arises is therefore how to define each person's share. The challenge of identifying each person's contribution to common goods presents communities with a coordination problem. This challenge was famously identified by Thomas Aquinas in his account of two ways that positive law can be derived from natural law.[18] First, some aspects of positive law are deductions from the basic precepts of practical reason; for example, the law against murder follows logically from the value of life. However, even in these cases, the moral rule in question must be further specified to become part of the positive law.

Second, some aspects of positive law fill in details that practical reason leaves indeterminate. For example, practical reason requires us to protect physical safety, but it does not tell us whether the speed limit on a certain road should be 65 as opposed to 70 kilometres per hour. It is part of the role of law to settle these kinds of issues authoritatively for the whole community. This kind of specification advances common goods.

Finnis argues that a strong conception of the authority of positive law is needed for it to fulfil the two roles identified by Aquinas. He recognizes a role for customary law in certain limited contexts, particularly international law; in general, though, he describes this as a clumsy solution to coordination problems.[19] Law, for Finnis, requires deference to the authority of rulers who are empowered by the community to settle coordination problems on their behalf.[20] He therefore contends that each person's duty to promote the common good translates into a duty to follow the positive law of their community.

Finnis's robust conception of legal authority partly explains why he regards the common good as a singular concept. The common good, as Finnis conceives it, is given shape by authoritative rule-makers through the mechanism of positive law. This implies that there can only be one determinative set of rules for each polity. Finnis's view assumes that positive law is the only feasible source of social norms that can solve coordination problems. However, as I have argued at length elsewhere,[21] many coordination problems are solved by informal norms or agreements rather than positive laws. Indeed, a strong

18 St Thomas Aquinas, *Summa Theologiae: Latin Text and English Translation, Introductions, Notes, Appendices and Glossaries* (Thomas Gilbey et al eds, Eyre & Spottiswoode 1963–74, CUP 2006) I–II.95.2.

19 Finnis (n 11) 245.

20 Finnis (n 11) 245–46.

21 Crowe, *Natural Law and the Nature of Law* (n 4) ch 6.

notion of legal authority can undermine social coordination by crowding out more effective informal solutions.

In any case, as Mark Murphy points out, even if we accept *arguendo* Finnis's premise that law is the best solution to coordination problems for the common good, this is not sufficient to make law authoritative.[22] For that to happen, members of the community would have to agree to give law authority over them for this purpose. Unless they do that, law cannot be said to be truly authoritative; at best, we have a moral duty to obey particular laws where this is the best way to promote the community interest.

The most compelling account of common good duties therefore does not posit a generic obligation to obey the positive law, but rather focuses on the role of social norms. We have a duty to follow these norms where they represent salient and reasonable modes of promoting common goods. The obligation to obey the law, on this account, depends on the three factors foreshadowed earlier: its salience, its reasonableness, and its link to common goods. The following sections of this chapter explore each of these factors in detail, focusing particularly on their role in assessing the moral obligation to follow unjust laws. I will begin, however, with some comments about the notion of injustice underpinning this discussion.

5. Justice and injustice

What does it mean to describe a law as unjust? Different conceptions of justice will yield diverse answers to this question. The conception of injustice at work in this chapter is informed by an account of justice I have developed at length elsewhere. I argued there that justice is best 'identified with whatever institutions would arise through a process of social evolution from ethical interpersonal dealings repeated consistently over time'.[23] I call this conception *small justice*, since it takes shape primarily at an interpersonal level.

Small justice, as I describe it, can be distinguished from the dominant paradigm of thinking about justice in legal and political philosophy, shaped by the work of John Rawls. For Rawls, as is well-known, justice is 'the first virtue of social institutions'.[24] Justice, on this view, provides 'a way of assigning rights and duties in the basic institutions of society'.[25] It follows that 'the primary subject of justice is . . . the way in which the major social institutions distribute fundamental rights and duties and determine the division of advantages'.[26]

22 Mark C Murphy, *Natural Law in Jurisprudence and Politics* (CUP 2006) 109–11.
23 Jonathan Crowe, 'The Idea of Small Justice' (2021) 34 Ratio Juris 224, 225.
24 John Rawls, *A Theory of Justice* (rev edn, Harvard University Press 1999) 3.
25 John Rawls, *A Theory of Justice* (rev edn, Harvard University Press 1999) 4.
26 John Rawls, *A Theory of Justice* (rev edn, Harvard University Press 1999) 6. See also 47.

I have argued that Rawls moves too quickly in identifying justice with the structure of social institutions. He calls the institutional framework of justice 'the basic structure of society'.[27] However, there is an important sense in which the basic structure of society is not its institutions but its interpersonal relationships. Institutions are grounded in interpersonal dealings, in the sense that they are causally, counterfactually, and explanatorily dependent upon them.[28] It is interpersonal interactions, in other words, that constitute institutions and therefore supply the primary subject matter of social or distributive justice.

My preferred conception of small justice, then, has two components.[29] The first is a theory of ethically sound interpersonal dealings. The second is a historically grounded account of the mechanisms by which interpersonal interactions give rise to institutions. The combination of these two components makes possible an ideal theory of justice whereby just institutions are those produced by ethically sound interpersonal relationships repeated consistently over time within a particular social environment.

Two features of small justice are germane for the present discussion. First, it is an ideal theory of justice (in the sense outlined by Rawls).[30] It identifies justice with an idealized set of social arrangements; actual societies will resemble these to a greater or lesser extent. Second, small justice is demanding. It identifies justice with the institutions arising from ethical interpersonal dealings; given that actual interpersonal relations are frequently unethical, small justice will inevitably diverge from actual social arrangements to a significant extent. Injustice, in other words, is pervasive in actual societies—as Shklar suggests.[31]

I have proceeded in this section by sketching a theory of justice; I have then defined injustice by contrast with this positive conception. This methodology flies in the face of Shklar's contention that injustice is not merely the absence of justice; it is an independent notion deserving its own analysis.[32] It is notable that Shklar's defence of this position relies heavily on phenomenological considerations; injustice, she points out, often provokes intense feelings and emotions,[33] particularly when it involves deliberate cruelty.

It is beyond the scope of this chapter to comprehensively evaluate Shklar's arguments on the priority of injustice. However, the phenomenological evidence she musters for this contention could equally be interpreted as favouring small justice, as opposed to a Rawlsian account of justice focused on institutions. Institutions are literally bloodless; Rawlsian justice, for this

27 John Rawls, *A Theory of Justice* (rev edn, Harvard University Press 1999) 6.
28 Crowe, 'The Idea of Small Justice' (n 23) 226.
29 Crowe, 'The Idea of Small Justice' (n 23) 235.
30 Rawls (n 24) 216.
31 Shklar (n 3) 22.
32 Shklar (n 3) 16.
33 Shklar (n 3) 21.

reason, lacks what Shklar calls 'emotional punch'.[34] Small justice, on the other hand, is concerned primarily with how people treat each other and secondarily with the institutional structures created over time by these forms of behaviour; it therefore engages more directly than the Rawlsian model with the everyday injustices Shklar so powerfully describes.

6. Injustice and salience

I have provided no more than a sketch of my preferred understanding of justice, but it lays the necessary groundwork for discussing the relationship between injustice and legal obligation. I have argued that the duty to promote common goods generates an obligation to follow salient social norms where these represent reasonable specifications of common goods. Each person has robust pro tanto reason to pursue common goods; the duty to follow social norms is also a robust pro tanto one. The duty arises because of the role social norms play in giving practical shape to common goods. They solve a significant coordination problem by clarifying what counts as each person's share of common good duties.

This duty only attaches to norms that are genuinely salient. Let us say a norm is *salient* if people generally prefer to follow it because they believe most other people in their reference group will follow it.[35] Salient norms play an important role in solving coordination problems. Coordination problems have a range of possible solutions, but to solve the problem effectively, the solution must be generally accepted within the group. Salient norms stand out from other solutions because members of the group recognize them as being generally accepted; this makes them plausible candidates to achieve social coordination.

Norms may become salient through either informal or formal mechanisms. Repeated interactions between members of a social group may dynamically produce shared norms that the members expect to be followed.[36] Alternatively, a recognized authority within the community may issue a norm; the source of the norm then bolsters its claims to salience. Some theorists argue that, in either case, the existence of some form of informal or formal sanction is important (if not essential) in entrenching norm-following expectations.[37] However, the importance of sanctions plausibly decreases over time; once the norm is entrenched in social practices, it may continue even if the consequences for breaching it diminish.[38]

34 Shklar (n 3) 105.

35 Compare Cristina Bicchieri, *Norms in the Wild: How to Diagnose, Measure and Change Social Norms* (OUP 2017) 19.

36 Bryan Druzin, 'Social Norms as a Substitute for Law' (2016) 79(1) Alb L Rev 67, 75.

37 See, eg, Bicchieri (n 35) 112.

38 Compare Elinor Ostrom, 'Design Principles of Robust Property-Rights Institutions: What Have We Learned?' in Gregory K Ingram and Yu-Hung Hong (eds), *Property Rights and Land Policies* (Lincoln Institute of Land Policy 2009) 25.

Finnis, as we saw previously, argues that positive law is necessary to reliably solve the coordination problems posed by the common good. He seems to think that the backing of positive law is necessary for norms to achieve and maintain salience; informal mechanisms will not suffice. However, as suggested previously, network effects can plausibly achieve similar results by informal methods, at least under certain conditions. The claim that positive law is necessary for social coordination therefore appears overstated.[39]

It is also important to note that positive law can be in tension with salient norms. Consider a community where the long-standing norm of conduct on a major road is for traffic to travel at 70 kilometres per hour. A new positive law proclaiming that traffic must stay under 60 kilometres per hour may struggle to gain salience. If most cars continue to drive at 70 kilometres per hour, then the others have reason to also travel at that speed, even if the law says otherwise. The positive law could, of course, supplant the existing norm if bolstered by sanctions, but it is hard to see why this shift would necessarily be an improvement.

The preceding example also illustrates the potential for positive law to crowd out more effective solutions to social coordination problems. Positive law has inbuilt advantages in attaining salience; it tends to be clearly promulgated and trades on the perceived generic authority of the legal system. It might also be backed by actual or threatened sanctions of sufficient weight to convert people from existing solutions. These factors can make positive laws salient regardless of their justice or reasonableness compared to evolved norms.

Salience, then, is at best a weak indicator of a rule's merits. Any indication it might provide of the benefits of a rule rests on the assumption that it involves a trial-and-error process that tends to weed out suboptimal solutions. However, even if this assumption sometimes holds for evolved social norms, it does not apply to positive laws that achieve salience through appeals to authority. Once a norm is salient, it gains a normatively privileged position, since only salient norms can be binding as specifications of common goods.

There is therefore a danger of unjust norms becoming salient through formal or informal social mechanisms and thereby gaining normative weight. These norms are not automatically binding, since they may not count as reasonable specifications of common goods. However, they at least become potential candidates to supply common good duties. Are there, then, any inherent safeguards against unjust standards attaining salience?

A law's injustice may undermine its salience by making it less likely to be generally accepted throughout the community. This possibility relies upon members of the community having a sense of justice that presents a barrier to unjust norms gaining acceptance. However, even if this empirical condition is met, it presents at best a presumptive obstacle that may be overcome by other

39 For further discussion, see Crowe, *Natural Law and the Nature of Law* (n 4) ch 6.

factors. Sanctions are one mechanism by which this may occur. Another is the kind of ubiquitous injustice that Shklar describes; this may have the effect of deadening people's sensitivity to unjust standards, leading to widespread 'passive injustice'.[40]

I have suggested elsewhere that there may be some putative laws that are so unjust they are not capable of gaining salience.[41] However, this claim covers at best a very small subset of the class of unjust laws. On the other hand, history teaches that even extremely unjust laws can gain wide social acceptance through various oppressive mechanisms, including propaganda and harsh sanctions. Injustice is therefore weakly relevant to salience but does not determine it. Unjust laws may still be effective in coordinating social behaviour.

7. Injustice and reasonableness

I argued in the previous section that unjust standards may nonetheless attain social salience, potentially allowing them to shape common good duties. However, this may not appear overly worrisome, given that common good duties are subject to two further conditions. Furthermore, those two conditions—reasonableness and connection to common goods—might seem like reliable safeguards to weed out unjust norms and prevent them from imposing moral obligations. However, appearances can be deceiving.

Let us turn next to reasonableness. Let us say a norm is *reasonable* if there is decisive reason, all things considered, to follow it. Salient norms, as explained previously, play an important coordinating role in giving practical shape to common goods, but this does not mean they should always be followed. Their salience provides a reason to follow them, but not a decisive one. There may be other reasons why they should not be obeyed; reasonableness is therefore an additional condition for their obligatory character.

A law's injustice will, in general, supply reason not to follow it; the strength of this reason will reflect the level of injustice. It is tempting to conclude that significantly unjust laws will not be reasonable and therefore ought not be followed. However, before drawing this conclusion, it is necessary to explore more deeply the factors that make rule-following reasonable. Reasonableness involves acting in accordance with the preponderance of normative (as opposed to motivational) reasons.[42] Importantly, reasonableness in this context incorporates both prudential and moral (roughly, self-regarding and other-regarding) reasons.

40 Shklar (n 3) 5.

41 Crowe, *Natural Law and the Nature of Law* (n 4) 173–77.

42 Normative reasons *justify* why people act in particular ways, while motivating reasons *explain* why they act in particular ways. See Crowe, *Natural Law and the Nature of Law* (n 4) 58.

Let us consider a significantly unjust law; for example, a law that perpetuates structural discrimination against a certain cultural group by distributing wealth in a way that ignores their historical disadvantage. Suppose this law is salient in coordinating social action; this gives at least a prima facie reason to follow it.[43] It is unjust; this gives a reason not to follow it. The balance of these reasons will depend on how integral the law is to the overall scheme of social coordination, on the one hand, and how unjust it is, on the other.

Suppose further that the law is backed by sanctions. This gives additional reason to follow it. A person has obvious reason to avoid sanctions insofar as they harm her personally. We might be disposed to regard this as a prudential reason, rather than a moral one. However, it is also a kind of moral reason, insofar as each person is properly for herself an object of moral consideration. Furthermore, a person will often have reason to avoid the sanction because it is harmful for others. It may harm her family (and perhaps her wider community), because it makes her less able to care for them and support them financially.

There are other possible considerations in play. A person's being subject to sanctions may harm her friends and loved ones, because it makes them worry about her. It may harm her work colleagues and clients, because she can no longer do her job. And it may harm society at large, because it imposes costs on the community (for example, if she is jailed, the community may bear the cost of housing, clothing, and feeding her). These reasons combine to make a compelling moral case for avoiding sanctions in many cases. The upshot may be that the balance of reasons favours obeying even a significantly unjust law.

The moral weight of sanctions, as outlined previously, forms an important part of the explanation for the ubiquity of injustice noted by Shklar. Law perpetuates manifold injustices, large and small. People often fail to confront these injustices and thereby passively perpetuate them.[44] In many cases, this is not just understandable; it is a normatively reasonable thing to do. It is part of the structural injustice of the law that it not only perpetuates injustices against specific classes of people but also makes other overlapping classes of people complicit in that injustice by supplying them with both prudential and moral reasons to support it.

8. Injustice and common goods

The reasonableness of a law, as discussed in the previous section, is not coextensive with its justice or moral content. Injustice is relevant to reasonableness but, as for salience, it is not decisive. It is therefore entirely possible that unjust

43 A prima facie reason is an epistemological notion. If A has a prima facie reason to ϕ, then A has presumptive reason to believe that A should ϕ. Compare Crowe, *Natural Law and the Nature of Law* (n 4) 101–02, 192.

44 Shklar (n 3) 5.

laws are both salient and reasonable guides to action. A person should do what is reasonable, all things considered, so the fact that it is reasonable to follow many unjust laws creates a significant moral hazard. Nonetheless, it might seem obvious that unjust laws cannot be regarded as serving common goods; we therefore should not regard them as giving rise to common good duties.

Unfortunately, matters are not so simple. As we will see, some unjust laws can plausibly be presented as genuinely serving common goods. The extent to which unjust laws may be regarded as serving common goods depends on how the moral limitations on common goods are conceptualized. I will suggest that some accounts of common goods—particularly the account defended by Finnis—are particularly susceptible to incorporating unjust standards. Other theories—such as those developed by Murphy and myself—are less open to this result. However, even these accounts do not rule out the possibility entirely.

Common goods, as noted previously, represent situations where all members of a community can flourish. Justice, as conceptualized in this article, concerns the distribution of goods (in the broad sense of things that make a person's life go well). A distribution of goods that perfectly manifested justice in a community would count as a specification of that community's common good. It would, to borrow a Finnisian term, be a *central case* of the common good—that is, a clear and obvious instance, one that could not reasonably be denied.[45]

Some unjust distributions of goods could never count as a specification of any genuinely common good. For example, there were many societies in history where salient social norms favoured slavery. Slavery was part of the way those societies distributed benefits and burdens; it was often integral to their social and economic institutions. However, a set of institutions including slavery can never be a specification of any common good, since it denies those who are enslaved any acceptable chance to flourish.

Some social distributions then are clearly compatible with a range of common goods whereas others clearly cannot qualify as fulfilling any truly common good. What should we say about the vast range of possibilities in between these two extremes? Where, in other words, should we draw the line between imperfect manifestations of common goods and distributions that cannot be regarded as realizing any common good at all?

Murphy usefully distinguishes three kinds of conceptions of the common good.[46] Instrumental conceptions regard common goods as instrumental to human flourishing; aggregative conceptions equate common goods with the situation where each person is flourishing; and distinctive conceptions treat common goods as distinctive values that are neither instrumental nor reducible to the flourishing of individuals.

45 Finnis (n 11) 9–11.
46 Murphy (n 22) ch 3.

Finnis's conception of the common good is instrumental, since he equates it with 'the securing of a whole ensemble of material and other conditions that *tend to* favour the realization [of each individual's] personal development'.[47] His theory also has elements of the distinctive conception, insofar as he argues that a genuine community arises only where people view the well-being of themselves and others as mutually supporting.[48] Murphy, by contrast, argues for an aggregative conception of the common good,[49] while I have developed a multidimensional account that incorporates aspects of all three conceptions.[50]

It is ambiguous whether Finnis's conception of the common good requires that all members of the community can *actually* enjoy flourishing lives or merely that they are provided with certain material conditions that are conducive to doing so. The latter possibility would seem compatible with significant injustice. It creates the prospect that a community could supply its members with certain minimal conditions that tend to promote fulfilment, but ignore structural features of the community's social and economic institutions that make members of some social groups significantly more likely to prosper than others.

The aggregative and multidimensional views, by contrast, make it clear the common good is not realized unless everybody actually enjoys access to human flourishing. This places a burden on the community to address structural barriers that may prevent some members from prospering even when provided with the same basic entitlements. Nonetheless, even this conception of common goods does not require perfect or even substantial equality of opportunities to thrive. One plausible idea is that common goods require everyone to enjoy a *reasonable* level of access to basic human goods relative to community standards.[51]

Small justice, as I defined it previously, is plausibly more demanding than even this conception of common goods. It equates justice with those institutions arising from ethical interpersonal interactions over time. Treating each person ethically rules out arbitrary discrimination based on racial, cultural, or other biases. Just institutions, then, will lack these kinds of structural inequalities. Common goods, by contrast, if defined by communal norms of reasonableness, will not necessarily meet this robust requirement. They may afford everyone a reasonable chance to flourish, but still treat some groups unfairly relative to others.

The idealized standard imposed by small justice is arguably impossible to achieve under actual social conditions, meaning that all actual institutions

47 Finnis (n 11) 154 (emphasis added).
48 Finnis (n 11) 143–44.
49 Murphy (n 22) 63–65.
50 Crowe, *Natural Law and the Nature of Law* (n 4) 88–90.
51 Compare Crowe, *Natural Law and the Nature of Law* (n 4) 111–15.

will be unjust to some extent. Some of these distributions might nonetheless count as reasonable specifications of common goods, even on the more demanding aggregative and multidimensional conceptions. They might therefore ultimately give rise to common good duties.

9. Injustice and moral harm

I have argued in the previous sections that at least some unjust laws may count as salient and reasonable specifications of common goods. These laws will impose common good duties; there will be a robust moral obligation to obey them. The notions of salience, reasonableness, and common goods all provide some level of safeguard against unjust standards, but none of them rules out unjust legal obligations entirely.

The ubiquity of injustice, as described by Shklar, therefore does not entail philosophical anarchism. We are left, however, with a more disturbing problem. Injustice of various kinds is endemic in legal institutions. People may be complicit in injustice in various ways. They may be forced to comply with it through sanctions or social pressure. They may be indoctrinated to accept it by government propaganda or social belief systems.

People may also be morally obliged to support injustice due to its incorporation into a specific community's specification of common goods. Common goods, as I mentioned previously, function by providing solutions to collective action problems. They instruct community members on how they can work together to ensure mutually beneficial institutions. This function confers important social benefits, but it also means salient specifications of common goods have the capacity to displace more just or efficient social arrangements.

The possibility that people may have common good duties to support unjust laws, I suggest, represents a serious and underacknowledged form of moral harm. The primary victims of this situation are, of course, those directly affected by the injustices. However, it also harms a second overlapping class of people: those who find themselves obligated to support unjust institutions. More broadly, it harms the fabric of society, by creating a cultural context where structural injustice is identified with the common good.

Why exactly is it harmful for people to be morally obliged to support unjust laws? I will offer three overlapping answers to this question. The first and most general answer relies on the idea that being complicit in injustice is inherently bad not just because it harms the victim of the injustice, but also because it harms the person who is complicit.[52] The thought is that participation in intrinsic human values, particularly what I have described

52 For related discussions of the notion of moral self-harm, see Crowe, *Natural Law and the Nature of Law* (n 4) 59–69; Jonathan Crowe, '"It Makes No Difference What We Do": Climate Change and the Ethics of Collective Action' (2021) 40 Univ QLJ 477, 487–88.

elsewhere as the goods of life and meaning,[53] is hindered by passive involvement in wrongdoing.

I have previously argued that the good of life, which involves an attitude of openness to human flourishing in all its forms, is one of the basic values for humans.[54] Inaction in the face of injustice sets back participation in this value. It makes a moral agent into someone who values human fulfilment inconsistently, rather than fully supporting all its varieties. This diminished mode of participation in human flourishing denies the full potential of the agent to embody a comprehensively life-affirming attitude.

Constituting oneself as a passive moral patient in the face of injustice, rather than an active and engaged moral agent, also sets back the good of meaning.[55] Pursuing basic value commitments through actively combating injustice enables individuals to create meaning in their lives by forging a robust moral self-identity. Ignoring such challenges, by contrast, sets back this good by missing an opportunity for positive self-definition. It also introduces incoherence and inconsistency into one's underlying value commitments, since these will effectively be upheld when they pertain to some people or groups, but not to others.

The forms of moral harm outlined here have both individual and collective dimensions. Individually, they hinder the goods of life and meaning. Collectively, they can create a social environment that devalues these goods, placing its members at risk of moral harm, and denying them opportunities for positive self-definition. It is significant here that basic human values are not only facilitated by the social environment, but also partly constituted by it.[56] A community that tolerates structural injustice therefore risks systematically impoverishing the forms of flourishing available to some, if not all, of its members.

The preceding argument suggests that all complicity in injustice harms those who are complicit. There are also at least two further forms of consequential harm that may attach to some, if not all, complicity in injustice. The first is a kind of psychological harm: namely, *moral injury*. Jeremy Jinkerson defines this concept as follows:

> Moral injury is a particular type of psychological trauma characterized by intense guilt, shame, and spiritual crisis, which can develop when one violates his or her moral beliefs, is betrayed, or witnesses trusted individuals committing atrocities. . . . Phenomenologically, moral injury represents a particular trauma syndrome including psychological, existential,

53 Crowe, *Natural Law and the Nature of Law* (n 4) ch 2.
54 Crowe, *Natural Law and the Nature of Law* (n 4) ch 2 39–41.
55 Crowe, *Natural Law and the Nature of Law* (n 4) ch 2 53–55.
56 Crowe, *Natural Law and the Nature of Law* (n 4) ch 2 36–39; Crowe, 'Intelligibility, Practical Reason and the Common Good' (n 17) 298–300.

> behavioral, and interpersonal issues that emerge following perceived violations of deep moral beliefs by oneself or trusted individuals (i.e., morally injurious experiences). These experiences cause significant moral dissonance, which if unresolved, leads to the development of its core symptoms.[57]

The notion of moral injury was developed to describe the trauma symptoms of war veterans.[58] However, it has broader applications. For example, it has been used to describe the trauma experienced by front-line health workers during the COVID-19 pandemic, where they had to provide care under conditions of structural injustice:

> Our societal and individual morality, grounded in what *should* happen, had drowned in the quicksand of what actually *did* happen. The mettle of physicians, nurses, and other essential personnel was shattered by the magnitude of human injustice. Our families and friends, inadvertently subsumed in our plight, magnified the psychological toll. All of our morals had been tested, distressed, and then finally injured. This was not just burnout, a condition of stress and fatigue from overextension causing reduced workplace productivity. No—this was deeper and more pernicious: a gross assault on our core ethics and morals as human beings in a world no longer rational or reasonable.[59]

Moral injury can be explained as a human reaction to being placed in a situation that forces people to think and behave contrary to their normative inclinations.[60] As Jinkerson observes, '[w]hen individuals experience moral conflict in ordinary situations, they tend to resolve conflicts consistently with their personal values, which avoids their perceiving transgressions'.[61] This reflects both our human inclination to reason morally and our instinct for psychological self-preservation. However, situations where we feel obliged to act contrary to our moral values cause 'cognitive dissonance between . . . morals and actions'.[62] This poses a serious and long-term threat to psychological well-being if left unresolved.

57 Jeremy J Jinkerson, 'Defining and Assessing Moral Injury: A Syndrome Perspective' (2016) 22 Traumatology 122, 126.
58 KD Drescher et al, 'An Exploration of the Viability and Usefulness of the Construct of Moral Injury in War Veterans' (2011) 17 Traumatology 8.
59 Venktesh R Ramnat, 'Moral Injury' (2021) 174 Ann Intern Med 1325.
60 For discussion of the moral relevance of normative inclinations, see Crowe, *Natural Law and the Nature of Law* (n 4) ch 1; Jonathan Crowe, 'Natural Law and Normative Inclinations' (2015) 28 Ratio Juris 52.
61 Jinkerson (n 57) 122.
62 Jinkerson (n 57) 122.

People who find themselves morally obliged to obey unjust laws may experience cognitive dissonance between their legal obligations and personal values. The attempt to resolve this potentially harmful dissonance could lead in either of two directions. They might cease to identify with law as a source of obligations, rather seeking to rely on their personal values. Alternatively, they might identify with the obligations imposed by positive law, realigning their personal values accordingly. Either of these strategies poses a potential threat to that person's moral integrity, as well as their community's institutions.

This point leads to a second kind of consequential harm that may attach to complicity in injustice. This is a type of sociological harm: namely, what Marc Hertogh terms *legal alienation*. Hertogh identifies that the proliferation of legal regulations in daily life, rather than increasing the social hegemony of law, can lead people to disconnect from legal institutions.[63] He describes four forms legal alienation may take.[64] Legal meaninglessness occurs where people are unable to understand and predict legal outcomes; the outcomes seem meaningless and arbitrary. Legal powerlessness occurs where people feel legal processes are outside their influence; they experience law as an impersonal mechanism to restrict and control them. Legal cynicism occurs where people view law not as a source of genuine norms but as lacking normative legitimacy. Finally, legal value-isolation occurs where people assign low value to legal standards, because there is a significant gap between these standards and their personal values.

Legal alienation is a possible outcome of legal injustice. People may cease to identify or care about law if they find it consistently unjust or arbitrary. However, there is also another troubling possibility, which I will call *moral alienation*. The common good duties described in this chapter are not merely legal standards but also moral obligations. A potential consequence of people experiencing moral obligations as regularly unjust is that people may become alienated not only from law but also from morality and common goods. These ideas may strike them as meaningless, outside their control, and lacking normative and personal resonance.

Shklar points out that public servants are particularly susceptible to passive injustice, 'being by training unwilling to step outside the rules and routines of their offices and peers'.[65] The resulting form of injustice is due to 'many hands in general',[66] making its causes difficult to pin down. Those perpetrating such injustice may feel they are acting correctly by fulfilling their role. And, in a sense, they may be right, as this chapter has shown; they

63 Marc Hertogh, *Nobody's Law: Legal Consciousness and Legal Alienation in Everyday Life* (Palgrave 2018) vi.

64 Marc Hertogh, *Nobody's Law: Legal Consciousness and Legal Alienation in Everyday Life* (Palgrave 2018) 55–56.

65 Shklar (n 3) 6.

66 Shklar (n 3) 6.

may, in some cases, be performing their moral duty. This makes it even more important that they possess and cultivate the ability to step outside their role and engage in a project of not merely performing their duties, but also reshaping the sources and content of those duties to bring them in line with justice. This point is by no means confined to government officials; it applies to everyone.

10. Conclusion

Common goods, according to the strand of legal and political theory engaged in this chapter, provide the moral fabric of legal and social existence. They are not merely abstract notions; rather, they capture the way in which a group supports and guides its members to lead meaningful and flourishing lives. The consequences of a situation where people come to view common goods, as expressed in legal and social norms, as sources of systemic injustice—rather than shared aspirations and values—are profoundly dire. However, it may be equally harmful if they simply accept the specifications of common goods on offer—and comply with the obligations they impose—without addressing the injustices they contain.

I have argued that unjust laws threaten precisely these consequences. Their injustice does not necessarily mean they do not impose moral obligations; as such, people may feel they have to choose between justice and common goods, both of which are crucial for healthy social institutions. We have, as such, no option but to make eradicating legal injustice an urgent and collective social project. This is for the sake not only of those who are treated unjustly but also of those who may be morally obliged to support unjust institutions. It is, more broadly, a critical aim for the moral well-being of society as a whole.

Chapter 9

Acting together to address structural injustice

A deliberative mini-public proposal

Ting-an Lin[1]

1. Introduction

Various contemporary social issues involve two types of moral wrongs: *interactional wrongs* and *structural injustice*.[2] Interactional wrongs are moral wrongs that are directly inflicted through interpersonal interactions. For example, consider the issue of sexual violence. There are interactional-wrong elements in this issue, namely those acts of sexual violation that are inflicted by a few individual perpetrators and constitute violations of the victims' moral rights. At the same time, it should also be noted that people are not impacted similarly by sexual violations. Rather, due to the impacts of social structure, which is formed through interactions among norms, schemas, and material conditions,[3] some groups of people (for example, women of colour and genderqueer people) are made unfairly prone to the threat of sexual violation. Such unfair structural impacts can be considered a structural-injustice element of sexual violence. Structural injustices exist when social structures expose some groups of people to disproportionate burdens (such as violence, exploitation, and alienation) while granting unearned benefits to others. These two types of moral wrongs can be found in many social issues other than sexual violence, such as colonization,[4] residential segregation,[5] labour

1 Earlier versions of this chapter were presented at the Political Theory Workshop at Stanford University and the Responding to Injustice conference at the University of Sydney. I am very grateful to all the participants of these events for their constructive feedback. Special thanks to Alex Guerrero for helpful discussions and detailed comments.

2 I discuss more details about the nature of these two types of moral wrongs and the relationships between them in Ting-an Lin, 'Sexual Violence and Two Types of Moral Wrongs' (2024) Hypatia <https://doi.org/10.1017/hyp.2023.105> accessed 22 June 2024.

3 Iris Marion Young, *Responsibility for Justice* (OUP 2011); Sally Haslanger, 'Distinguished Lecture: Social Structure, Narrative and Explanation' (2015) 45 Can J Philos 1.

4 Catherine Lu, 'Colonialism as Structural Injustice: Historical Responsibility and Contemporary Redress' (2011) 19 JOPP 261.

5 Clarissa Rile Hayward, 'Responsibility and Ignorance: On Dismantling Structural Injustice' (2017) 79 J Polit 396.

DOI: 10.4324/9781032676159-10

injustices in global sweatshops,[6] health inequalities,[7] and the biased impact of artificial intelligence (AI).[8]

Although the ways to address interactional wrongs are relatively well established, ideas for addressing structural injustice are less clear. For example, to address the interactional-wrong element of sexual violence, we know that individual perpetrators should be held responsible for the harm they impose on the victims. Accordingly, we enforce legal or moral sanctions against them. What about the structural-injustice elements involved in sexual violence? Who should be responsible for an unjust social structure? What does it mean to be responsible for it? How should the responsibility for structural injustice be implemented? The answers to these questions are still unclear.

Over the past few decades, inspired by Iris Marion Young's work,[9] increased scholarly attention has been paid to the issue of responsibility for structural injustice. According to Young's influential *social connection model*, all of the agents whose actions contribute to the reproduction of such wrongful social structures together bear a *shared responsibility* for structural injustice, and such shared responsibility can only be discharged through collective action.[10] Even though the idea of collective action is theoretically attractive, its practical implementation often encounters various forms of practical challenges, which have prevented the realization of mature forms of collective action from adequately and smoothly taking place.[11] To address structural injustice effectively, we need to gain clarity on the practical challenges that are involved and explore possible means of implementing shared responsibility. This chapter thus aims to contribute to the study of addressing structural injustice in the following two ways. First, building on previous studies, I categorize three forms of practical challenges that have been encountered by existing proposals

6 Maeve McKeown, 'Global Structural Exploitation: Towards an Intersectional Definition' (2016) 9 Glob Just Theory Pract Rhet 155; Brian Berkey, 'Sweatshops, Structural Injustice, and the Wrong of Exploitation: Why Multinational Corporations Have Positive Duties to the Global Poor' (2021) 169 J Bus Ethics 43.

7 Ryoa Chung, 'Structural Health Vulnerability: Health Inequalities, Structural and Epistemic Injustice' (2021) 52 J Soc Philos 201.

8 Ting-an Lin and Po-Hsuan Cameron Chen, 'Artificial Intelligence in a Structurally Unjust Society' (2022) 8 FPQ <https://doi.org/10.5206/fpq/2022.3/4.14191> accessed 22 June 2024.

9 Iris Marion Young, 'Responsibility and Global Justice: A Social Connection Model' (2006) 23 Soc Phil & Pol'y 102; Young, *Responsibility for Justice* (n 3).

10 Young, 'Responsibility and Global Justice' (n 9); Young, *Responsibility for Justice* (n 3).

11 Jade Schiff, *Burdens of Political Responsibility: Narrative and the Cultivation of Responsiveness* (CUP 2014); Hayward (n 5); Robin Zheng, 'What Is My Role in Changing the System? A New Model of Responsibility for Structural Injustice' (2018) 21 ETMP 869; Tamara Jugov and Lea Ypi, 'Structural Injustice, Epistemic Opacity, and the Responsibilities of the Oppressed' (2019) 50 J Soc Philos 7; David Jenkins, 'Understanding and Fighting Structural Injustice' (2021) 52 J Soc Philos 569; Anne Schwenkenbecher, 'Structural Injustice and Massively Shared Obligations' (2021) 38 J Appl Philos 23.

for discharging shared responsibility for structural injustice. Second, I offer an alternative proposal, which I will refer to as the *deliberative mini-public proposal*, and argue that it has the potential to mobilize structural change and better overcome the identified practical challenges.

This chapter proceeds as follows. In section two, I clarify the notion of shared responsibility for structural injustice and note the multifaceted moral demands to which such responsibility should aim to respond. In section three, I point out three categories of practical challenges to implementing shared responsibility for structural injustice—psychological and epistemic barriers, lack of platforms for coordinating collective action, and a daunting amount of work. I also argue that two types of existing proposals on implementing responsibility for structural injustice fail to overcome these practical challenges. Clarifying the moral demands and common practical challenges facilitates the exploration of better alternatives for discharging shared responsibility. In section four, I outline my proposal for implementing shared responsibility for structural injustice; it is based on a form of political institution known as *deliberative mini-publics*, which involve a diverse group of people convening to deliberate on issues of public concern. In section five, by evaluating its potential to overcome the practical challenges and satisfy the moral demands of addressing structural injustice, I argue that my proposal based on deliberative mini-publics is a promising alternative for mobilizing the desired form of collective action.

2. Moral demands for addressing structural injustice

Before exploring the practical methods for addressing structural injustice, we need to obtain a more precise grasp of the moral nature of structural injustice and the moral demands related to addressing it. Who should be responsible for structural injustice? What goals or tasks should the responsibility for structural injustice aim to achieve? This section briefly overviews the theoretical background upon which this chapter builds.

When holding people responsible for interactional wrongs, in both moral and legal contexts, the following two criteria are usually required: (1) *cause condition*—the agent's action can be shown to have causally contributed to the wrong; and (2) *control condition*—the action was performed by an agent voluntarily and with sufficient knowledge of the consequences of their actions. This conventional model of ascribing responsibility is often referred to as the *liability model*.[12] An agent whose action satisfies these two conditions bears responsibility for interactional wrongs in the liability sense, which usually means that legal sanctions (such as imprisonment or fines) or moral sanctions (such as blame) can be imposed upon them.

12 Young, *Responsibility for Justice* (n 3); Hayward (n 5).

However, these two conditions of ascribing responsibility in the liability model usually cannot be satisfied when considering structural injustices; in other words, the liability model alone is usually unable to ground the responsibility for structural injustice. Recall that structural injustices exist when the impacts of social structures constitute unfair power relations between different groups of people, exposing some to disproportionate burdens while granting unearned benefits to others. It is important to note that the social structure exists only in dynamic practices and is formed and shaped through the interaction between norms (such as institutionalized laws and social norms), schemas (associated symbols, meanings, and values), and distributions of resources.[13] In other words, structural injustice is a collective result to which various participants of the social structure contribute. This feature makes it difficult to meet the cause condition, as it is almost impossible to single out a few agents as the main contributors or trace the exact causal contribution of each agent's action on the social structure. Furthermore, agents often contribute to the reproduction of the social structure through their everyday practices without being aware of the consequences of their actions.[14] For example, consumers buying garment products might not know how they contribute to the reproduction of a social structure in which women in the Global South are exposed to poor working conditions. The fact that the practices contributing to structural injustice are often regarded as 'normal' or 'morally permissible' under the existing norms makes the control condition challenging to meet.

In response to the limitations of the liability model for ascribing responsibility for structural injustice, Young famously proposed a different conception of responsibility that she called the *social connection model*.[15] She suggested that the social connection model supplements the liability model: whereas the liability model is suitable for responsibility for interactional wrongs, the social connection model is a more appropriate conception of responsibility for structural injustice. In contrast to the two conditions used in the liability model, the social connection model suggests that the moral grounds for ascribing responsibility for structural injustice are based on one's *connections* to the related social structure or when one's actions contribute to the reproduction of that social structure. As the everyday practices of the participants of the social structure usually fuel its reproduction, the social connection model suggests that *almost all* participants, regardless of their position in the social structure, are responsible for the related structural injustice.

13 Young, *Responsibility for Justice* (n 3); Haslanger (n 3).

14 Young, *Responsibility for Justice* (n 3); Hayward (n 5); Robin Zheng, 'What Kind of Responsibility Do We Have for Fighting Injustice? A Moral-Theoretic Perspective on the Social Connections Model' (2019) 20 Crit Horiz 109.

15 *Young, 'Responsibility and Global Justice' (n 9); Young, Responsibility for Justice (n 3).*

What does being responsible for structural injustice entail? First, the responsibility for structural injustice is a *shared responsibility*, one that each relevant agent personally bears but does not bear alone. Young drew from Larry May[16] to contrast shared responsibility with *collective responsibility*, which is attributed to a collective of persons, such as organizations, corporations, and societies, without being distributed to its constituent individuals. Structural injustice, in contrast, as the wrongful social structure is a collective result produced and maintained by multiple agents through everyday practices, necessitates the assignment of responsibility to each of them, and they bear this responsibility together. Therefore, one implication of this shared responsibility is that it cannot be discharged alone but only through collective action with other responsible agents.

Second, the content of such shared responsibility is open; in other words, bearing a shared responsibility does not directly specify what one should do. As Young pointed out, responsibility is different from duty.[17] When one has a duty, morality dictates the specific actions that one needs to perform. In contrast, responsibility points out specific ends that one should bring about without specifying the detailed actions that should be taken. The specifics of assuming responsibility are thus left to the discretion of each agent, who must decide what to do to approach such ends.

What, then, should be those ends of such shared responsibility? Young suggested that the goal is primarily forward-looking and is about transforming structural processes—or reducing unjustified power imbalances—to make them more just in the future.[18] I will refer to this forward-looking goal as *structural transformation*. For example, by challenging patriarchal norms, disputing rape myths, conducting legal reforms, or educating people to use interventions in problematic scenarios, the social structures that sustain the prevalence of sexual violence against women of colour could be shaped into a more just form.[19]

In addition to the forward-looking demands, I argue that there are also backward-looking demands, such as *structural reparation*, involved in addressing structural injustice. After all, while structural transformation might help prevent people from encountering structural injustice in the future, it does not address the wrongful structural impacts that have already been imposed. Reparations, as one form of backward-looking moral demand, pay attention to the victims' experience and aim to do justice by acknowledging the wrong done, repairing the harm, and holding relevant agents accountable for the reparation. Considering the nature of structural injustice, reparations

16 Larry May, *Sharing Responsibility* (University of Chicago Press 1992).
17 Young, *Responsibility for Justice* (n 3).
18 Young, *Responsibility for Justice* (n 3).
19 Lin, 'Sexual Violence and Two Types of Moral Wrongs' (n 2).

should be provided to all who inhabit vulnerable positions within the social structure. Measures of structural reparation need to recognize the harmful effects, such as restricted options and compromised well-being, that are imposed on these groups of people and work to rectify the wrongs by compensating for those harmful effects and helping people transition away from vulnerable positions.[20]

In summary, Young's social connection model provides a distinct moral ground for responsibility attribution regarding structural injustice. Reflecting on the intertwined relations between individuals' everyday practices and the impact of social structure reminds us that we, as participants in the social structure, are 'structurally complicit'[21] in many issues of structural injustice. All participants in a wrongful social structure bear a shared responsibility and are required to join in collective action to provide reparations for those who are wronged and to transform the social structure, making it less unjust in the future.

3. Practical challenges encountered for responsibility implementation

Although Young's social connection model helps clarify the moral nature of shared responsibility for structural injustice, questions about the implementation of such responsibility naturally follow. How should this shared responsibility for structural injustice be implemented? How might the right sort of collective action for structural transformation proceed? In this section, after identifying two types of proposals for addressing structural injustice in the literature (in subsection a), I identify three categories of common challenges that both of the proposals encounter: psychological and epistemic barriers, lack of platforms for coordinating collective action, and a daunting amount of work (in subsection b).

a. Two types of proposals for implementing responsibility for structural injustice

Two types of proposals for implementing the responsibility for structural injustice can be found in the literature: one provides guidelines for moral reasoning (*Type 1 proposal*), while the other appeals to the power of disruptive politics (*Type 2 proposal*).

20 I discuss the need to consider the backward-looking reparation for structural injustice in Ting-an Lin, *Addressing Structural Wrongs: From Moral Theory to Implementation* (Rutgers, The State University of New Jersey, School of Graduate Studies 2022) <https://rucore.libraries.rutgers.edu/rutgers-lib/67881/> accessed 22 June 2024.

21 Corwin Aragon and Alison M Jaggar, 'Agency, Complicity, and the Responsibility to Resist Structural Injustice' (2018) 49 J Soc Philos 439.

Young is a proponent of the Type 1 proposal, which provides guidelines for moral reasoning for addressing structural injustice. Noting that shared responsibility does not imply that all relevant agents should share the responsibility equally, nor does it suggest that all agents should act similarly, Young proposed what she calls the *parameters of reasoning*, which each agent can use to decide their actions and the role that their actions may play in the collective action.[22] She pointed out four parameters of reasoning derived from the situated social positions—*power, privilege, interest*, and *collective ability*—and sketched some guidelines for contributing to the collective action according to the associated resources. Agents with power are those who have a greater capacity to shape structural processes (such as government officials or, in the case of global sweatshops, large multinational corporations) and should use their influence accordingly. Agents with privilege are those who have benefited from the wrongful social structure (such as consumers in the social structure of the global apparel industry or White men in a White supremacist and patriarchal society), and they should use the ample resources available to them to change their habits and make extra efforts to support collective action. Victims suffering from structural injustice are a group of people with particular interests in transforming the social structure, and they can contribute to the collective action by broadcasting their knowledge and experience of suffering from structural injustice. Lastly, agents with collective ability, such as those in a position to mobilize unions or religious organizations, should exercise their ability.

Young's parameters of reasoning are not the only form of the Type 1 proposal. For example, Robin Zheng proposed alternative guidance for moral reasoning, the *role-ideal model*, which suggests that agents should decide what actions to take by reflecting on their social roles, such as that of parent, colleague, employer, and citizen.[23] Considering the relationships that such social roles concern and the expectations associated with them, Zheng suggested that social roles provide us with a more precise guide for identifying the actions one should take.

Both Young's parameters of reasoning and Zheng's role-ideal model implicitly assume a picture in which all or most agents are on board with the idea that they are responsible for structural injustice and are genuinely interested in identifying the specific actions they should take to contribute to the collective action. However, such an assumption is highly problematic. Feminist epistemologies and critical race theorists working under the theme of epistemologies of ignorance have pointed out that ignorance is often actively constructed by privileges and serves the purpose of maintaining the structure

22 Young, *Responsibility for Justice* (n 3).
23 Zheng (n 11).

of power imbalance.[24] Thus, while the ideal situation, as described in the Type 1 proposal, is that the privileged would use the resources and benefits conferred on them to change their practices and make extra efforts to support collective action, wilful ignorance often prevents this from happening.

Motivated by such concerns, the Type 2 proposal appeals to the power of disruptive politics, such as boycotts, protests, and sit-ins, to ignite collective action. Clarissa Rile Hayward is one of the proponents in this camp.[25] According to Hayward, whereas the Type 1 proposal highlights the moral reasoning of the privileged, the alternative emphasizes the political power of the oppressed. By organizing disruptive politics, the oppressed have the power to interrupt (perhaps a subset of) the privileged people's motivated ignorance and compel them to pay attention to the issues. In his critique of Young's lack of specification of the content of collective action, David Jenkins also emphasized the value of disruption in mobilizing the collective action required for structural transformation.[26] Drawing from empirical studies in politics, sociology, and social psychology on social change, both Hayward and Jenkins suggest that a significant part of enacting social change has to do with political disruption, which is usually initiated by the oppressed and then joined by others.

b. Three categories of practical challenges

In what follows, I identify three categories of practical challenges that concern the implementation of responsibility for structural injustice and argue that both types of proposals mentioned above do not succeed in overcoming them. This examination aims to provide a theoretical ground for identifying the desiderata of a satisfactory proposal and explore alternatives for implementing such shared responsibility.

Challenge 1: psychological and epistemic barriers

If the shared responsibility for a structural injustice is to be implemented, the responsible agents must first regard the issue as morally problematic and acknowledge responsibility for it. However, many psychological and epistemic barriers often prevent relevant agents from doing so. It is true that in the cases of interactional wrongs, an agent might also fail to recognize

24 Linda Martín Alcoff, 'Epistemologies of Ignorance: Three Types' in Shannon Sullivan and Nancy Tuana (eds), *Race and Epistemologies of Ignorance* (State University of New York Press 2007); Charles Mills, 'White Ignorance' in Shannon Sullivan and Nancy Tuana (eds), *Race and Epistemologies of Ignorance* (State University of New York Press 2007).

25 Hayward (n 5).

26 Jenkins (n 11).

responsibility; still, the nature of structural injustice, namely the difficulty of tracing causal connections and knowing how one's everyday practices contribute to the wrongful social structure, makes these barriers even more severe. The wilful ignorance mentioned in subsection a is an example of such a barrier. Moreover, Jade Schiff provides a detailed analysis of three dispositions that problematize individual acknowledgement of implications in structural injustice: thoughtlessness (an incapacity to think, partly produced by one's socio-political conditions), bad faith (a form of lying to oneself), and misrecognition (a kind of collective bad faith that fails to see how people's suffering is related to us).[27] These dispositions support each other, making it more difficult for agents to confront their responsibilities. It is thus impractical to expect that the privileged would naturally conduct moral reasoning and take on their share of responsibility accordingly, as suggested by the Type 1 proposal.

The circumstances of structural injustice exacerbate epistemic barriers not only for the privileged but also for the oppressed. Tamara Jugov and Lea Ypi categorized victims of structural injustice into three different categories based on their levels of awareness of their own oppression: the *epistemically aware* (those who understand the existence of injustice as well as its structural nature and how it affects them); the *partially epistemically opaque* (those who rightly observe the existence of injustice and know that they are impacted by it but do not fully understand its structural nature); and the *totally epistemically opaque* (those prevented from adequately understanding the structural nature of their oppression).[28] To enact a Type 2 proposal, which appeals to the power of the oppressed to conduct disruptive politics, there needs to be a sufficient number of oppressed people who are epistemically aware or at least partially epistemically opaque. While this consideration of the epistemic conditions of the oppressed does not entirely rule out the potential to appeal to disruptive politics, it does raise concerns that there are limited circumstances in which this proposal is plausible.

Challenge 2: lack of platforms for coordinating collective action

If an agent has overcome the psychological and epistemic barriers and thus recognizes the existence of an issue of structural injustice and acknowledges their connections to it, this agent will quickly encounter another challenge. The nature of shared responsibility means that one cannot discharge responsibility alone but needs to do so with others through participation in collective action. But how does such collective action happen?

27 Schiff (n 11).
28 Jugov and Ypi (n 11).

Anne Schwenkenbecher has helpfully distinguished two types of collective action by unorganized groups: *distributive action* and *cooperative action*. For distributive action to be possible requires only shared plans that inform individuals of the roles they can play to contribute to the collective goal. The actions that individuals need to take in such scenarios are usually relatively straightforward and simple.[29] For example, in public health campaigns to reduce the impact of a pandemic, individuals can contribute to the goal by getting vaccinated. However, given the complicated nature of structural injustice, as Schwenkenbecher pointed out, merely appealing to distributive action is insufficient; rather, cooperative actions are also required.[30] For cooperative actions to be possible, the agents involved need to have more knowledge, which includes: (a) knowledge of a shared plan P, (b) knowledge of one's role in P, and (c) knowledge that most of the other agents also know about P. In order for agents to acquire the full gamut of knowledge, some form of platform for coordination is also required. However, in our current society, there is a lack of such a platform for facilitating the desired epistemic conditions, and neither the Type 1 nor 2 proposals provide us with any clues on how to approach it.

Challenge 3: the daunting amount of work

The idea of joining in collective action with others further raises another practical challenge: the daunting amount of work that such action requires. One unfortunate reality is that there are multiple issues of structural injustice in the contemporary world—racial and sexual violence, global sweatshops, homelessness, and unemployment, to name just a few—and many of us are implicated in many of them. For an agent to take on responsibility for every issue of structural injustice, they need to invest time and effort in coming up with a shared plan P, clarifying their role in P, and acting in accordance. Although shared responsibility suggests that the agent does not need to do all of this on their own, given the multiple issues of structural injustice in which each of us is implicated, the demands would add up to a daunting amount of time and effort for each agent.

Currently, both Type 1 and Type 2 proposals fail to accommodate this challenge. The Type 2 proposal, which appeals to the power of the oppressed to disrupt ordinary people's ignorance, is essentially silent on this issue. Disruptive politics might function to raise awareness of the issues; however, it does not explain how people should navigate the process of defining the next steps. On the other hand, although Type 1 proposals provide agents with

29 Schwenkenbecher (n 11).
30 Schwenkenbecher (n 11).

some guidance related to responding to an issue (for example, reflecting on one's situated positions or one's social roles), given the unfortunate reality that many of us are implicated in multiple issues of structural injustice, these proposals bump squarely into the problem of the daunting amount of work. Given the difficulties and amount of work required, individuals might rationally feel overwhelmed and paralyzed regarding their share of responsibility.

Overall, although the social connection model provides a helpful theoretical analysis of shared responsibility for structural injustice, the reflections in this section have identified three categories of practical challenges that would prevent the smooth implementation of such shared responsibility. Various psychological and epistemic barriers block individuals' recognition of structural injustice and their connections to it; the lack of a suitable platform for individuals to organize and coordinate a shared plan makes the more sophisticated type of collective action difficult to enact, and given the unfortunate reality of our involvement in multiple issues of structural injustice, the decision to join collective actions with others imposes a daunting amount of work on each agent, leading to them feeling overwhelmed by the demands. To effectively implement the responsibilities for structural injustice, we need to take these challenges seriously.

4. The turn to institutional design

The analysis in the last section reveals that it is impractical to expect the desired form of collective action to arise naturally from unorganized groups of people in our current society. How could such circumstances be changed? In this section, I suggest that the exploration of institutional design is a promising route.

In presenting her proposal to appeal to the power of disruptive politics to address structural injustice while highlighting the power of those politics to create 'political openings for structural change',[31] Hayward also recognized that their influences are partial and impermanent. Reflecting on historical experience, she notes that a more common way to utilize the momentum for structural change is to influence the reluctant actors through extrinsic motivation, which includes but is not limited to moral responses (for example, praise or blame) and material incentives (for example, monetary cost or opportunities such as jobs or promotions). After all, many individual practices that contribute to the reproduction of social structures are at the level of *habit*, which is acquired without individuals' regular conscious thoughts and decisions. Thus, instead of appealing to moral suasion that makes claims about what people *ought* to do, Hayward suggests that a more effective way to shape and maintain a habit is to change the incentive structure that

31 Hayward (n 5) 408.

is favourable to that habit. Making recycling an almost costless option or charging for plastic bags are two examples of this approach.

I suggest that the idea of shaping incentive structures to change habits is not only relevant when considering changing individuals' practices in accordance with structural change but is also insightful when considering changing individuals' practices in approaching issues of structural injustice. Currently, people are usually presented with moral demands to address structural injustice as independent agents and are asked to take the initiative in forming or joining collective actions. Such an experience is often accompanied by a sense of loneliness or of being overwhelmed, which adds another layer of barriers to the three categories of practical challenges mentioned earlier. Changing the circumstances by reducing the effort required to join collective action might help to incentivize engagement.

Although there is potentially more than one way of achieving this goal, in the following sections I sketch a proposal based on a form of political institution known as *deliberative mini-publics*, in which a diverse group convenes to deliberate issues of public concern and produces some form of result that the greater public can use as guidance when addressing those issues. After briefly introducing the idea of deliberative mini-publics in subsection a, I discuss the details of my proposal to utilize deliberative mini-publics to address structural injustice in subsection b. In the following section (five), I discuss how this proposal provides an incentive structure that complements the two existing types of proposals for implementing shared responsibility for structural injustice and better mobilizes the desired form of collective action.

a. Deliberative mini-publics: a brief introduction

Deliberative mini-publics are an institutional mechanism in which an assembly of people who are demographically representative of the larger population is brought together to learn about and deliberate on a topic of public issue in order to form a considered result.[32] There are two core features of deliberative mini-publics. First, it is *mini-public*, a demographically representative microcosm of the public, which is achieved through random selection or similar methods. Second, it is *deliberative*, that is, participants engage in a careful discussion about an issue after receiving relevant information. The concepts of random selection and deliberation can be traced to ancient Athenian democracy, but they regained contemporary attention around

32 Robert A Dahl, *Democracy and Its Critics* (Yale University Press 2008); Oliver Escobar and Stephen Elstub, 'Forms of Mini-Publics: An Introduction to Deliberative Innovations in Democratic Practice' (newDemocracy Foundation 2017) <www.newdemocracy.com.au/2017/05/08/forms-of-mini-publics/> accessed 22 June 2024; John S Dryzek and others, 'The Crisis of Democracy and the Science of Deliberation' (2019) 363 Science 1144.

three decades ago when political scientist Robert Dahl coined the term 'mini-populous'[33] and inspired a 'new wave of deliberative democracy'.[34]

In the past few decades, hundreds of deliberative mini-publics have been created worldwide to consider various topics of public concern.[35] Among the varieties of these deliberative mini-publics, five main forms can be observed: *citizens' juries, planning cells, consensus conferences, deliberative polls*, and *citizens' assemblies*. These sub-types of mini-publics differ in many aspects, from the number of people recruited, the number of meetings, the selection method, and the activities involved to the form of the result and how it is incorporated into the existing political system. Which sub-forms of mini-publics should be adopted and how they should be designed depends on the issue of concern, the nature of the organizer, and the purpose of such an assembly.[36] For example, when the purpose is to obtain a representative survey of the opinions of the public, deliberative polls (which incorporate larger groups of participants and fewer meetings) are often selected. In contrast, when the purpose is for the participants to create more detailed reports or recommendations, citizens' juries or citizens' assemblies (which utilize relatively smaller groups but a more extended series of meetings) are usually preferred.

Two relatively recent examples of deliberative mini-publics can provide a brief overview of the design and impact of this mechanism. From 2012–2014, the Irish government established an Irish Constitutional Convention (a form of citizens' assembly) to discuss and propose amendments to the Irish Constitution. The assembly consisted of 99 randomly selected members: 66 citizen representatives plus 33 representatives from Ireland's political parties. The members convened for plenary sessions on Saturdays to discuss eight topics within 12 months, and they produced reports sent to Parliament. Later on, Parliament responded to their reports and put three proposals to the referendum—one was about permission for same-sex marriage, and it was subsequently passed, which marked a transformative change in a traditionally Catholic country.

On the other side of the spectrum, America in One Room is an example of the recent use of deliberative polls. America in One Room took place over a long weekend in 2019, and it gathered, through stratified random sampling, 526 American registered voters to discuss issues of the 2020 presidential election related to five areas: immigration, the economy, healthcare, the

33 Dahl (n 32).

34 Claudia Chwalisz, 'A New Wave of Deliberative Democracy' (2019) 26 Carnegie Eur 1.

35 For more details on these deliberative mini-publics, visit the Sortition Foundation <www.sortitionfoundation.org/> accessed 22 June 2024; and Participedia <https://participedia.net/> accessed 22 June 2024.

36 See Escobar and Elstub (n 32) for a detailed comparison between these five main forms of deliberative mini-publics.

environment, and foreign policy.[37] At the beginning of the process, the participants were surveyed about their views on these issues, and the results were later contrasted with their views (collected via confidential questionnaires) after participating in the deliberation. The general purpose of deliberative polls is to see what the public would think if given sufficient time and opportunity to gather well-balanced information and deliberate with a diverse cohort. One interesting finding of America in One Room is that the deliberative process can significantly reduce polarization. In all five topic areas, the partisan differences between Republicans and Democrats dramatically decreased after they participated in the deliberation process. Even though the result of America in One Room was not directly used to guide voting in the 2020 presidential election, it received wide media coverage, as it revealed some positive results about how to overcome the differences and polarization in society.

b. A deliberative mini-public proposal for addressing structural injustice

Deliberative mini-publics, as a form of institutional innovation, are often advocated for their potential to overcome some of the problems of the current democratic system, which relies on elections to select representatives, and to further strengthen the value of democracy.[38] Here, I want to instead argue for the potential of using deliberative mini-publics to address structural injustice; I call this the *deliberative mini-public proposal*. The proposal, briefly, is to establish multiple deliberative mini-publics and to make it a civic duty to serve on them to address some issue(s) of structural injustice.[39] The participants of each of the deliberative mini-publics would be provided with relevant information and sufficient time, and they would be tasked with

37 James Fishkin and others, 'Is Deliberation an Antidote to Extreme Partisan Polarization? Reflections on "America in One Room"' (2021) 115 APSR 1464.

38 For example, see Alexander A Guerrero, 'Against Elections: The Lottocratic Alternative' (2014) 42 Philos Public Aff 135; Hélène Landemore, *Open Democracy: Reinventing Popular Rule for the Twenty-First Century* (Princeton University Press 2020). One rare exception that focuses on the usage of deliberative mini-publics for social movement is discussed in James Wong, 'Deliberative Mini-Publics for Social Movement: A Case from Hong Kong' (European Consortium for Political Research General Conference, Montreal, August 2015).

39 One potential analogy is jury service in the US, which is regarded as part of civic duty. Jury service is mandatory, and the person who is summoned must attend (except for some cases of exemptions and excuses), some reimbursement for the service can be provided, and there are some protections (eg, employers must allow their employees time off to serve on a jury and cannot fire an employee who is summoned for jury service). For more details about US jury service, see <www.uscourts.gov/services-forms/jury-service> accessed 22 June 2024. I should emphasize that the exact rules of qualifications, exemptions, reimbursement, and protection for attending deliberative mini-publics need not be like jury service in the US; I mention jury service just to be used as an analogy for further exploration.

producing some forms of results that would be helpful for the greater public to use as guidance in addressing those issues.

Before moving into more details about the deliberative mini-public proposal, two notes should be emphasized. First, there is no one-size-fits-all design of deliberative mini-publics for addressing structural injustices. Instead, depending on the target issue, multiple aspects of the design choices may be needed. Although more details about the design and implementation of the deliberative mini-public proposal remain as yet unexplored, my goal is to provide a theoretical ground for approaching some core design choices.

Second, deliberative mini-publics do not have to be used as a sole method; instead, they can be combined with other proposals, including those presented earlier. For example, the occurrence of disruptive politics (Type 2 proposal) can be regarded as indicative of a need to establish deliberative mini-publics on relevant issues. Thus, whereas disruptive politics create political openings, deliberative mini-publics sustain the momentum to proceed with structural change. Furthermore, in the kind of deliberative mini-publics that aim to develop a shared plan or provide actionable guidance for individuals who wish to contribute to the plan, the principles suggested by the Type 1 proposal might be useful. These, of course, are just a few potential ways to envision the relationships between these different proposals. The takeaway here is that the deliberative mini-public proposal presented as follows is not and should not be regarded as a silver bullet for addressing structural injustices. Rather, my goal is to argue that this proposal bears several advantages that can complement existing proposals; thus, it should be recognized as a promising alternative in the toolbox for addressing structural injustice.

Typically, deliberative mini-publics proceed in five stages: (1) planning and recruitment, (2) learning phase, (3) deliberative phase, (4) decision-making phase, and (5) follow-up.[40] In the rest of this section, I discuss how the nature of structural injustice informs the design of deliberative mini-publics during these five stages.

In the first stage, *planning and recruitment*, deliberative mini-publics identify the topic and recruit an assembly of people. To use deliberative mini-publics to address structural injustice, an issue with a specific scope, such as sexual violence on college campuses in the US, must first be identified.[41] Participants can then be recruited through random selection or

40 Escobar and Elstub (n 32); Dryzek and others (n 32).

41 Questions about how to carve out different issues of structural injustice might need more attention. One consideration has to do with the fact that many issues of structural injustice are intricately interrelated, interwoven, and intersecting with each other. Thus, while drawing distinctions to some extent is required for the deliberation to be effective, it needs to be aware of the complicated dynamics in the larger context. Thanks to Nannerl O Keohane and Valerie Soon for raising this important concern.

quasi-random selection methods to ensure representativeness.[42] Because all the participants of the wrongful social structure bear a shared responsibility for the issue of structural injustice, the scope of participant recruiting should correspond to the social structure of the target. For example, if the issue is on a domestic level, then people within that national boundary should be the potential pool from which to recruit; when the wrongful social structure goes beyond the state boundary (such as with the issues of global sweatshops and transnational migration), the recruitment pool should expand accordingly.

In the second stage, the selected participants enter the *learning phase*, where they will be given relevant information about the topic from diverse perspectives. They might, for example, be given information packages in advance and then exposed to a wide range of evidence, views, and testimonies from diverse angles (including experts, officials, activists, and so on). In some cases, there will also be opportunities for the participants to raise questions and consult directly with the selected experts. The point of the learning phase is to inform participants using the best available relevant knowledge. Some questions can be raised about the implementation of this stage: what kind of qualification should be used to consider someone an expert? Among the multiple experts (as well as officials, activists, and so on), who should be selected to join the process? Who should be making these decisions? These crucial questions are still under scholarly debate, and the answers to these questions might differ depending on the issues of focus.[43] However, I want to emphasize that when using deliberative mini-publics to address structural injustice, it is especially important to count those who are oppressed by the given social structure as a type of expert. As feminist epistemologists have long pointed out, one's standpoint or situated positions hugely influence how one sees the world, and the situated positions of the oppressed may impart some special epistemic advantage regarding the dynamics of oppression.[44] From this perspective, the oppressed bear expertise that comes from experience and have much to contribute to deliberation on how to address these structural injustices. In addition to epistemic value, inviting the oppressed as

42 There are different ways of recruiting for various issues of structural injustice: purely random sampling, stratified random sampling, discursive representation (or opinion representation), target groups, or a mixture of these approaches. For more discussions, see Clodagh Harris, 'Mini-Publics: Design Choices and Legitimacy' in Stephen Elstub and Oliver Escobar (eds), *Handbook of Democratic Innovation and Governance* (Edward Elgar Publishing 2019).

43 Guerrero (n 38); Jennifer J Roberts and others, 'Experts and Evidence in Deliberation: Scrutinising the Role of Witnesses and Evidence in Mini-Publics, a Case Study' (2020) 53 Policy Sci 3.

44 Patricia Hill Collins, 'Learning from the Outsider within: The Sociological Significance of Black Feminist Thought' (1986) 33 Soc Probl 14; Sandra Harding, *Whose Science? Whose Knowledge?: Thinking from Women's Lives* (Cornell University Press 1991); Alison Wylie, 'Why Standpoint Matters' in Robert Figueroa and Sandra G Harding (eds), *Science and Other Cultures: Issues in Philosophies of Science and Technology* (Routledge 2003).

experts further satisfies the moral demands of addressing structural injustice; I will discuss this point in section 5.a.

After the learning phase, participants move into the *deliberative phase*, during which they engage in diverse, small-group deliberation about the presented information. Usually, trained facilitators play a crucial role in this phase, as they ensure that the deliberation dynamics are respectful and that participants have equal opportunities to contribute.[45] Given that power imbalance is a key issue underlying structural injustice, how to mitigate problematic impacts and ensure that participants can have equal footing in the deliberative process is crucial. It should be noted that, despite the efforts of trained facilitators, concerns have been raised regarding whether active facilitation in deliberative mini-public settings is sufficient to ensure these values. Some studies suggest that certain groups of people, such as women, less educated participants, and those with a lower economic status, tend to be disadvantaged in contributing to the process,[46] whereas other empirical studies have not found such a gap between different groups.[47] The kind of facilitation that would better ensure the desired dynamics and reduce unjustified power imbalances in deliberative mini-publics remains an active topic under research.

In the fourth stage, the *decision-making phase*, based on the discussions and information learned in the previous stages, the participants produce outputs together, and such outputs can be used by the greater public as guidance in addressing structural injustices. Depending on the issue of focus, deliberative mini-publics might be designed in different ways and with different kinds of expected outputs. For example, for issues about which there is less consensus or more tension among the public, it might be more appropriate to begin with some survey-oriented mini-publics, such as deliberative polls. In such a setting, the ultimate goal is to examine how people's positions might change after the learning and deliberative phases, and the survey opinions can be used by the greater public to signal the potential for evolution of viewpoint—the degree to which a perspective might realistically change in the short term. In contrast, for cases where there is more general recognition of a moral problem with the issue and a shared vision to address it, models such as citizens' juries and citizens' assemblies, where

45 Claudia Landwehr, 'Facilitating Deliberation: The Role of Impartial Intermediaries in Deliberative Mini-Publics' in Kimmo Grönlund, André Bächtiger, and Maija Setälä (eds), *Deliberative Mini-Publics: Involving Citizens in the Democratic Process* (ECPR Press 2014).

46 Maija Setälä, Kimmo Grönlund, and Kaisa Herne, 'Citizen Deliberation on Nuclear Power: A Comparison of Two Decision-Making Methods' (2010) 58 PSR 688; Christopher F Karpowitz and Tali Mendelberg, *The Silent Sex* (Princeton University Press 2014).

47 Alice Siu, 'Deliberation & the Challenge of Inequality' (2017) 146 Daedalus 119; Marlène Gerber and others, 'Deliberative Abilities and Influence in a Transnational Deliberative Poll (EuroPolis)' (2018) 48 Br J Polit Sci 1093.

the expected output would be recommendations for actions or analysis of the pros and cons of different proposals, may be most appropriate. It should be noted that the form of deliberative mini-public that is appropriate for a given issue is context-sensitive and might change over time. In societies around the world, for example, some social issues (for example, the prevalence of sexual violence and its disproportionate impacts on some populations) that once went unrecognized now garner much more awareness and consensus about their moral seriousness. At the same time, these deliberative mini-publics might also play a role in shaping the public's awareness and perception of certain issues.

Lastly, the results produced by the deliberative mini-publics will be shared through relevant networks and used as helpful guidance for the greater public when approaching issues of structural injustice. Methods through which to follow up on the implementation or communication of the results are needed to better ensure its effectiveness.[48] How exactly the results produced by the deliberative mini-publics should be used is another issue under heated debate. Some scholars suggest that significant power should be conferred to the mini-publics and that the results produced from them can be used to shape public policies directly,[49] while others suggest that deliberative mini-publics should be given rather restrictive power and limited to, for example, indirectly shaping the greater public's opinion instead of directly deciding public policies.[50] While this issue warrants further consideration in the implementation of mini-publics to address structural injustice, engaging more fully in this issue will go beyond the scope of this piece. For the purposes of this chapter, I will only note the following: since the social structure is a collective result, addressing any issues of structural injustice comprehensively would require the participation of a sizable portion of the greater public. Therefore, discussion of the role of deliberative mini-publics in this context will need to incorporate the dynamics between the participants of the mini-publics and the rest of the public. No matter how much power the mini-publics are given, some forms of communication of the reasons behind the results will need to be properly presented to achieve an adequate uptake by the rest of the public.

48 Escobar and Elstub (n 32).

49 James S Fishkin and Robert C Luskin, 'Broadcasts of Deliberative Polls: Aspirations and Effects' (2006) 36 BJPolS 184; Robert E Goodin and John S Dryzek, 'Deliberative Impacts: The Macro-Political Uptake of Mini-Publics' (2006) 34 PAS 219; Archon Fung, 'Minipublics: Deliberative Designs and Their Consequences' in Shawn W Rosenberg (ed), *Deliberation, Participation and Democracy: Can the People Govern?* (Palgrave Macmillan 2007).

50 Cristina Lafont, 'Deliberation, Participation, and Democratic Legitimacy: Should Deliberative Mini-Publics Shape Public Policy?' (2015) 23 JOPP 40; Cristina Lafont, *Democracy without Shortcuts: A Participatory Conception of Deliberative Democracy* (OUP 2019).

5. Evaluating the deliberative mini-public proposal

I have now sketched a proposal for addressing structural injustices based on deliberative mini-publics, but why should we think this proposal is worth considering? In this section, I evaluate the deliberative mini-public proposal from two perspectives: the potential to satisfy the multifaceted moral demands for addressing structural injustice (subsection a) and the feasibility of overcoming practical challenges and facilitating the proper form of collective action (subsection b).

a. Considerations regarding the fulfilment of moral demands

Let's first consider the potential of the deliberative mini-public proposal to fulfil the moral demands for addressing structural injustice. Recall that in section two, I pointed out the twofold moral demands: forward-looking structural transformation and backward-looking structural reparation. The former concerns making changes in social structures to reduce unjustified power imbalances between members of society in the future, while the latter focuses on rectifying the harmful impact that has been imposed on groups of people through recognizing the wrongs, compensating for the harmful impact, and holding relevant agents accountable. How promising is the deliberative mini-public proposal in meeting these moral demands?

First, the deliberative mini-public proposal shows promise regarding holding the relevant people accountable for issues of structural injustice. As mentioned earlier, the fact that structural injustice is a collective result and responsibility is shared among broad groups of people often obscures the issue, allowing people to avoid recognizing their connections to issues of structural injustice. The establishment of various deliberative mini-publics for addressing structural injustice and making participation in these mini-publics part of civic duty has the potential to dispel these myths. The establishment of these mini-publics would make clear that, beyond interactional wrongs, some structural-injustice elements require public awareness. Furthermore, making participation in these mini-publics part of civic duty conveys the message that the broader community bears a shared responsibility. Even though each individual only needs to serve on a few deliberative mini-publics, the fact that the selection is made randomly sends the message that the responsibility for these issues of structural injustice is shared collectively (by those selected and not selected). In this way, the whole process of regularly establishing deliberative mini-publics on some issue of structural injustice urges people to recognize the wrongful impact of these structural injustices, confront their responsibility for them, and gather collective attention to address them.

Second, the deliberative mini-public proposal is promising to ensure a fairer distribution of responsibility for addressing structural injustice. Currently, the burden of raising public awareness about some issues of structural injustice, urging changes, or even driving the movement to bring about some large-scale transformation often unfairly falls on the shoulders of the oppressed. This unfortunate reality is in part because those who are oppressed by the existing social structures do have an interest in changing them, while those who are currently conferred benefits by the social structures tend to be less aware of the problem or lack the motivation to change it.[51] The design of the deliberative mini-public proposal, specifically making participation in mini-publics part of civic service, helps partially solve the paradox. Even though the establishment of deliberative mini-publics would sometimes be prompted by disruptive politics, which often rely on the efforts of the oppressed, once they are established, the mini-publics provide a mechanism to distribute the responsibility for addressing structural injustices more fairly and systematically. The deliberative mini-publics would recruit participants from all positions of the social structure to learn, deliberate, and produce outcomes related to the assigned case of structural injustice. In some cases, the produced outcomes would further guide people with different social roles or positions to contribute to the collective efforts.

Third, by inviting the oppressed to act as experts in the process, the deliberative mini-public proposal has the potential to further empower those who are disadvantaged by structural injustices. In section 4.b, based on studies of feminist epistemologists and standpoint scholars,[52] I pointed out the epistemic value of inviting the oppressed to act as experts and share their experiences. In addition to the epistemic value they contribute, sharing their experiences at deliberative mini-publics also empowers them. By incorporating their expert feedback on how they have been and are impacted by the current social structure, the process better recognizes the unfair impacts that society has imposed on them, pays attention to their experience, shows appreciation for their contribution, and ensures that their voices are heard and treated seriously while identifying directions for future growth of the social structure. In this way, this process respects the agency of the oppressed, empowers them, and contributes to the forward-looking goal of reducing the unjustified power imbalances embedded in society.

Lastly, the deliberative mini-public proposal shows promise regarding fulfilling the moral demands of addressing structural injustice by facilitating *relational transformation*,[53] the needed relational change among members

51 Such a phenomenon is described as a 'paradox of the participation of the privileged'. See more detailed discussions in Sally J Scholz, *Political Solidarity* (Penn State Press 2008).

52 Collins (n 44); Harding (n 44); Wylie (n 44).

53 I borrowed the term *relational transformation* from Colleen Murphy, *The Conceptual Foundations of Transitional Justice* (CUP 2017). In Murphy's original usage in considering the goal of transitional justice, she uses 'relational transformation' to refer to changes in relationships among citizens and between citizens and officials in order to manifest the value of reciprocity and respect for agency. I believe that the broader sense of 'relational

of society. Through bottom-up participation in deliberative mini-publics for addressing structural injustices, people in different social positions can interact and better understand each other's perspectives. Even though each individual only directly participates in a few mini-publics, the results and information exchanged throughout the process will be communicated to the greater public. This serves an educational function for the general public and encourages more sensitivity towards the related considerations. Thus, through direct participation in deliberative mini-publics and learning about the results from other deliberative mini-publics, members of society are provided with opportunities to establish mutual trust and respect, which are ineliminable components for the needed relational transformation.

Overall, the deliberative mini-public proposal has the potential to fulfil the moral demands of addressing structural injustice. The design of deliberative mini-publics directs people's attention to the structural-injustice elements of some social issues, making it more evident that the responsibility for structural injustices is shared among all participants of the social structure. Instead of putting an unfair burden on the oppressed to drive the needed changes, it distributes the responsibility to broader groups of people; at the same time, by inviting the oppressed to participate as a type of expert, the deliberative mini-public respects the agency of the oppressed and empowers them. Furthermore, through bottom-up participation in a small number of mini-publics and learning about the results from other conveners, the greater public is given opportunities to transform their relations with each other, which is essential for reshaping our unjust social structure.

b. Considerations regarding practical feasibility

After examining the promise of deliberative mini-publics, the focus now shifts to the examination of their practical feasibility. Recall that in section 3.b, I pointed out three categories of practical challenges encountered in the implementation of shared responsibility for addressing structural injustice (psychological and epistemic barriers, a lack of platforms for coordination, and the daunting amount of work) and argued that the existing two types of proposals for implementing responsibilities for structural injustice (one that provides guidelines for moral reasoning and another that appeals to the power of disruptive politics) fail to provide effective ways to overcome these challenges. In this section, I discuss the potential of deliberative mini-publics to overcome the aforementioned three categories of challenges

transformation', namely the fundamental change of relations between members of a society, is crucial not only for societies dealing with transitional justice but for all societies aiming to address structural injustices, although some specific values and practices might look different in these different contexts.

while considering some of their limitations and potential concerns. Given the diverse nature of issues of structural injustice, there might be circumstances in which the proposal of deliberative mini-publics would be more likely to succeed. Through the following reflection on its potential and limitations, my goal is to show that the deliberative mini-public proposal is worth further exploration; at the same time, being aware of its limitations highlights the necessity of caution in design and may guide future studies in identifying conditions that are suitable for its implementation.

First, the deliberative mini-public proposal shows the potential to address the epistemic and psychological barriers that prevent individuals from recognizing the moral problems of structural injustice and their responsibility for it. Several empirical studies have revealed the potential of deliberative mini-publics to motivate and facilitate public engagement.[54] By exposing the public to diverse perspectives and information that might not be accessible to them in their everyday lives, deliberative mini-publics help people to overcome polarization, grow respect and trust towards those holding opposing views, and form a more considered judgment.[55] Being exposed to the narrative of the oppressed (both in the learning phase, where disadvantaged individuals are invited to share their experience as experts, and in the deliberative phase, where some participants might be situated in the more oppressed positions) encourages acknowledgement of structural injustices and motivates ordinary people to confront their responsibility for them.[56] Furthermore, since the output of these deliberative mini-publics will be communicated and shared with the greater public, those who do not attend the deliberations can still have access to the exchange of ideas among the participants, which may motivate them to reflect on their connections to these issues.

The advantages supported by the empirical evidence offered here mostly occur when people are put into a deliberative mini-public setting; thus, questions might be raised regarding how to motivate people to participate in deliberative mini-publics in the first place. Since the proposal that I advocate here is to make participation in deliberative mini-publics part of one's civic duty (based on the grounds that the responsibility for addressing structural

54 James Fishkin, *When the People Speak: Deliberative Democracy and Public Consultation* (OUP 2009); Christopher F Karpowitz, Chad Raphael, and Allen S Hammond, 'Deliberative Democracy and Inequality: Two Cheers for Enclave Deliberation among the Disempowered' (2009) 37 PAS 576; Kimmo Grönlund, Maija Setälä, and Kaisa Herne, 'Deliberation and Civic Virtue: Lessons from a Citizen Deliberation Experiment' (2010) 2 EPSR 95; Simon Niemeyer, 'The Emancipatory Effect of Deliberation: Empirical Lessons from Mini-Publics' (2011) 39 PAS 103; Robert C Luskin and others, 'Deliberating across Deep Divides' (2014) 62 PSR 116; Kevin M Esterling, Archon Fung, and Taeku Lee, 'How Much Disagreement Is Good for Democratic Deliberation?' (2015) 32 Polit Commun 529.

55 Luskin and others (n 54).

56 Schiff (n 11).

injustice is shared among all participants of the social structure), it would be generally obligatory to participate in some small number of mini-publics, excepting justified absences. While this might face resistance at the beginning of its implementation, I suggest that once people recognize that participation is part of a civic duty that applies to everyone, they will become more receptive to this new approach to structural injustice.

Some might still worry that merely making *attendance* at mini-publics obligatory cannot ensure that participants will display the appropriate amount of motivation needed to participate in the whole process. What if people are there but are unwilling to engage? Indeed, depending on the issues of focus, different levels of resistance might be encountered. However, reflecting on the hundreds of deliberative mini-publics that have been implemented all over the world in the past few decades[57] should give us confidence that people are generally interested in joining in deliberation on difficult social issues with others. At the same time, to ensure an effective implementation of the deliberative mini-public proposal, future research can examine and identify factors that might influence motivations for such participation.

Second, in response to the challenge of the lack of platforms for coordinating the collective action required for addressing structural injustice, the deliberative mini-public proposal provides a way to make more sophisticated forms of collective action possible. In fact, the deliberative mini-publics serve as a platform for the exchange of ideas and collaboration among participants. With the help of proper facilitation, participants engage in the process of informed deliberation with others and may produce certain detailed plans about how to address the issue of structural injustice, which will be further communicated to the greater public.[58] The shared plan and guidance for people occupying a variety of societal roles provide an epistemic foundation conducive to more sophisticated forms of collective action.

Although actionable changes would still depend on the general public's uptake of the overall plan, a few features of this shared plan might increase general motivation to engage. Knowing that this plan is made by participants

57 For more details, visit the Sortition Foundation (n 35) and Participedia (n 35).

58 While some suspicions might be raised about the quality of the plan produced by the deliberative mini-publics, there are actually reasons to think that the outcome can be fairly good. According to the *diversity trumps ability* principle, groups of agents with high cognitive diversity usually outperform groups of individually high-performing agents (namely, experts). As the assembly of people recruited through random selection in deliberative mini-publics would have high cognitive diversity, there are good reasons to believe that the proposed results would be even better than the results proposed by a few experts or generated by individuals reasoning independently. For more discussions on the diversity trumps ability principle, see Lu Hong and Scott E Page, 'Groups of Diverse Problem Solvers Can Outperform Groups of High-Ability Problem Solvers' (2004) 101 Proc Natl Acad Sci U S A 16385.

of the deliberative mini-publics instead of a group of elite politicians might help the public to believe that their perspectives were represented and taken into account during production of the plan. Furthermore, considering that successful structural change is only possible when sufficient numbers contribute to joint efforts, the public nature of the shared plan can bolster belief that individual efforts made in accordance will not be in vain, and thus should motivate the populace to act according to that plan. How effectively these factors contribute to collective agency is a topic worth further exploration in future studies.

Lastly, responding to the challenge of the daunting amount of work caused by the unfortunate reality that we are all inevitably implicated in various issues of structural injustice, the deliberative mini-public proposal provides a form of division of labour to lessen the overall burden. Instead of asking all agents to understand every single issue in which they are structurally complicit and to laboriously reason with others to figure out a shared plan to address it, each individual agent can focus on just a few issues when they are randomly selected to serve as participants in the deliberative mini-publics. Regarding additional issues, they can defer to others for clarification, an overall plan to address them, and guidance for ways in which the greater public can contribute to that plan. In this way, although the deliberative mini-public proposal cannot reduce the moral responsibility for structural injustice that each individual bears, it provides a helpful mechanism of division of labour that reduces the overall work for all individuals. Furthermore, with the publicity of the shared plan, everyone gains grounds to hold each other accountable and reasons to believe that their efforts are in accordance with the plan that is most likely to bring about the desired change.

Overall, despite some limitations, I argue that the deliberative mini-public proposal exhibits promise regarding shaping people's habits when approaching issues of structural injustice and overcoming the three practical challenges to implementing shared responsibility for structural injustices. By exposing people to an environment in which they can hear narratives of the oppressed and deliberate with people of diverse perspectives, the deliberative mini-public proposal motivates people to overcome psychological and epistemic barriers and better recognize structural injustices and their connections with them. To make possible the sophisticated form of collective action necessary to address structural injustice, deliberative mini-publics serve as a platform for coordination, and the shared plans produced by the mini-publics provide guidance in how the greater public can contribute to the joint efforts. Lastly, even though the proposal cannot reduce each individual's responsibility for various issues of structural injustice, it provides some mechanism of division of labour to reduce the amount of work that each person needs to take on in order to discharge the shared responsibility.

6. Conclusion

Situated in a world with multiple issues of structural injustice, we, together with others, bear a shared responsibility to join collective actions to address the unfair restrictions imposed by social structures. Various challenges make it impractical to expect the desired form of collective action to happen naturally among unorganized groups of people. To change the way people respond to structural injustice, we need to change the incentive structure. In this chapter, I have proposed a deliberative mini-public proposal, according to which multiple deliberative mini-publics should be established in order to address various issues of structural injustice; responsible agents should be randomly selected to serve on these deliberative mini-publics, where they will convene with diverse participants and produce outcomes that can be used as guidance for the greater public. By examining its potential to fulfil the moral demands of addressing structural injustice and its practical feasibility in implementing shared responsibility, I have argued that the deliberative mini-public proposal provides a promising incentive structure that is conducive to the desired form of collective action. Like all measures, this proposal has limitations and might be more attuned to success under certain circumstances; future research is thus required to better identify those circumstances and tailor the design of deliberative mini-publics to different contexts. Furthermore, since the issue of unjustified power imbalances is at the core of structural injustice, while designing and implementing deliberative mini-publics for addressing structural injustices, caution should be constantly paid to avoid creating new forms of unwarranted hierarchies.[59]

One might still ask: how, then, can we get from here to there? In other words, how do we move from our current society into the world depicted by the deliberative mini-public proposal, where deliberative mini-publics are established on an ongoing basis for the purpose of addressing structural injustice? Although we are definitely not there yet, observing that hundreds of deliberative mini-publics have been established over the past few decades, I suggest that we are progressing steadily towards that reality. My hope is that this chapter provides evidence that the deliberative mini-public proposal is worth further exploration—and the more people who share that thought, the closer we will get to that world.

59 Relevant cautions are recently raised through the urge of 'decolonizing deliberative mini-publics'. For more detailed discussion, see Azucena Morán and Nicole Curato, 'Decolonizing Deliberative Mini-Publics' <www.youtube.com/watch?v=r6aGb57d8Z0> accessed 22 June 2024.

Index

Note: Page numbers in **bold** indicate a table on the corresponding page and page numbers followed by n indicate a note.

FSC
www.fsc.org
MIX
Papier | Fördert
gute Waldnutzung
FSC® C083411

Kolibri 360 GmbH
Ferdinand-Jühlke-Straße 7
99095 Erfurt, Deutschland
produktsicherheit@kolibri360.de